Kimberly Hartz

Master Photographer, Photographic Craftsman & Certified Professional Photographer

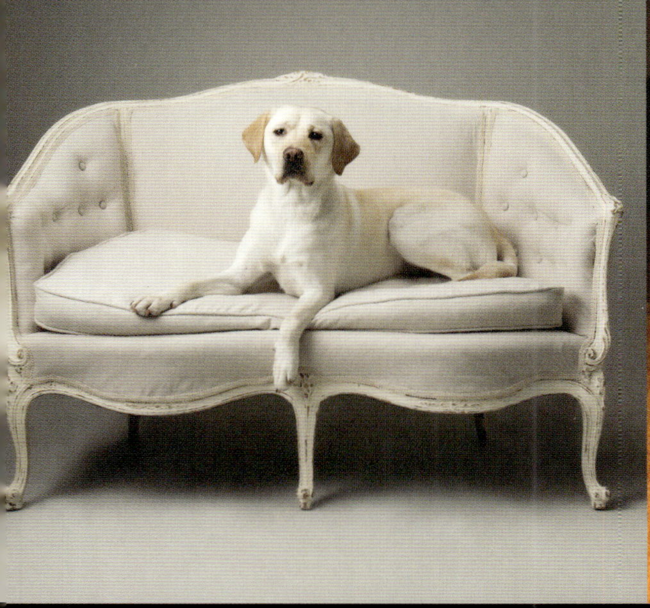

Art of Dog Photography

Pro Techniques for Everybody

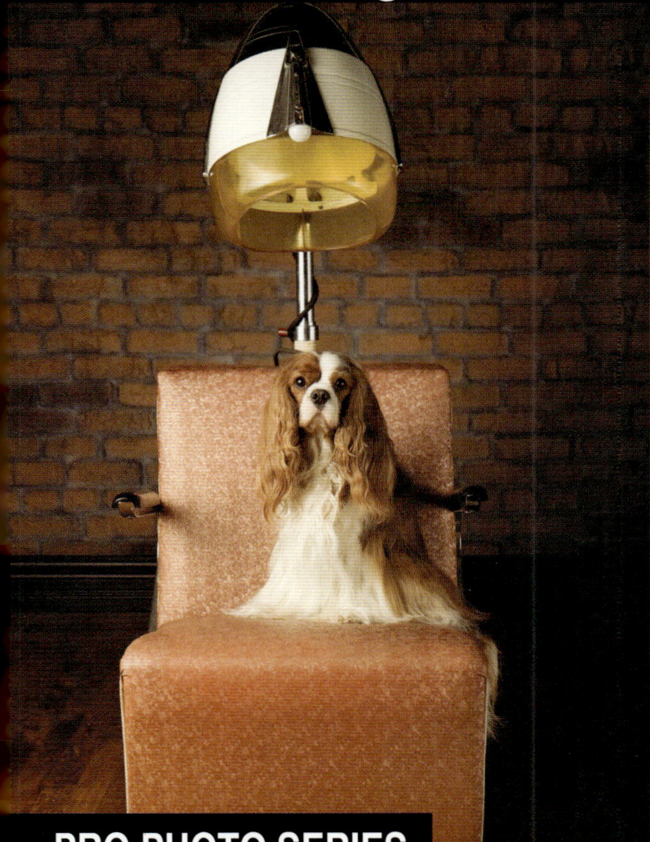

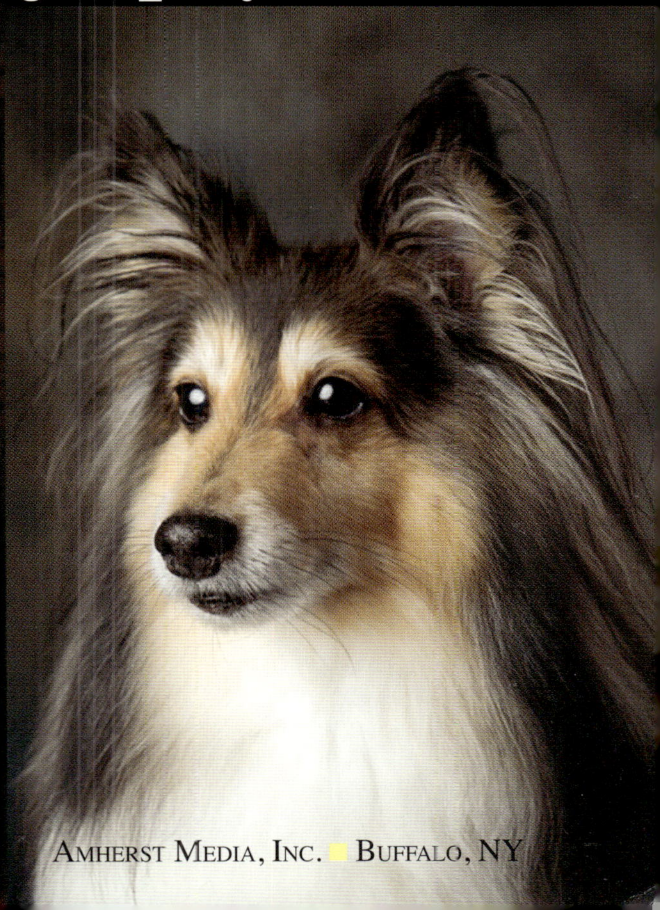

PRO PHOTO SERIES

Amherst Media, Inc. ■ Buffalo, NY

DEDICATION

To all of the photographers out there who want to do what they love and create beautiful portraits of pets. I hope this helps you!

Published by:
Amherst Media, Inc.
PO BOX 538
Buffalo, NY 14213
www.AmherstMedia.com

Publisher: Craig Alesse
Associate Publisher: Katie Kiss
Senior Editor/Production Manager: Barbara A. Lynch-Johnt
Senior Contributing Editor: Michelle Perkins
Editor: Beth Alesse
Acquisitions Editor: Harvey Goldstein
Editorial Assistance from: Carey A. Miller, Roy Bakos, Jen Sexton-Riley, Rebecca Rudell
Business Manager: Sarah Loder
Marketing Associate: Tonya Flickinger

ISBN-13: 978-1-68203-438-5
Library of Congress Control Number: 2020934970
Printed in the United States of America
10 9 8 7 6 5 4 3 2 1

Contents

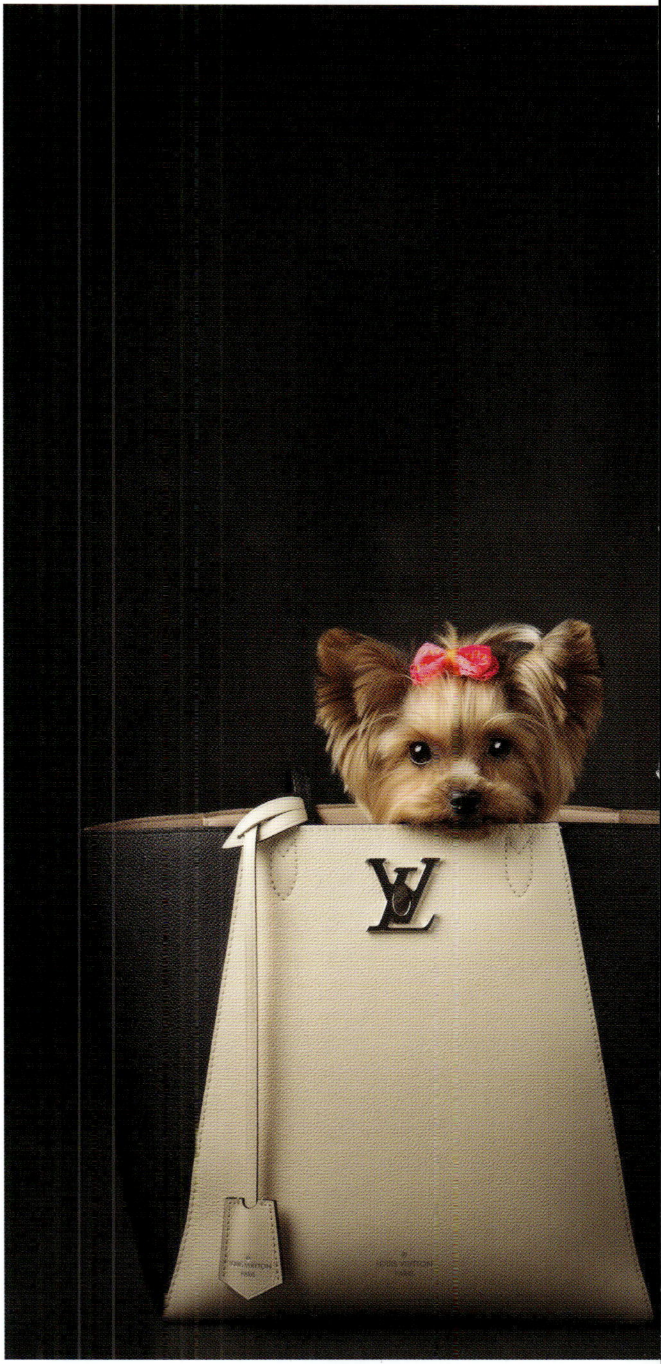

About the Author

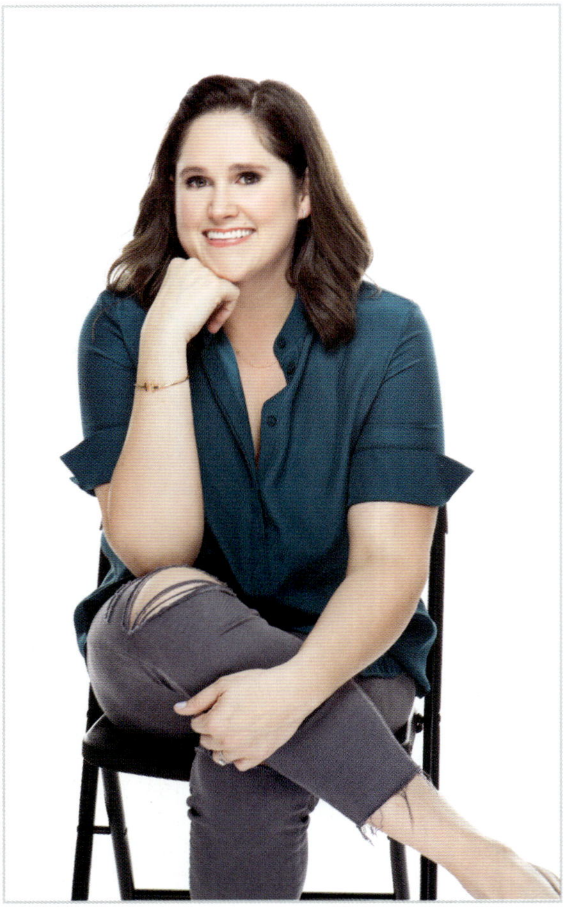

Kim Hartz has always been an animal and photography lover. Over the years, she has honed her art, specializing in pet photography, gaining recognition within the photography industry, and producing award-winning images.

The images Kim takes for her clients capture the unique essence of each subject, and she produces works of art that are both timeless and precious.

Kim teaches pet photography workshops and consults with studios all over the country. She is dedicated and experienced in instructing students on the creative process and building a successful photography business.

Kim is a Master Photographer, Photographic Craftsman, and Certified Professional Photographer.

Introduction

I took this image *(below)* of my parents' dog, Agador, when I was in photography school, and it was my first attempt at a pet portrait. It took this one portrait to make me want to be a pet photographer. Of course, at the time, pet photography was not really a "thing"; it wasn't as popular as it is today. When I proposed the idea of photographing pets, I was laughed at over and over. However, I saw a real opportunity to build a business and craft a niche for myself. It's almost ten years later, and I'm still photographing pets full time. It was a risk I was willing to take, and I couldn't be happier!

Take the time to read through each of the lessons in this book, and practice your craft. Create and find beautiful light. You can turn your passion into a hobby, part-time job, or full-time career.

Let's get started.

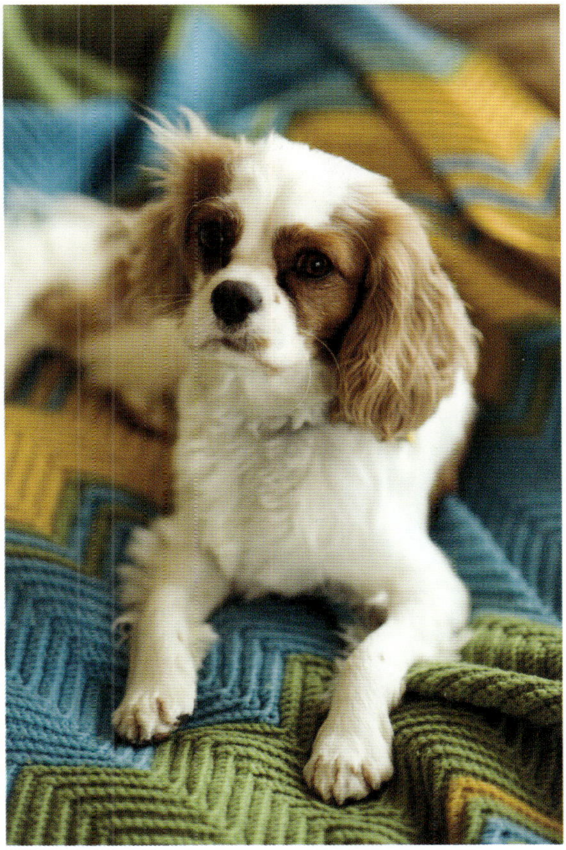

CHAPTER ONE

Working with Dogs

Before we delve into working with dogs in the studio and on location, I want to cover a few housekeeping items you need to be aware of when working with canines (and other pets).

First, you need to make sure that you and your studio are covered when it comes to vaccinations and preventative medications for pets. I work with several rescue groups, and one brought me a

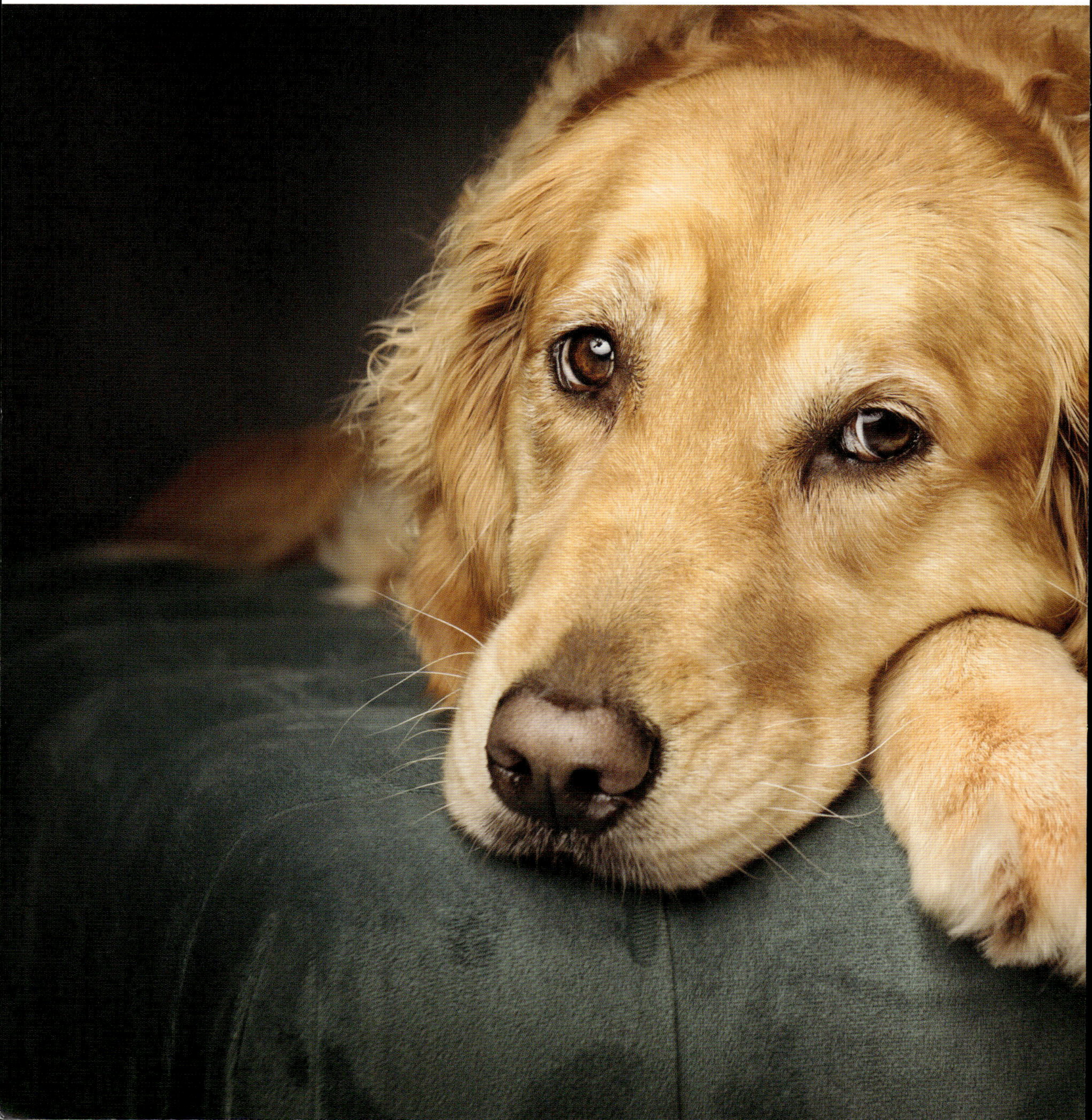

dog with fleas, which meant my studio got fleas. This is a huge problem if you photograph other animals and people in your studio. Make sure your contract outlines that all animals must be up to date on their vaccinations and meds.

There are also some tools you will need to have on hand to be a successful pet photographer. Those include show leads, lint rollers, Nature's Miracle for accidents, treats, and lots of noisemakers! Some of my favorite noisemakers include a squirrel call and an empty water bottle. I also wear lanyards that hold

"Make sure your contract outlines that all animals must be up to date on their vaccinations."

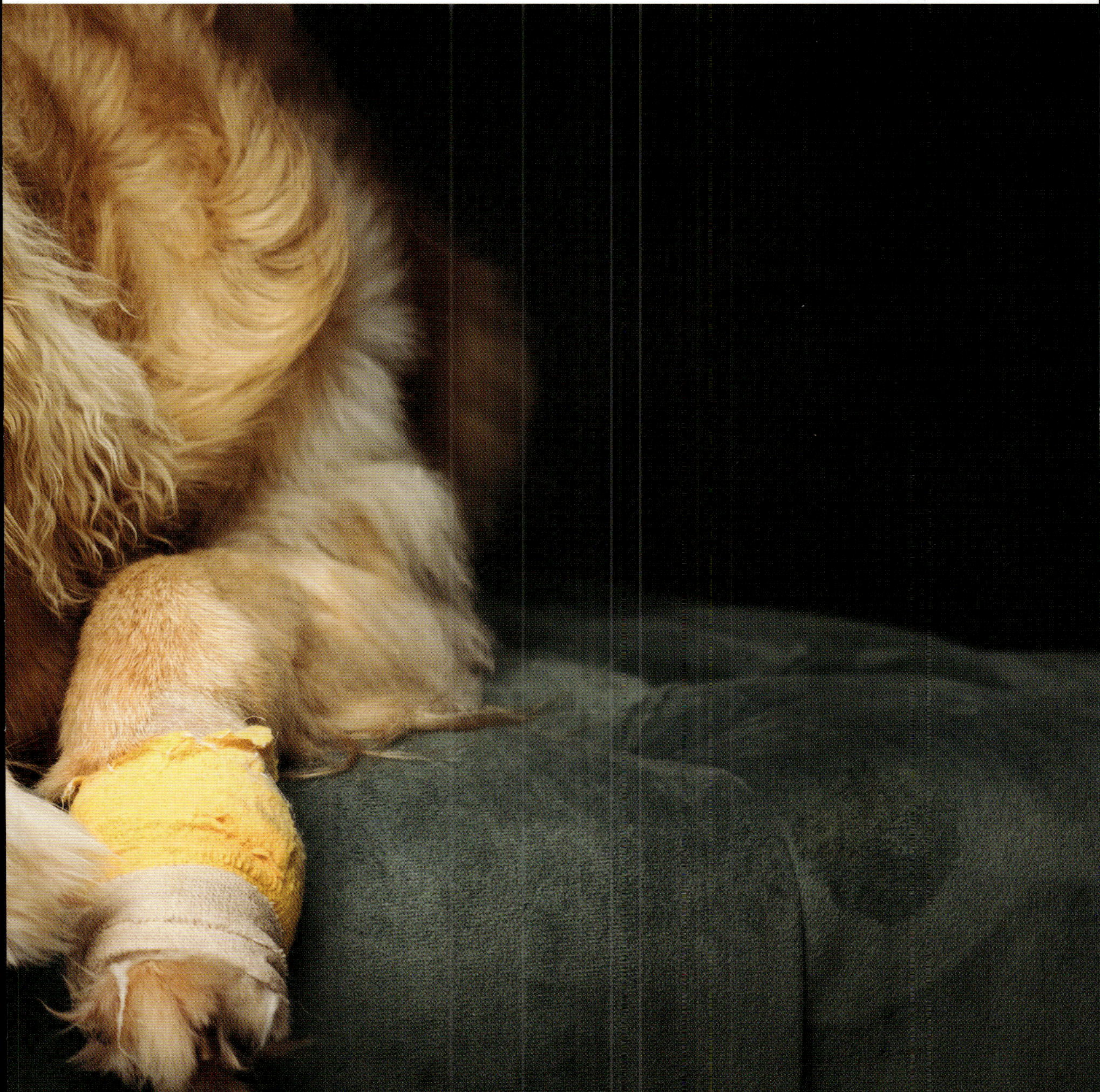

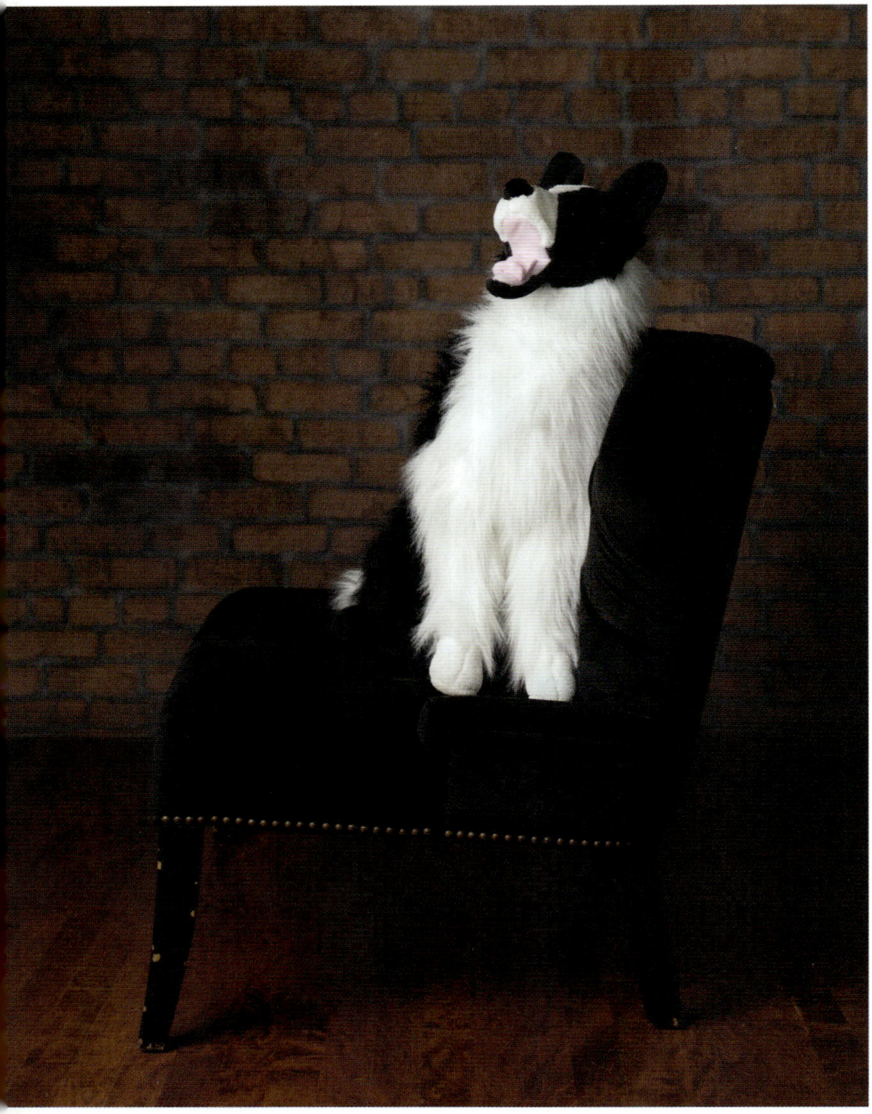

too, and sometimes just jiggling a treat bag or the pup's collar can work, too.

It's also a good idea to get a model to practice with in order to really perfect your lighting. My go-to model is Rozita *(left)*. She is great because she doesn't move! I see more and more pet photographers picking up this type of model because it allows them to work on their lighting without having to wrangle a live animal. I chose this version (there are lots of breeds to choose from!) because she has both black and white fur, which can be a challenge to photograph.

"Always be on the lookout for fun new noises."

lots of animal calls like pheasant, duck, quail, and much more. You can find a lot of these hunting calls at sporting goods stores. Always be on the lookout for fun new noises. Kids' toys—like kazoos and train whistles—are great,

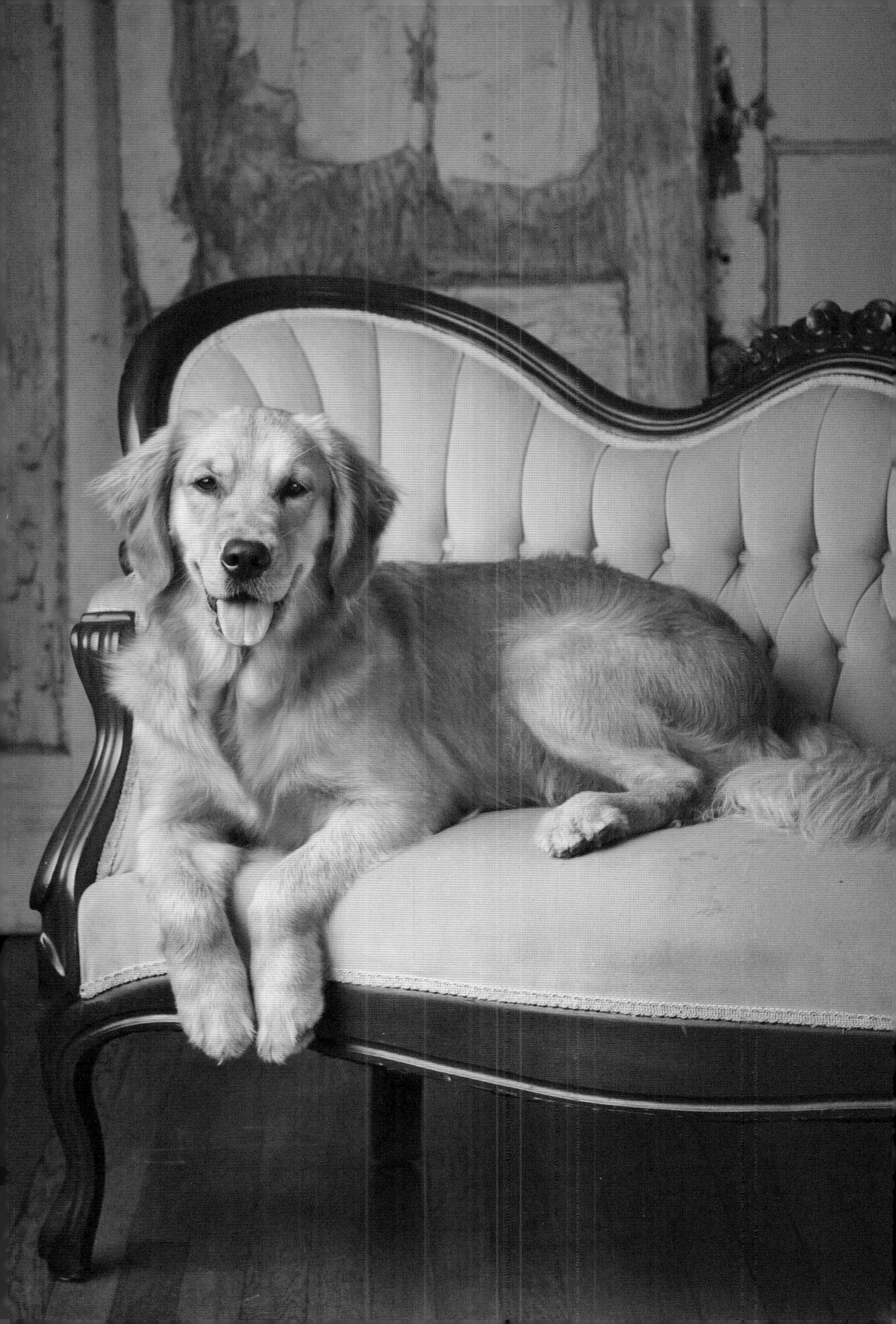

Safety

If you're photographing a dog on location, you need to have them on-leash, for the entire shoot, when outdoors and on location in unfenced areas. The last thing you want is for a pet to get loose and run. This may seem like a no-brainer, but you would be surprised how many people don't practice safety on location. I use show leads; you can also use a retractable leash. Both are easy to remove in postproduction.

" Keep dogs on-leash at all times when outdoors and on location in while in unfenced areas."

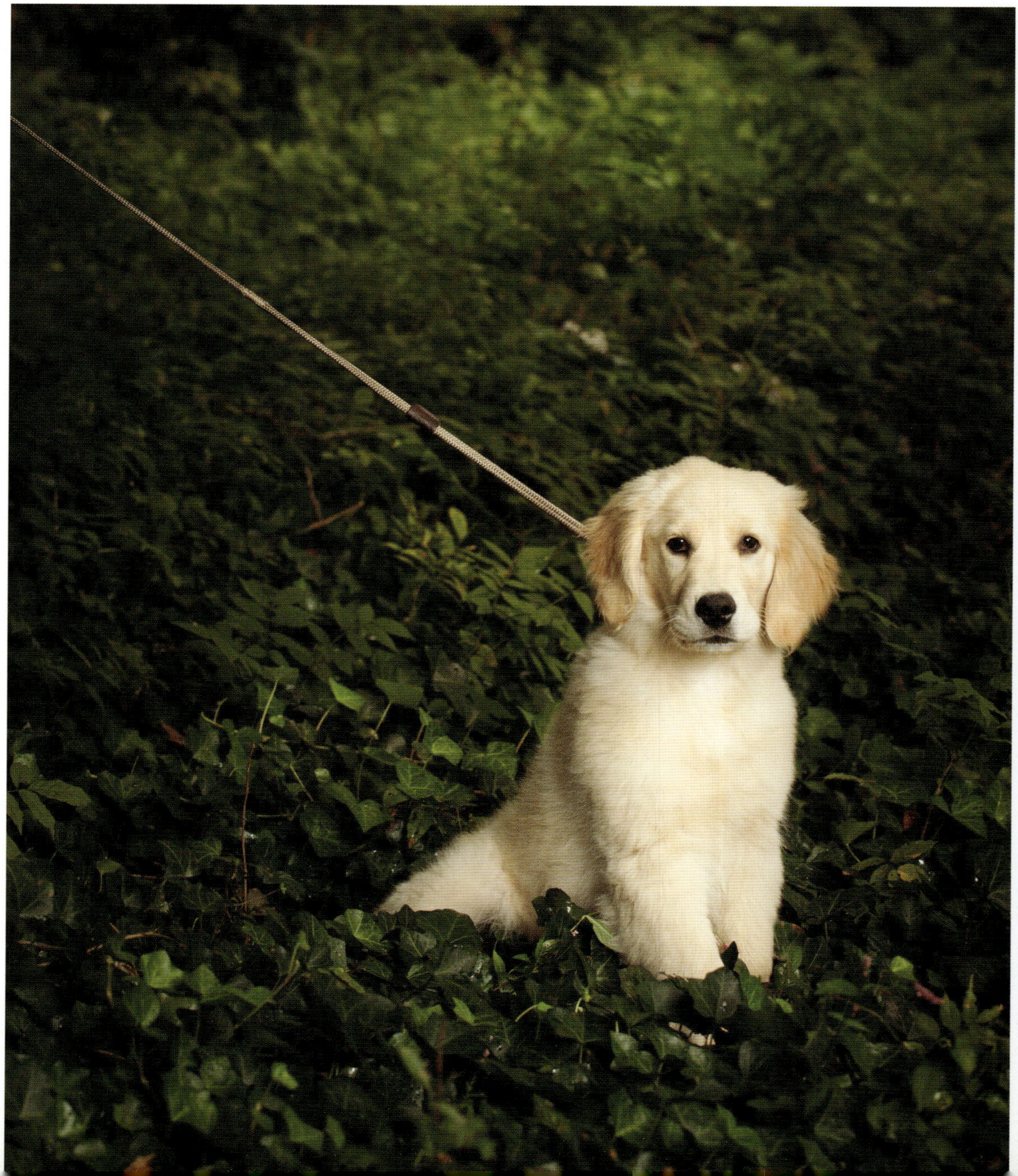

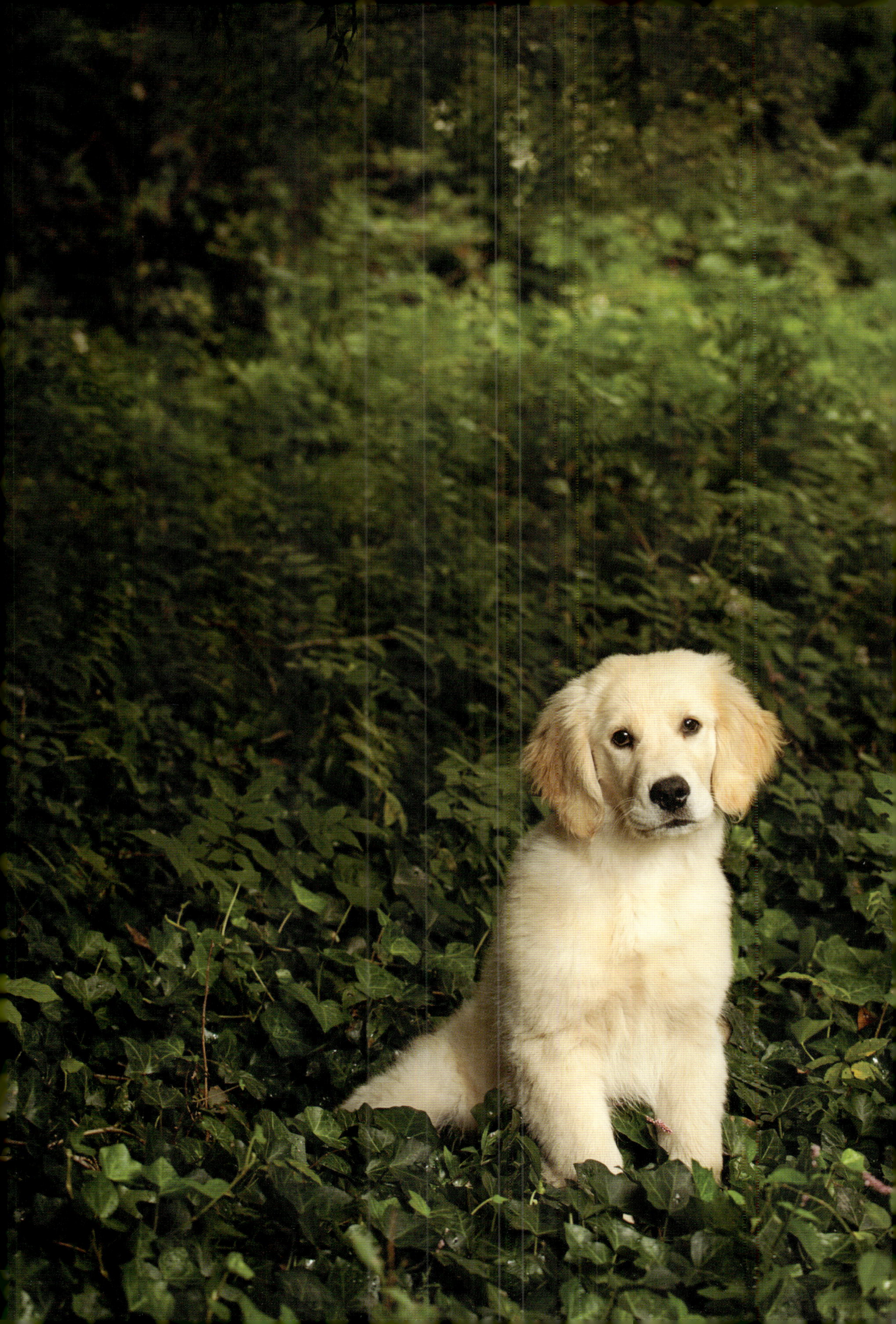

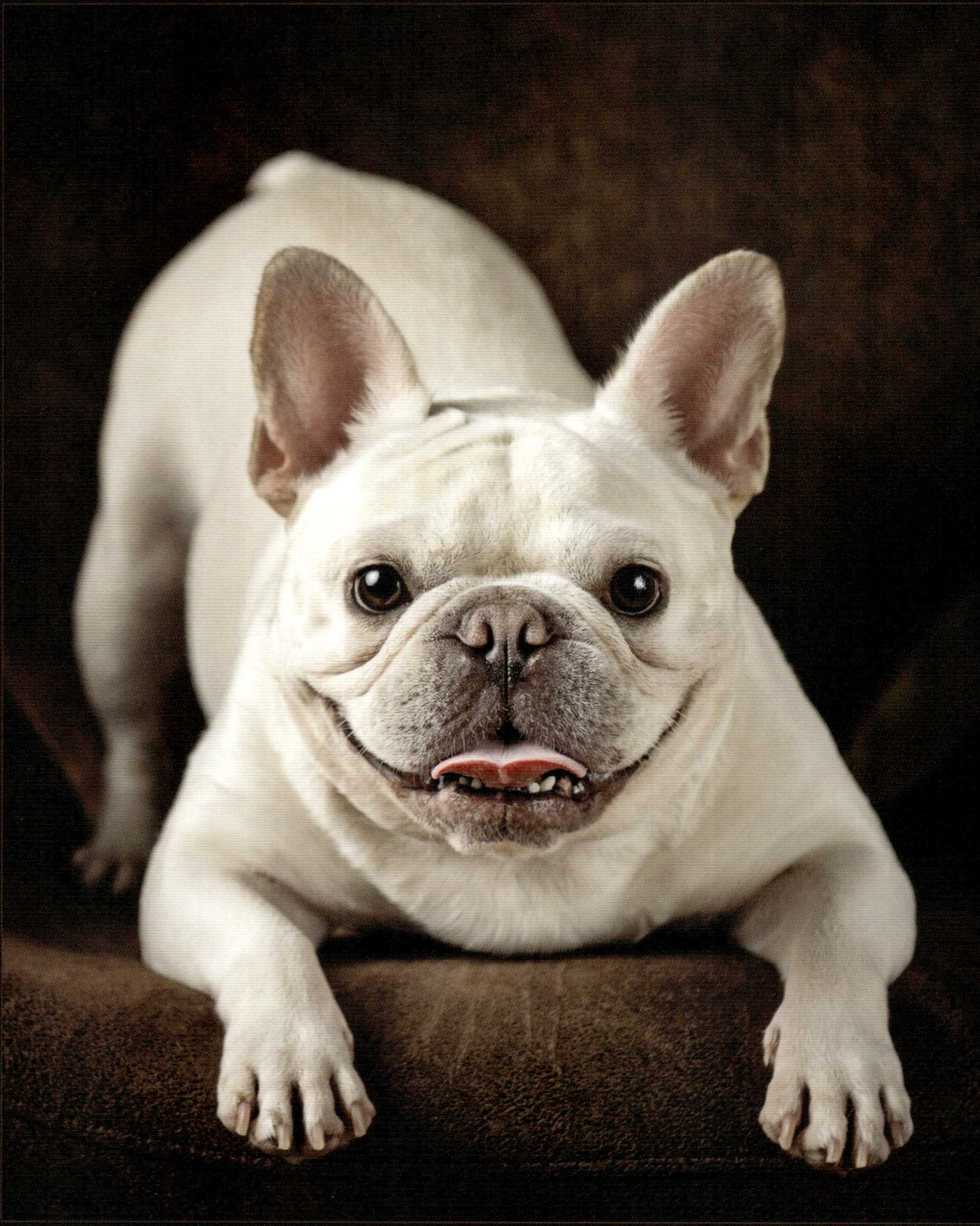

Planning Sessions

My #1 tip for getting great expressions is, conduct a planning session. This book is mainly about photographing pets with artificial light in-studio and on location, but if you can't get great expressions, you won't get a great image, even if your lighting is spot-on.

A planning session is critical for pet photographers because it allows you to gather all of the information you need for a successful session.

During the planning session, you meet with the owner and dog and can learn about the pet: what they like, dislike, are afraid of, and respond to. You can also gauge the dog's obedience level, which will help you determine how tough your session will be. You can hone in on keywords the dog may respond to during the shoot. I've heard some random keywords from pet parents, but knowing them will make it much easier to get the pet's attention.

"For great expressions, conduct a planning session."

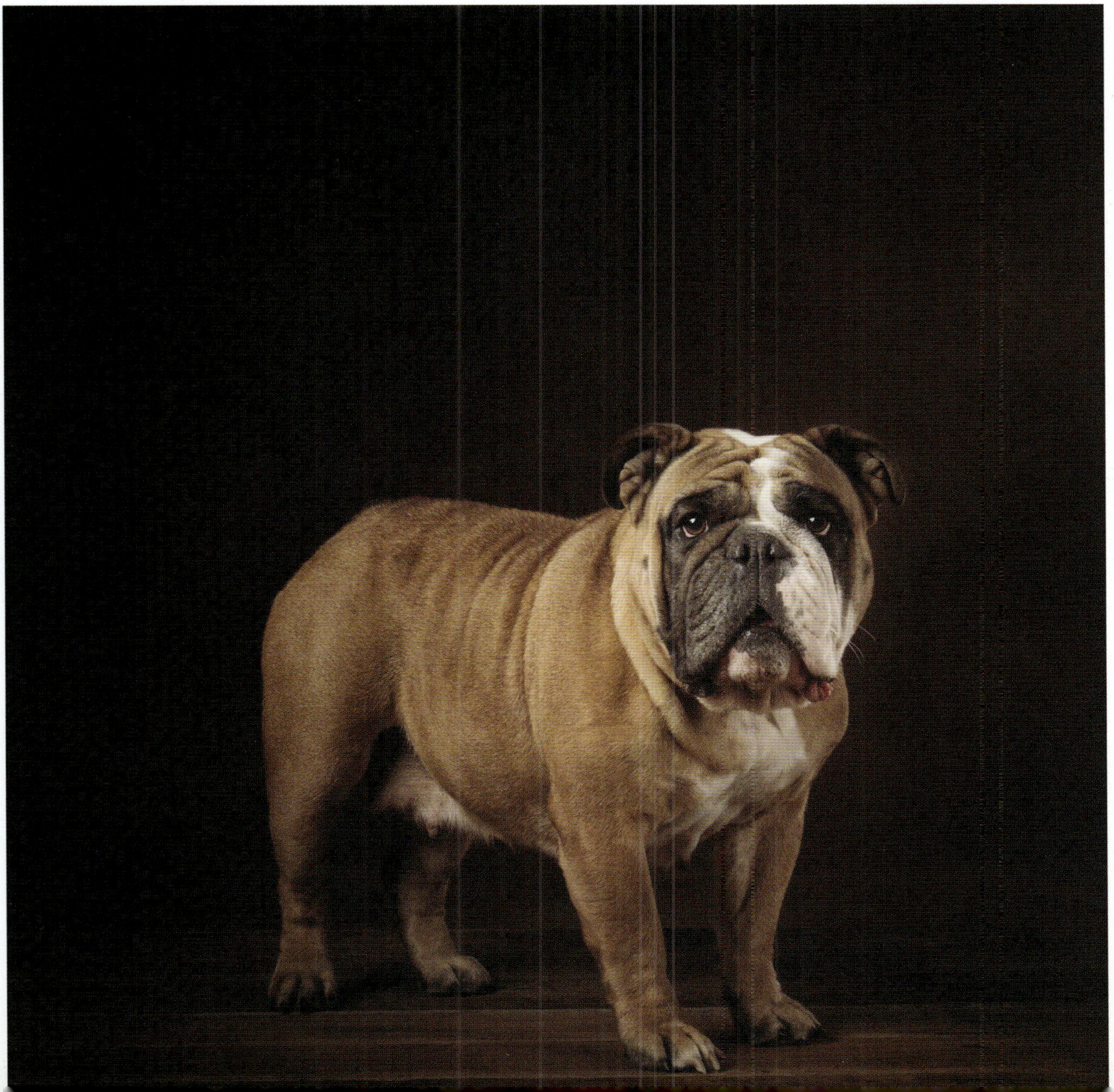

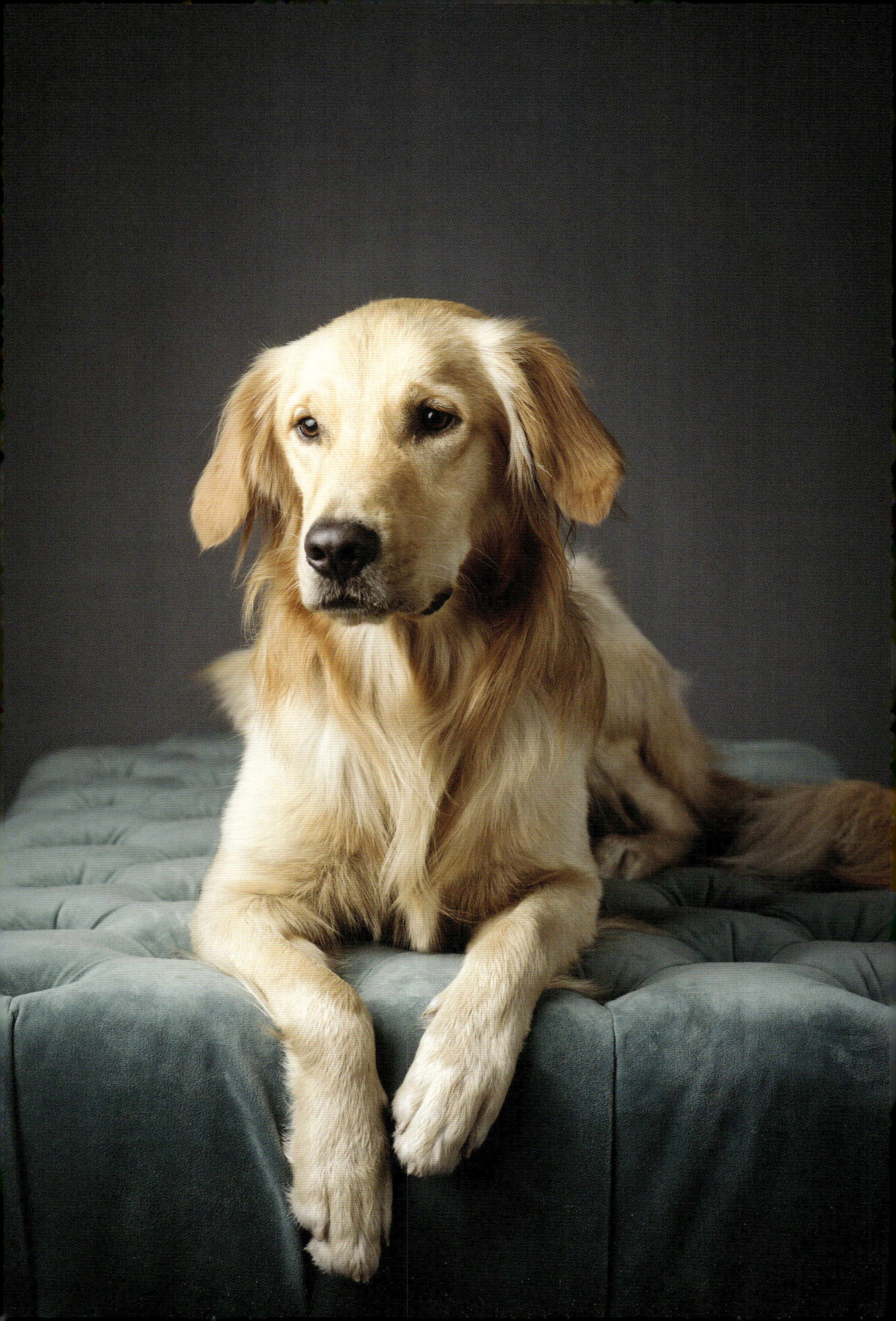

For example, I photographed this Golden Retriever in-studio. He was scared of the equipment but was ball obsessed. Everything I tried, from treats to toys, did nothing—but once I pulled out a ball, he was ready to sit and pose. That second of distraction allowed me to snag the image on the top right, which I love!

Do your homework. Find out what your subject responds to. It makes a big difference in how your final images will turn out.

Here's a great trick: to get a dog to look off-camera, roll something, like a tennis ball, in that direction. Just be prepared for the dog to jump and run after it.

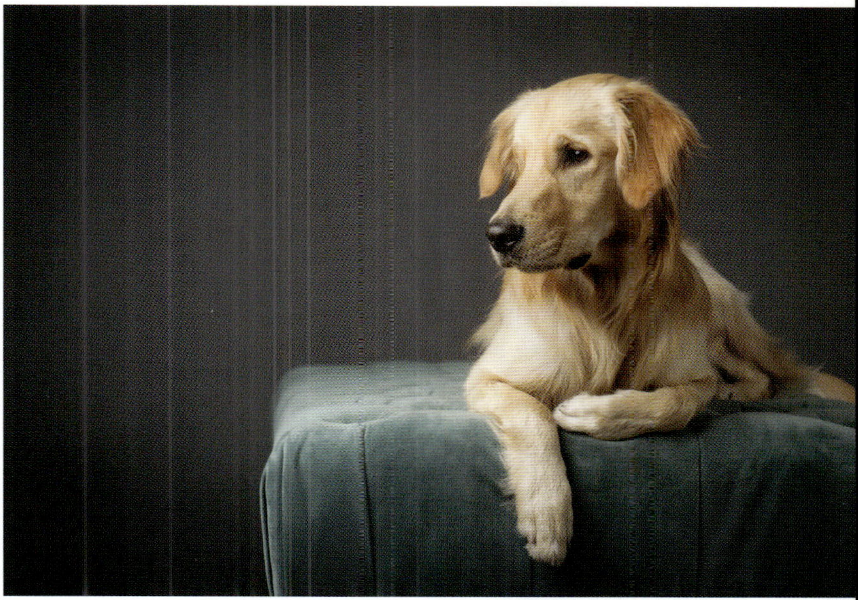

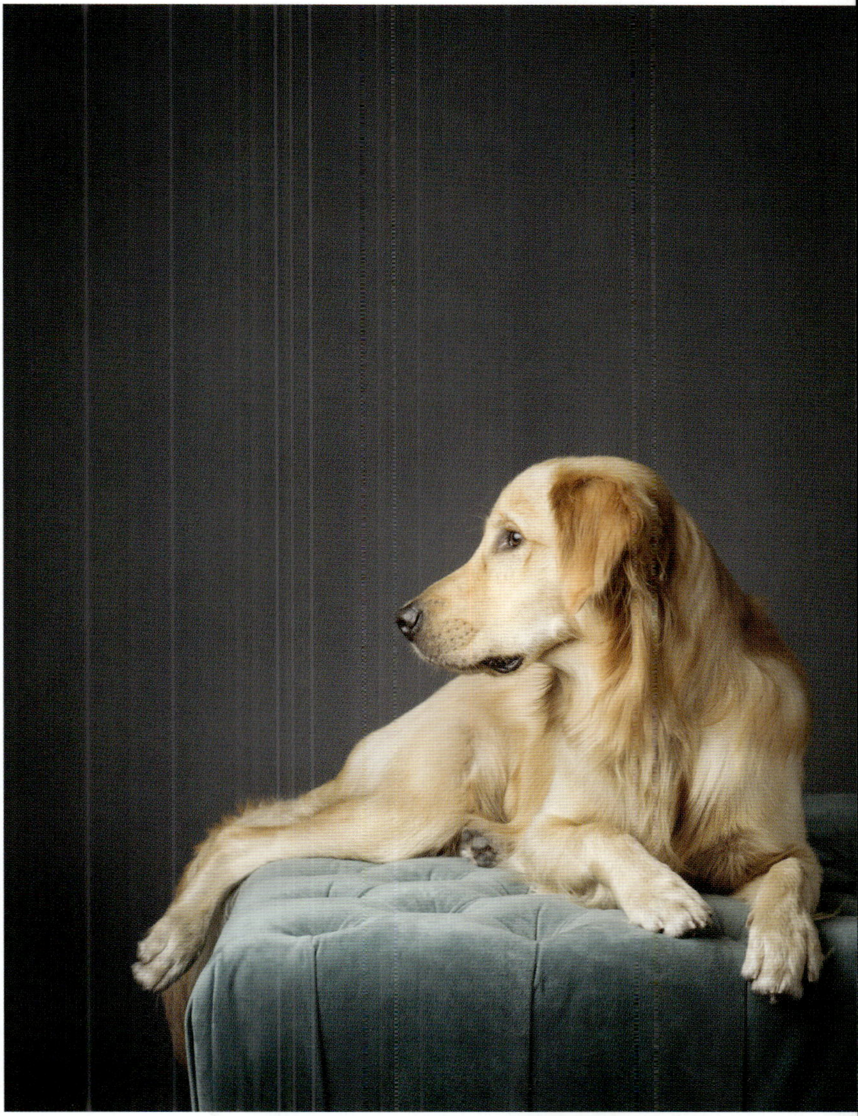

"Do your homework. Find out what your subject responds to."

CHAPTER TWO

In the Studio

Why would you want to add artificial lighting to your pet photography toolbox? Well, adding this technique can set you apart from the thousands of other pet photographers competing for the same client. It can also take your images from okay to professional in one click! Even if you don't have a studio, adding in a light on location (either outdoors or in a client's home) can add so much depth and professionalism to your images. The key is to learn how to balance your flash outdoors, which we will talk about in a later chapter.

The majority of the images you see in this book have been minimally retouched. Some doggie drool may have

"Add artificial light to set your work apart."

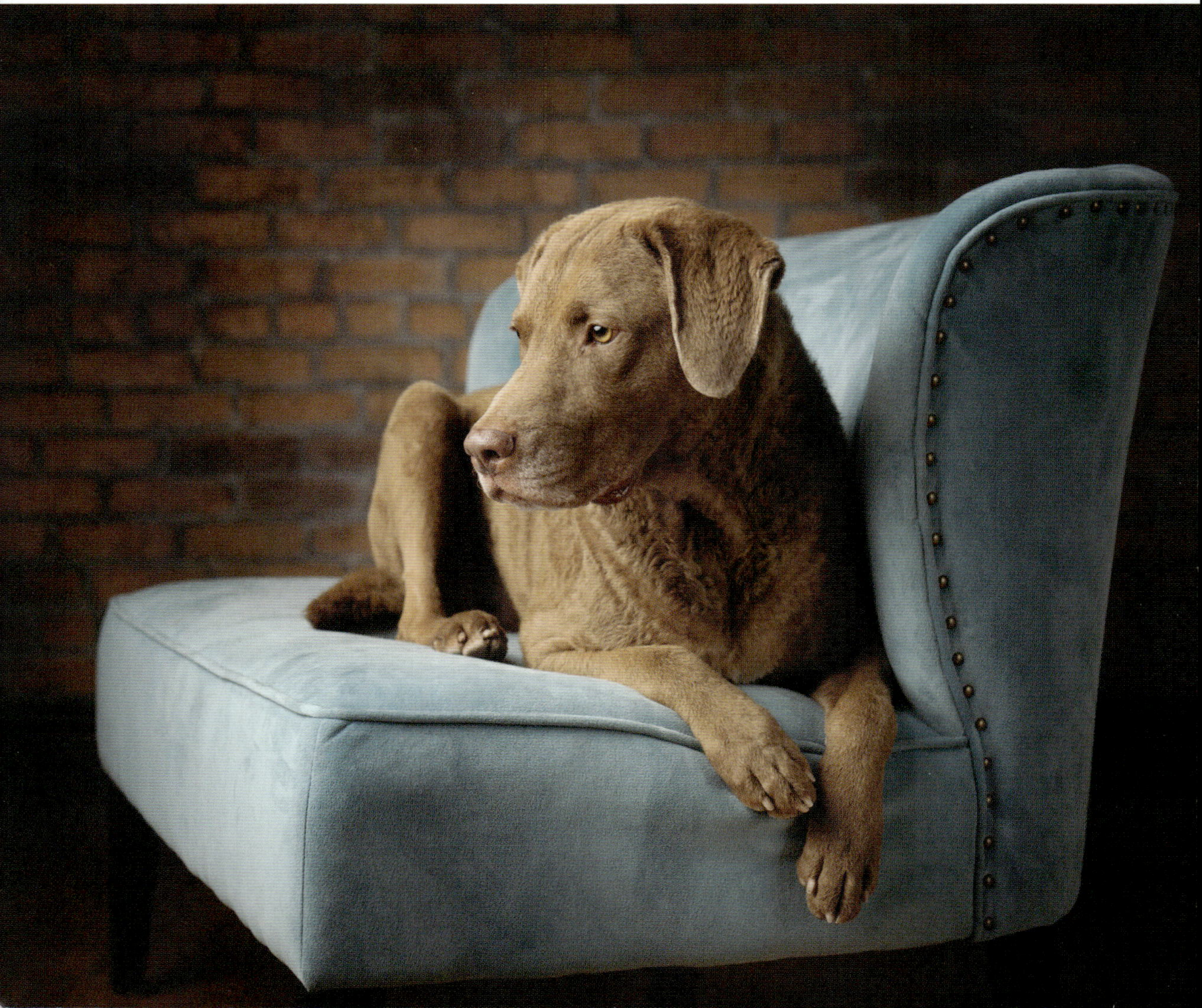

been removed, and fur has been retouched out from the furniture or floor, but the light you see on the pet is straight out of the camera. I am not a big fan of sitting in front of my computer, retouching images. I prefer to light as best I can so I have minimal retouching work to do later. Everything I teach in this book is about achieving the perfect light in-camera.

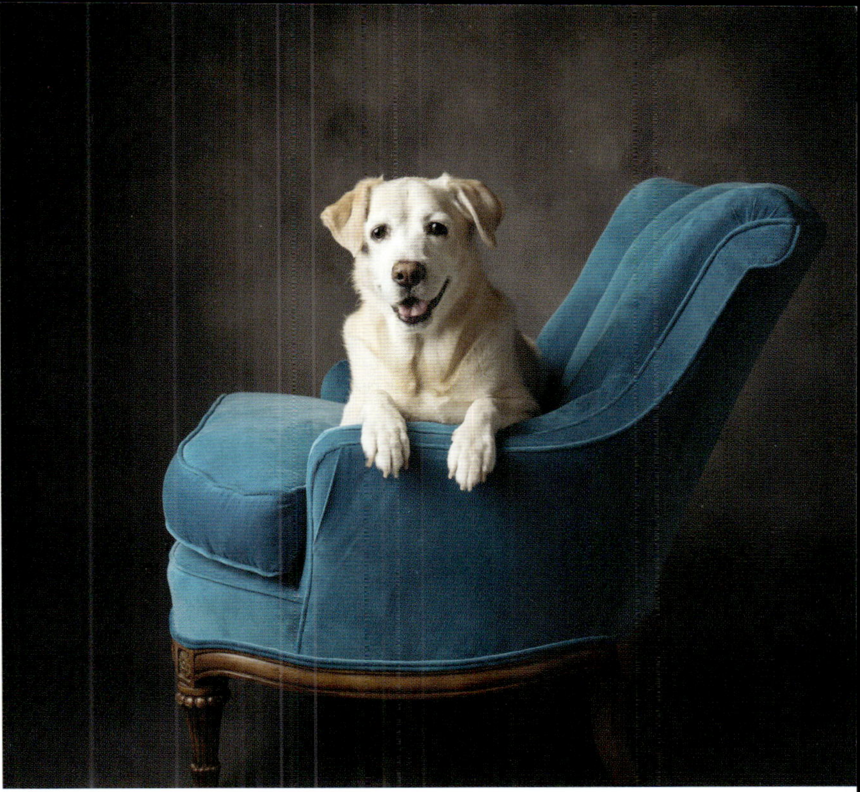

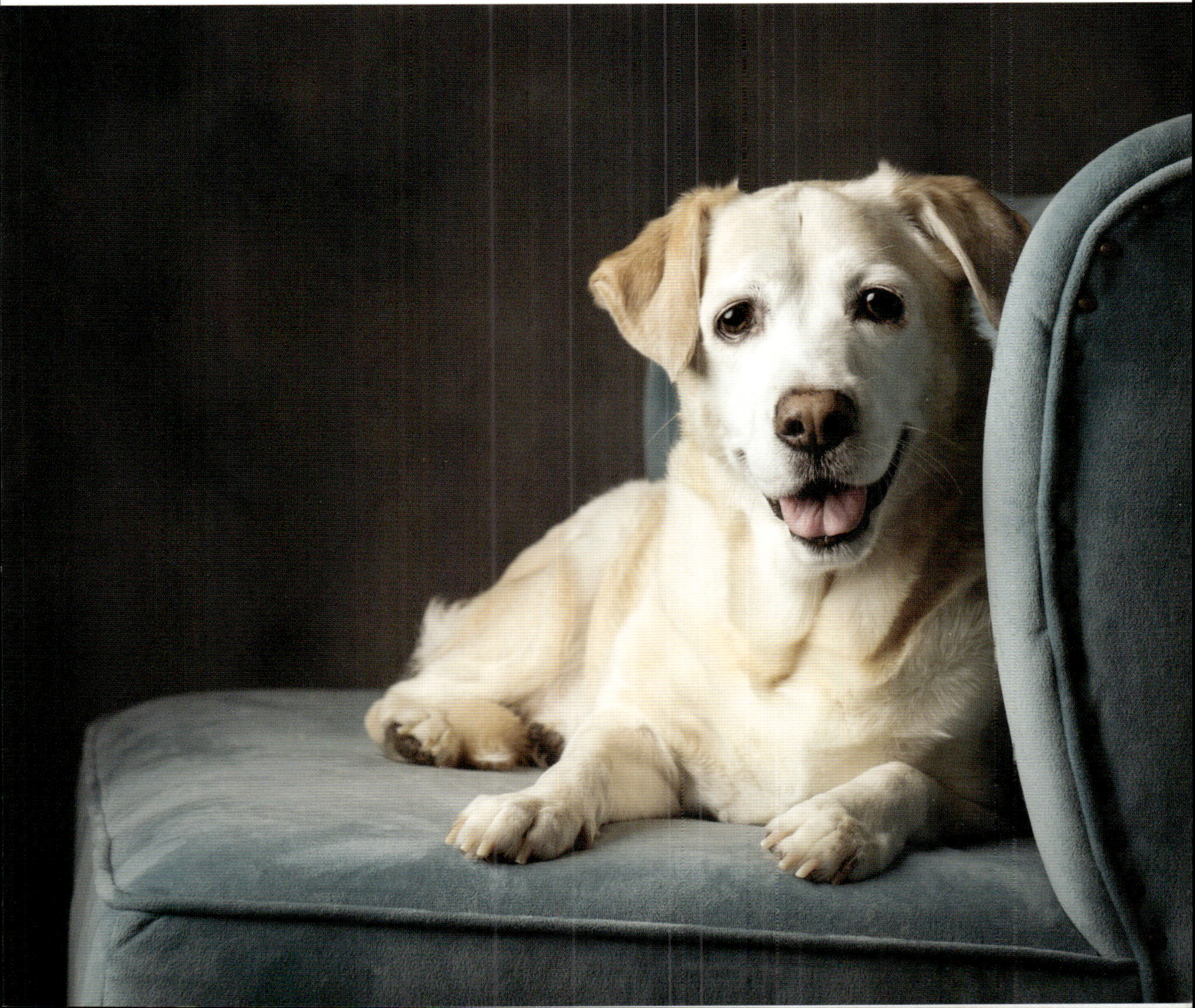

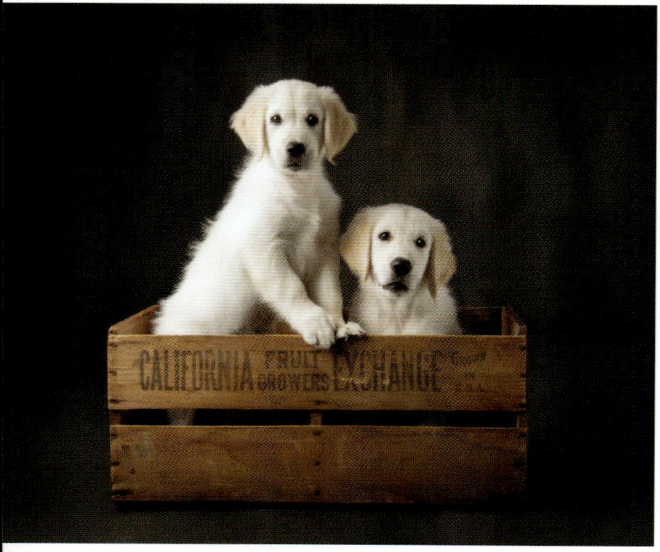

Before we get into the nuts and bolts of lighting dogs in the studio and techniques for using off-camera flash on location, we need to touch on some of the equipment you will need. There are a lot of different options for lighting equipment, but I'm going to limit my discussion to what works best for dogs and what will be easiest for you, the photographer. This is not a book about lighting equipment. There are tons of titles on that topic if you need a better background on lighting options.

When working in the studio with pets running around, you want to keep things as clean as possible. You don't want cords lying on the floor for puppies to chew.

I have found that working with monolights—self-contained flash units, each with independent power supply and controls—are ideal. Monolights are easy to adjust and move around your studio space. There are a wide range of monolights on the market, and you have a lot of options when it comes to price range, as well.

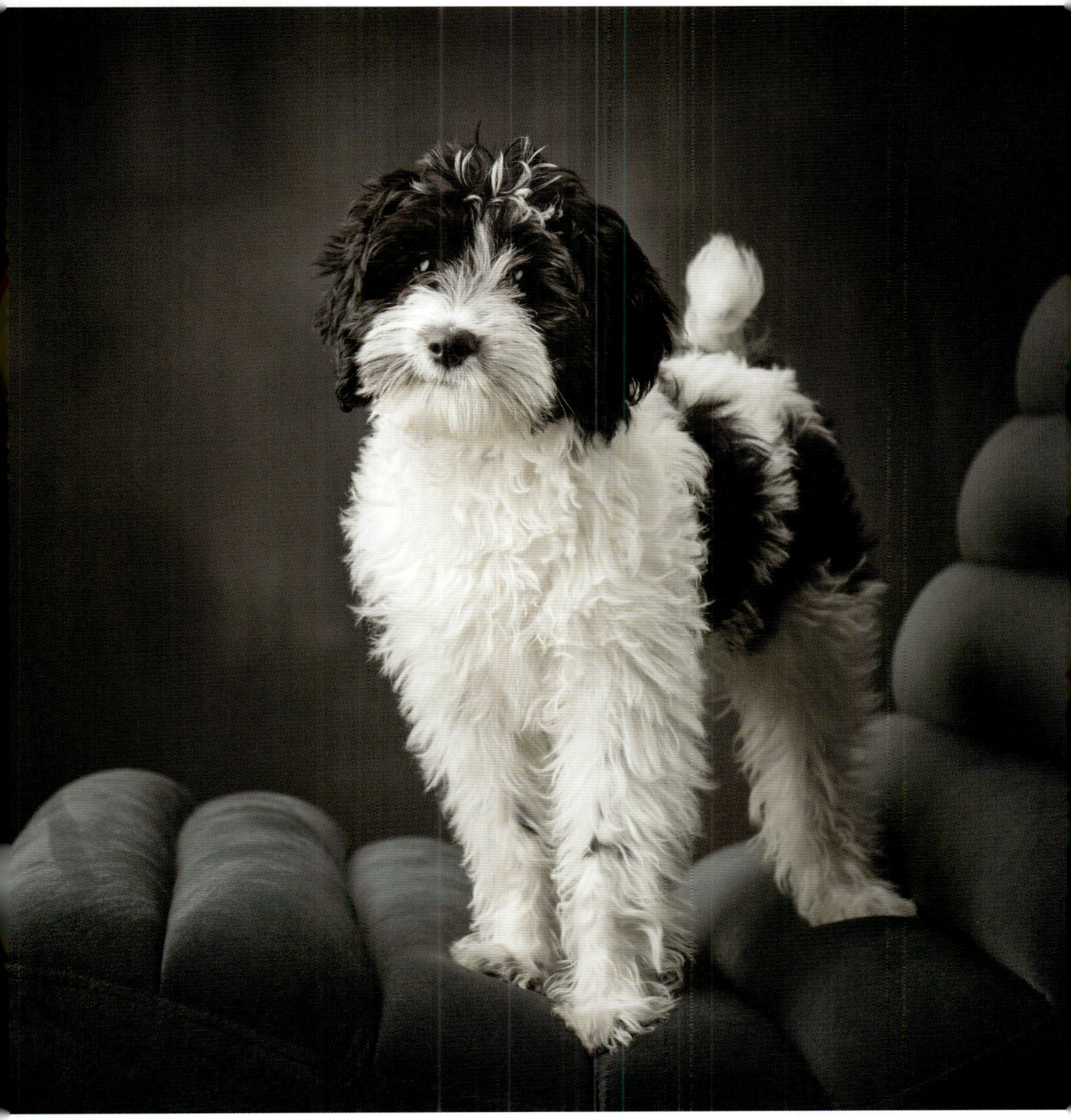

"Keep your studio space clean and well-organized to ensure everyone's safety."

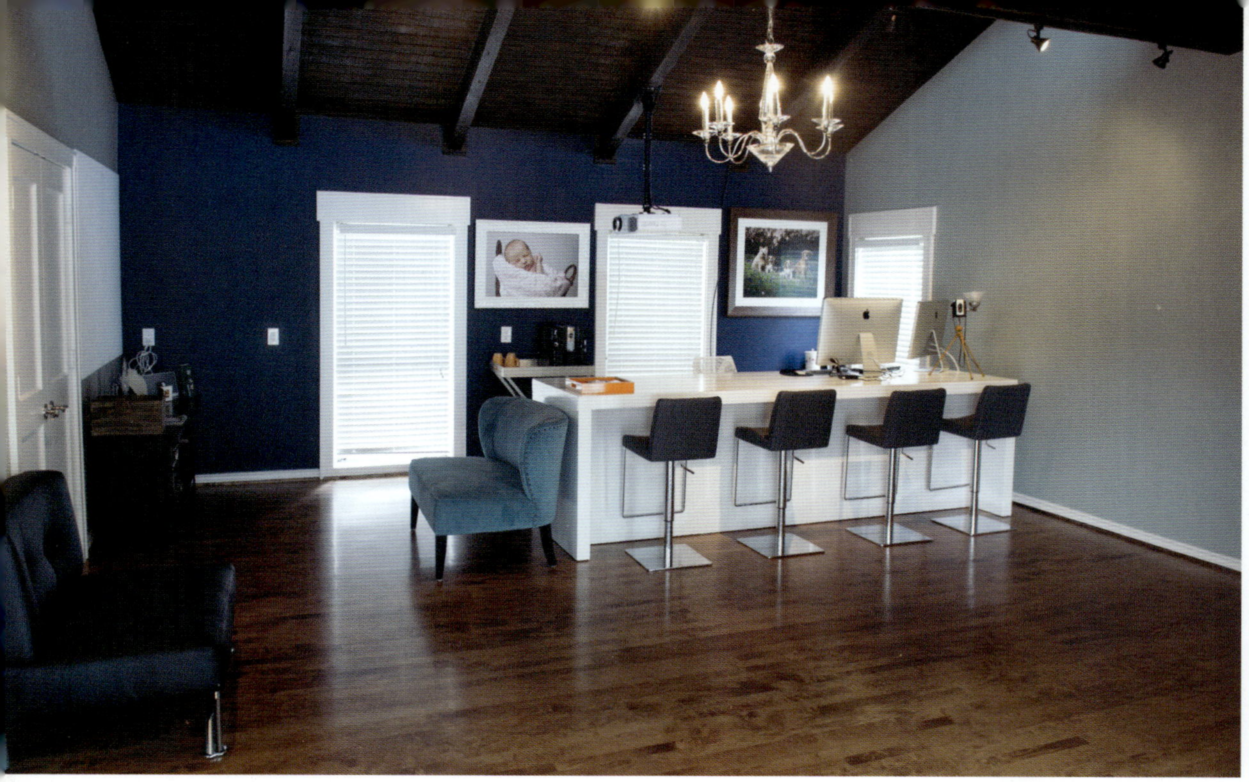

Throughout my career as a pet photographer, I've used everything from power packs to monolights. I currently work with one or two monolights in my studio, depending on what I'm trying to achieve in my photograph.

If you can mount your lights to your ceiling and get everything off of the floor, that is ideal; however, my studio space just doesn't allow for that, as it has vaulted ceilings. So, I keep everything tucked away as neatly as possible.

Do your own research when it comes to selecting equipment. Determine what best suits your needs and fits your budget.

When you are first starting with studio lighting for pets, you don't need to go crazy. There's no need to splurge on lighting kits or to buy multiple lights. You can create beautiful pet images with just one light. Most of my studio pet portraits are made with just one light, as are the majority of my on-location shots. The key is understanding where to position the light, how to best position the subjects in relation to the light, and getting that perfect expression. There are, of course, cases where you may want to use more than one light. I will cover that in a later chapter as well.

"Don't go crazy buying lighting kits or multiple lights. You can create a beautiful image with just one light."

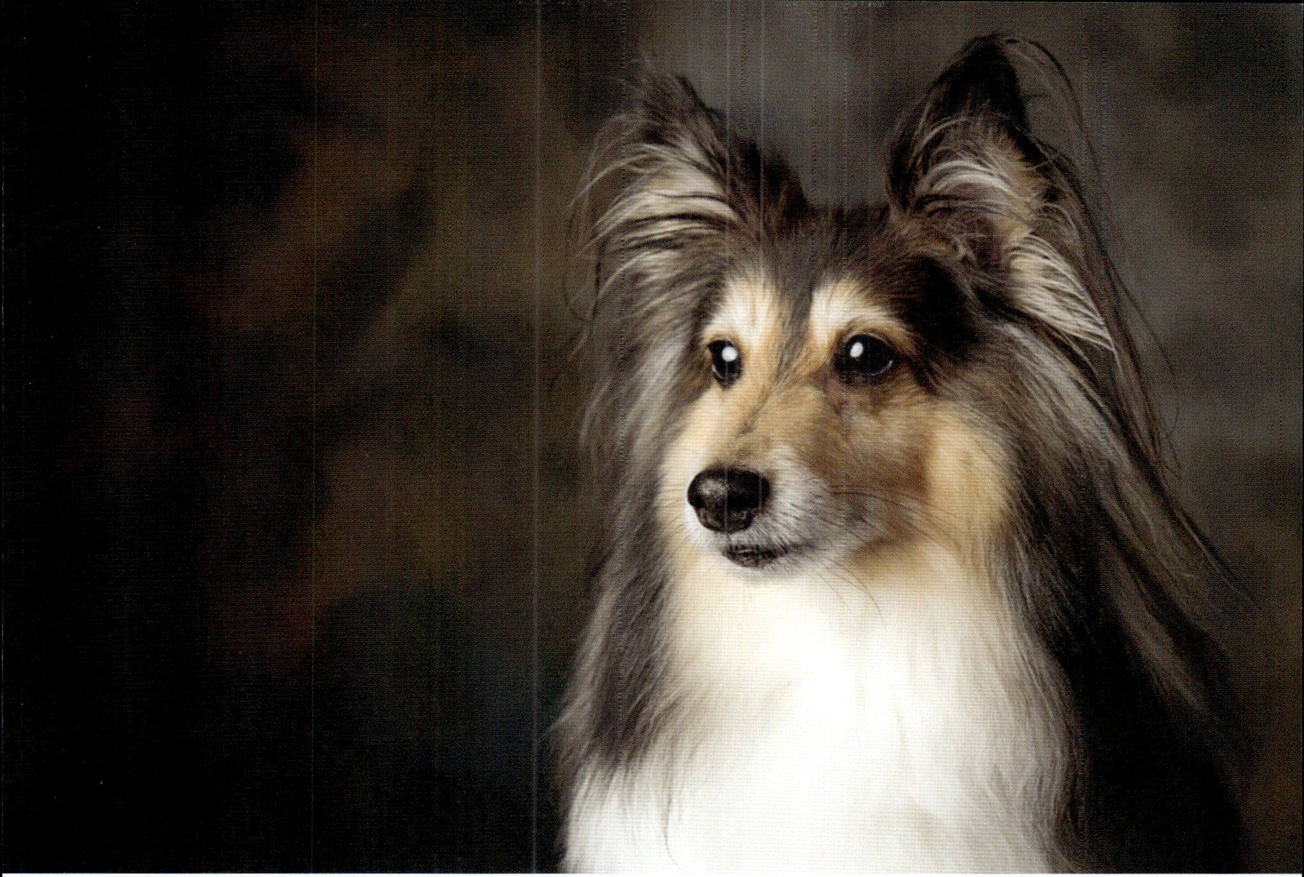

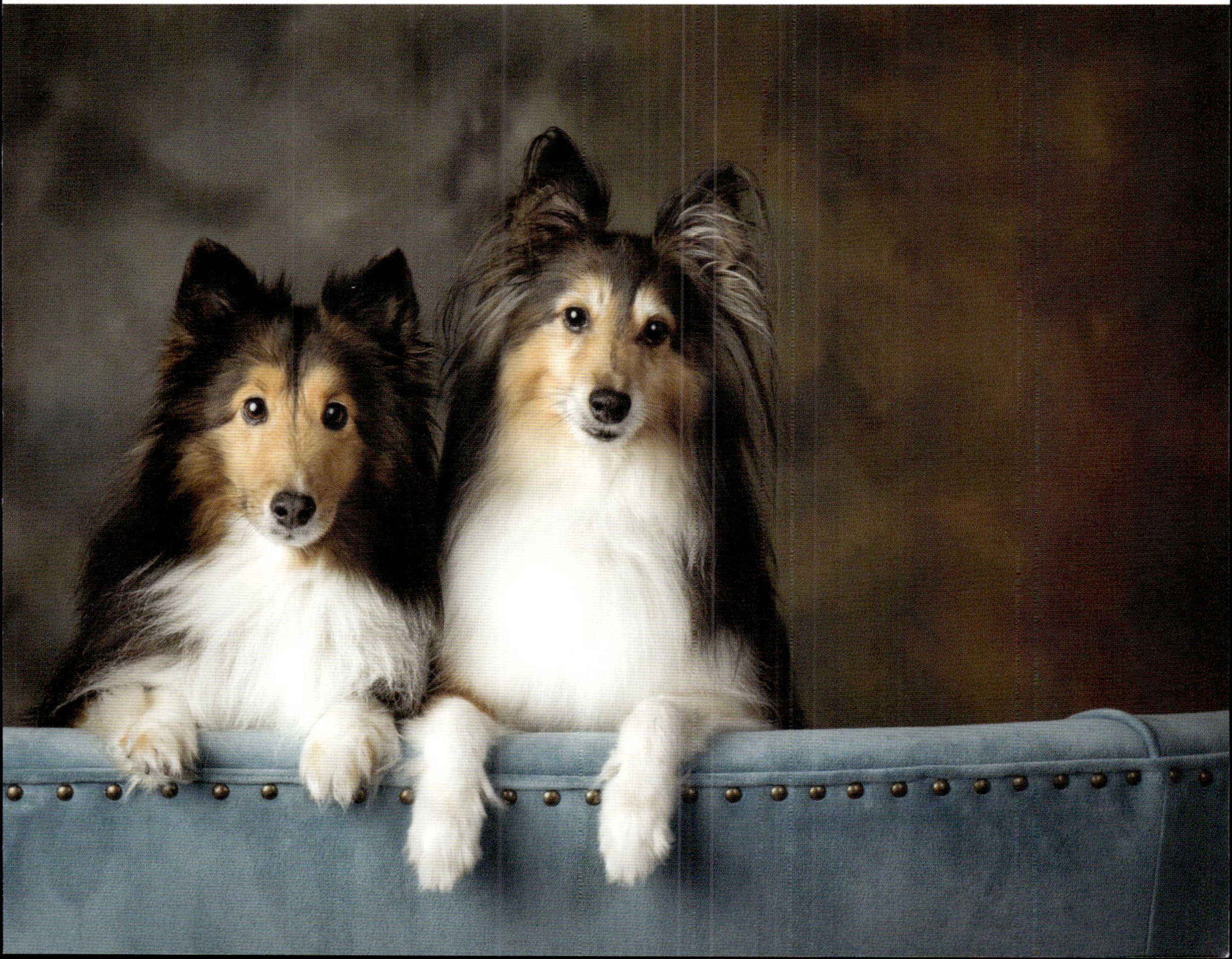

You will also want to consider using some tools called light modifiers to achieve perfect lighting for your pet portraits. I have used many different light modifiers throughout my career, but the thing they all have in common is that they are a pretty decent size.

When I opened my studio, I used a 4x6-foot Larson softbox, which I worked with for years. I paired it with a 42x72-inch silver reflector on a stand, also from Larson. Later, I switched to a 7-foot octabox, which turned out to be a little too big. These days, I use a 5-foot octabox from Profoto. The key is, the bigger the better (in most cases!).

The size of the dog doesn't matter when choosing a modifier. I use my 5-foot octabox for all sizes of pups, from a tiny Frenchie to a giant Mastiff.

A large modifier is important because we want nice, soft, diffused light. Also, and more importantly, we want a little wiggle room if our subject moves around, which is inevitable when you're photographing pets. With a large softbox, you have a little room to continue photographing, even if your subject moves. The key is to position the pet at the back of the softbox, or toward the back edge of it, so you will get decent light on them even if they move toward you.

"Select a large modifier for soft, diffuse light."

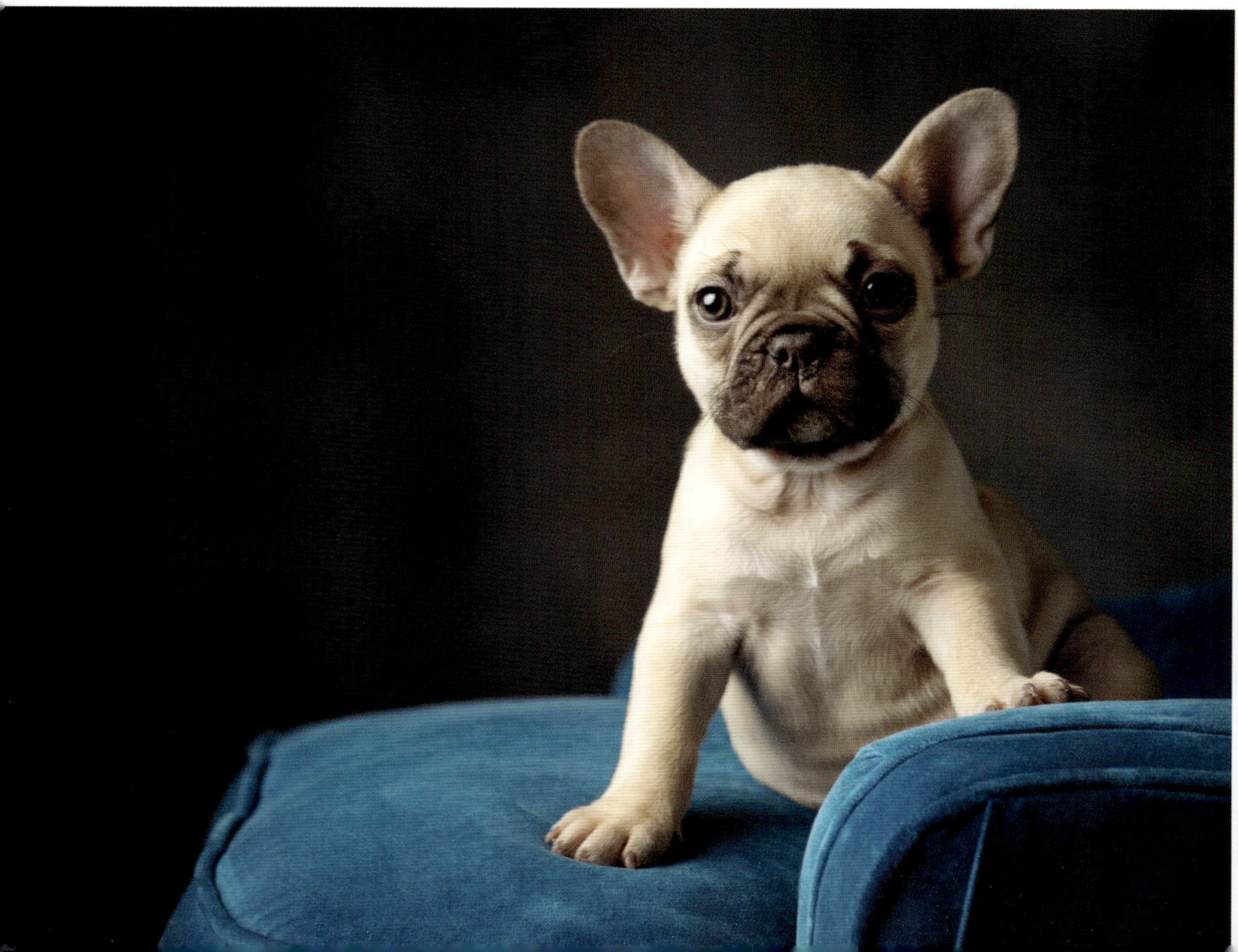

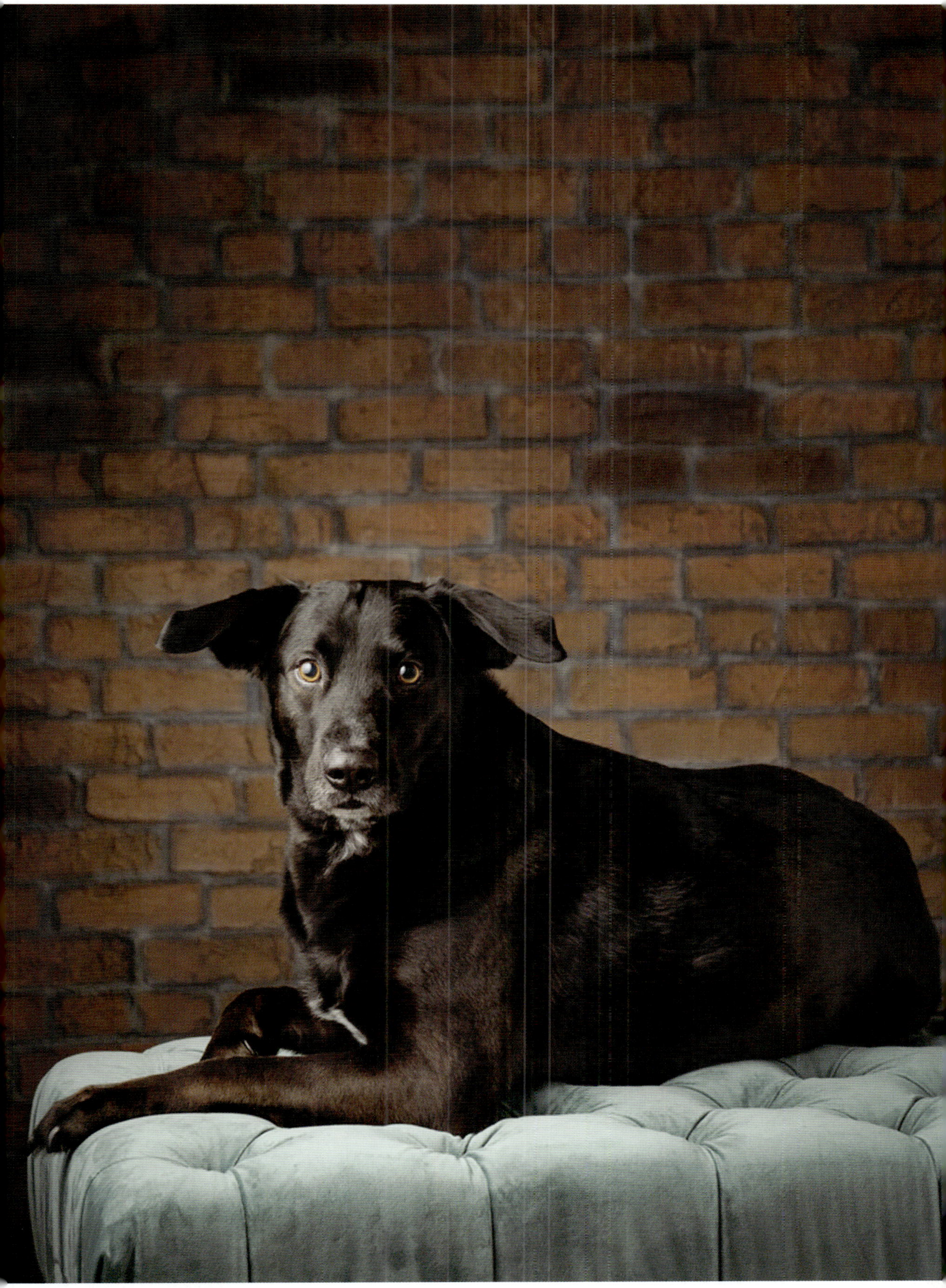

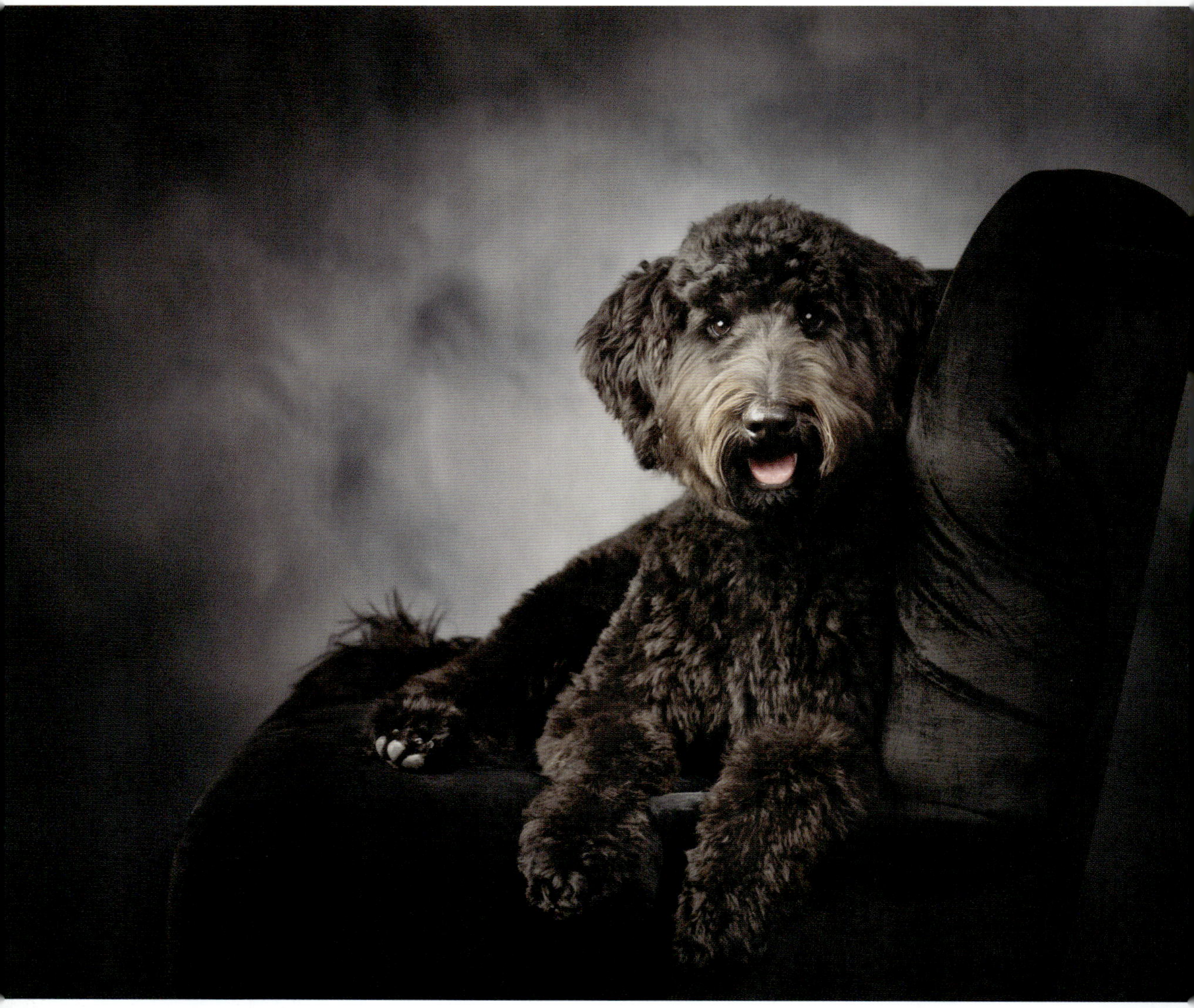

There are other light modifiers you may want to consider, as well. If you do decide to use two lights, you may want to look into an umbrella or a strip softbox. An umbrella is a more cost-effective option, but it doesn't shape the light as much as you may want. You will have more control over where the light goes if you invest in a strip softbox, or a smaller softbox, to use as a fill light.

I use a 12x24-inch strip softbox as a hair light and a fill light when needed in my studio. I typically use it as a hair light if I have dog whose fur is a similar color to my backdrop, like in the image above. You really don't want the dog's fur to blend in with the background.

"Add a strip softbox or a smaller softbox if you use a two-light setup."

I love darker, mid- to low-key images, and I achieve this look by using a gobo, or a flag—a device used to block light from striking the background, or any other area that you want to restrict light in. You can invest in a commercial gobo or flag, but a piece of cardboard or any other device that blocks light will do.

Notice that the left side of this image is darker, making the background less important. That was done with a gobo.

You can see where the gobo goes in relation to the light and the background in the diagram below.

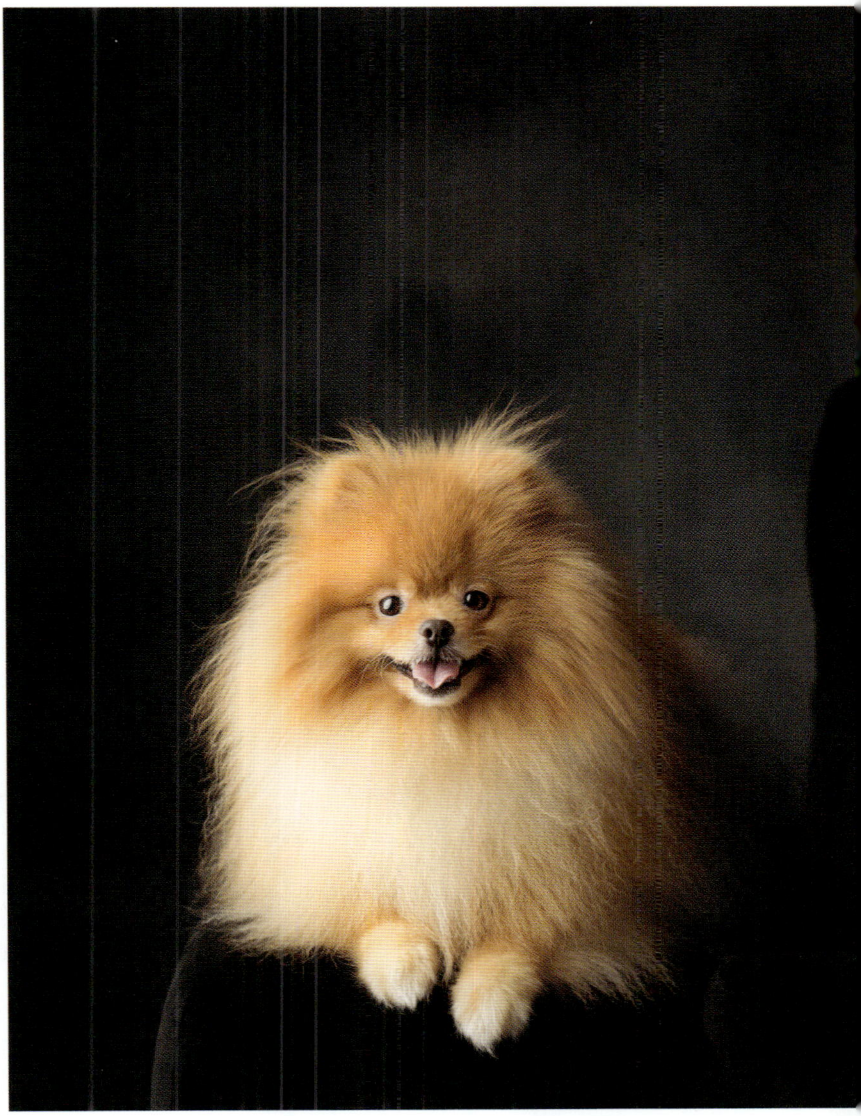

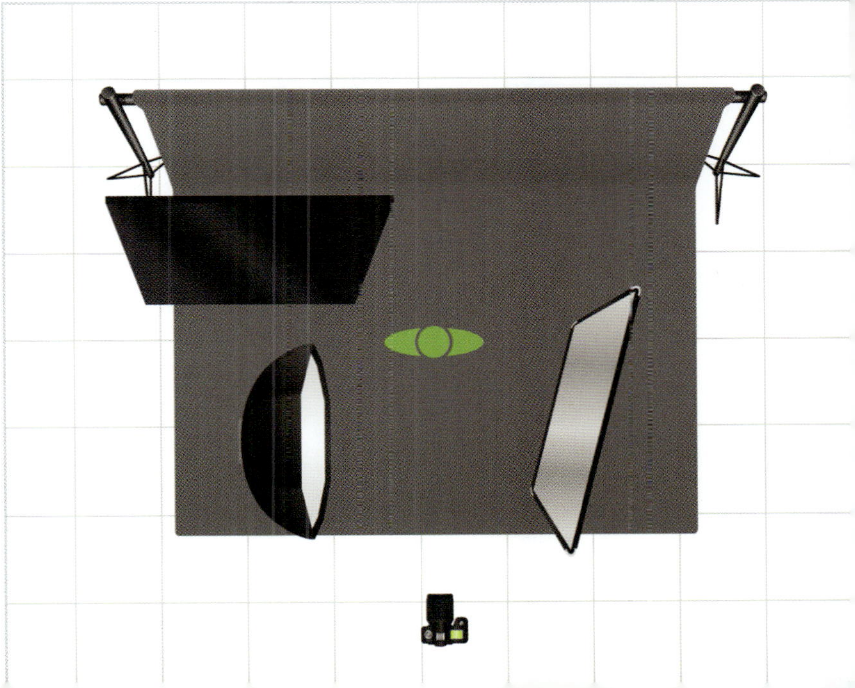

White Balance

Different types of flashes have slightly different color temperatures, which may create a color cast on fur. Before every session, I set my white balance in-camera using a gray target. Check your camera's manual to see how to do it on your specific camera. If you prefer, you can simply take a photo of your gray target or card and then, with one click in Lightroom, you can color balance all of your images.

Setting the white balance is a good habit to get into because, when you do, you can ensure the whites in the dog's fur are actually white.

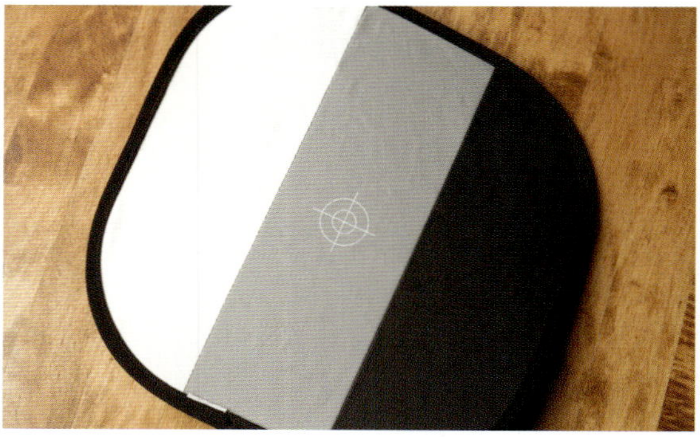

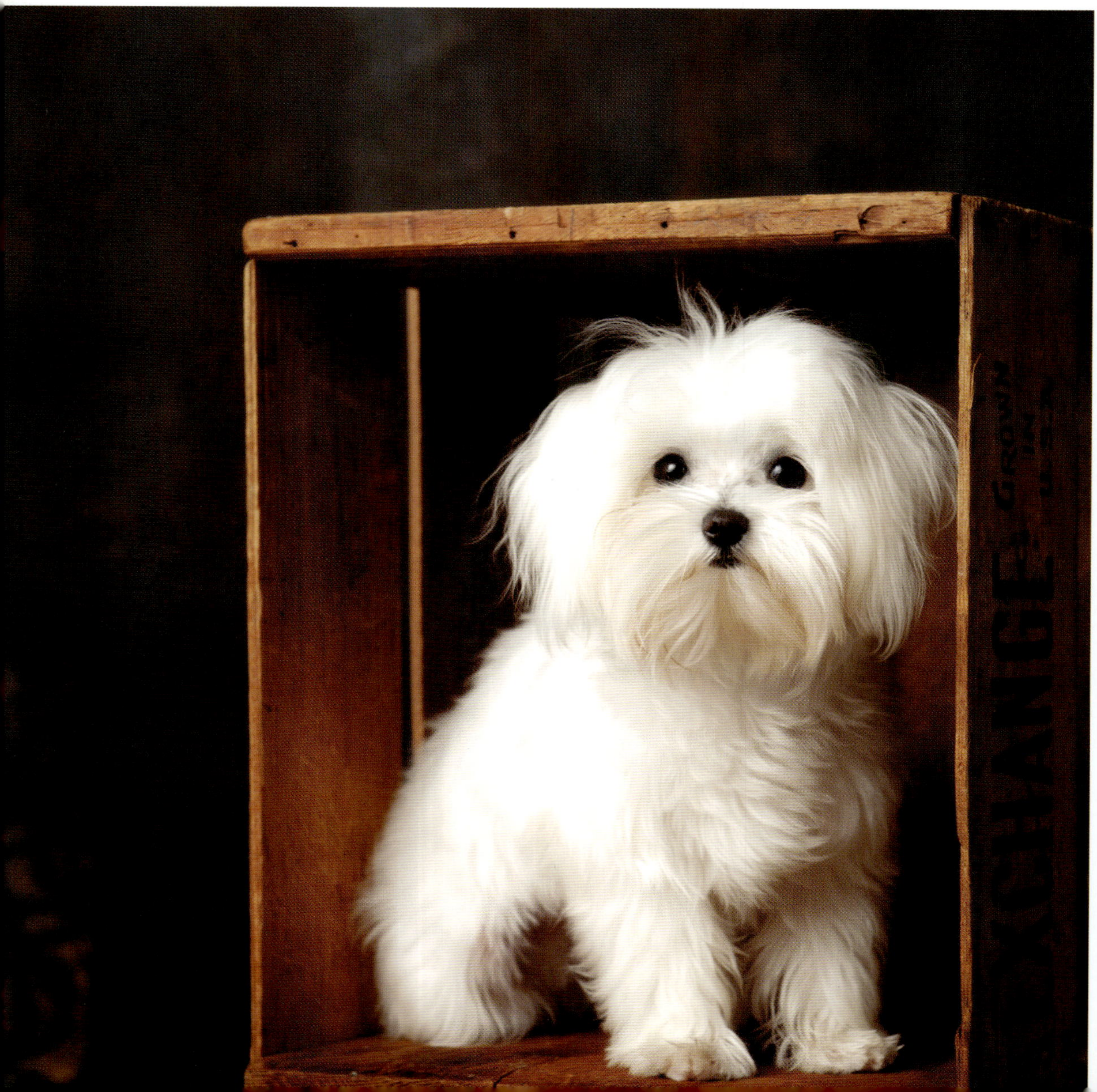

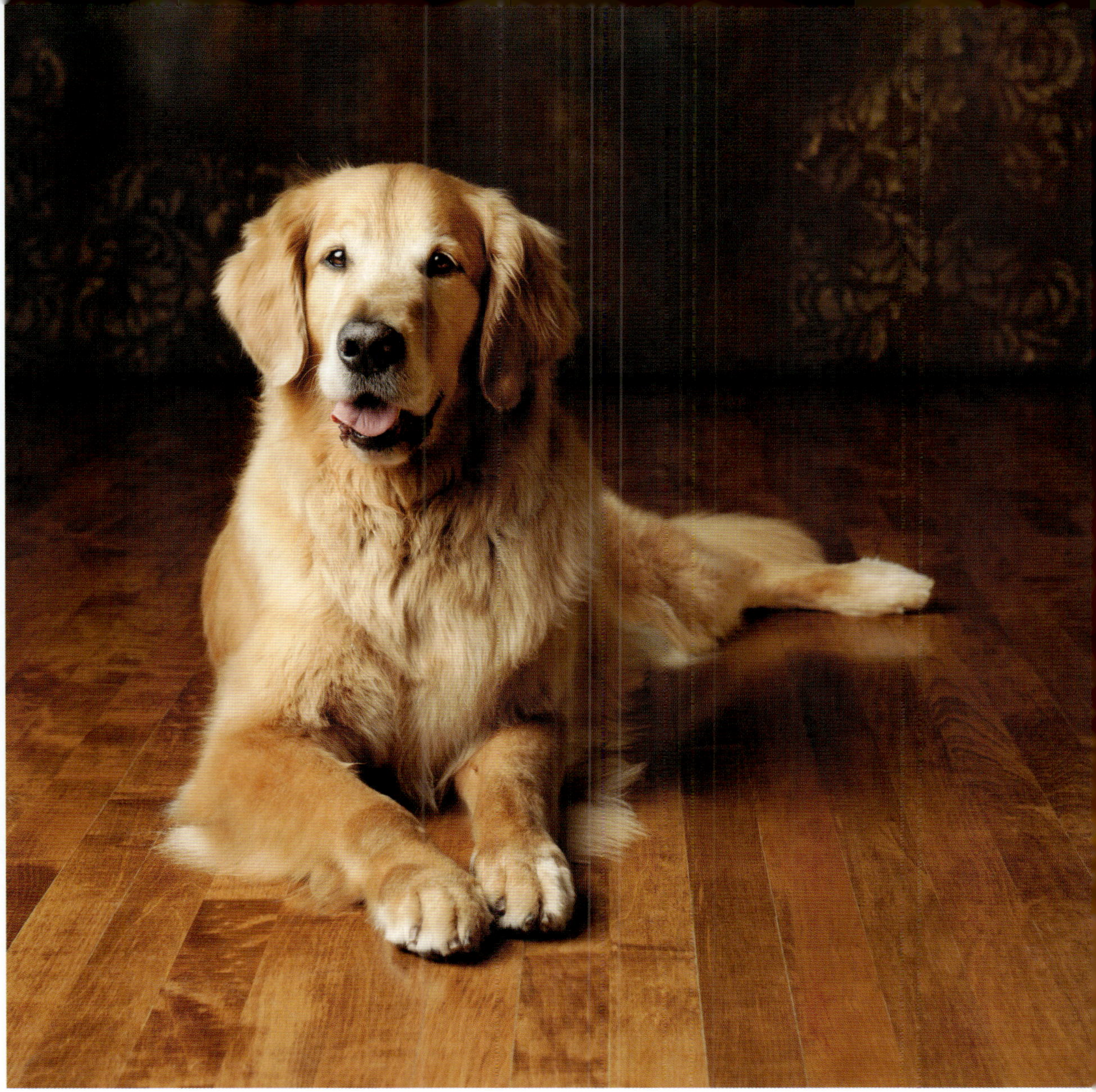

The Angle of the Light

Finding the right angle of the light to your subject will dramatically increase the dimension, depth, and texture in your image. The light spill on the background will also change because you will add or subtract light as you move the source. The sharper the angle of the light to your subject, the more texture will be apparent in the fur. I use a strong angle of light in most of my images, because I don't want the fur to be flat, I want to make the viewer want to reach out and pet the dog.

"Position your light at a strong angle for great detail in the fur."

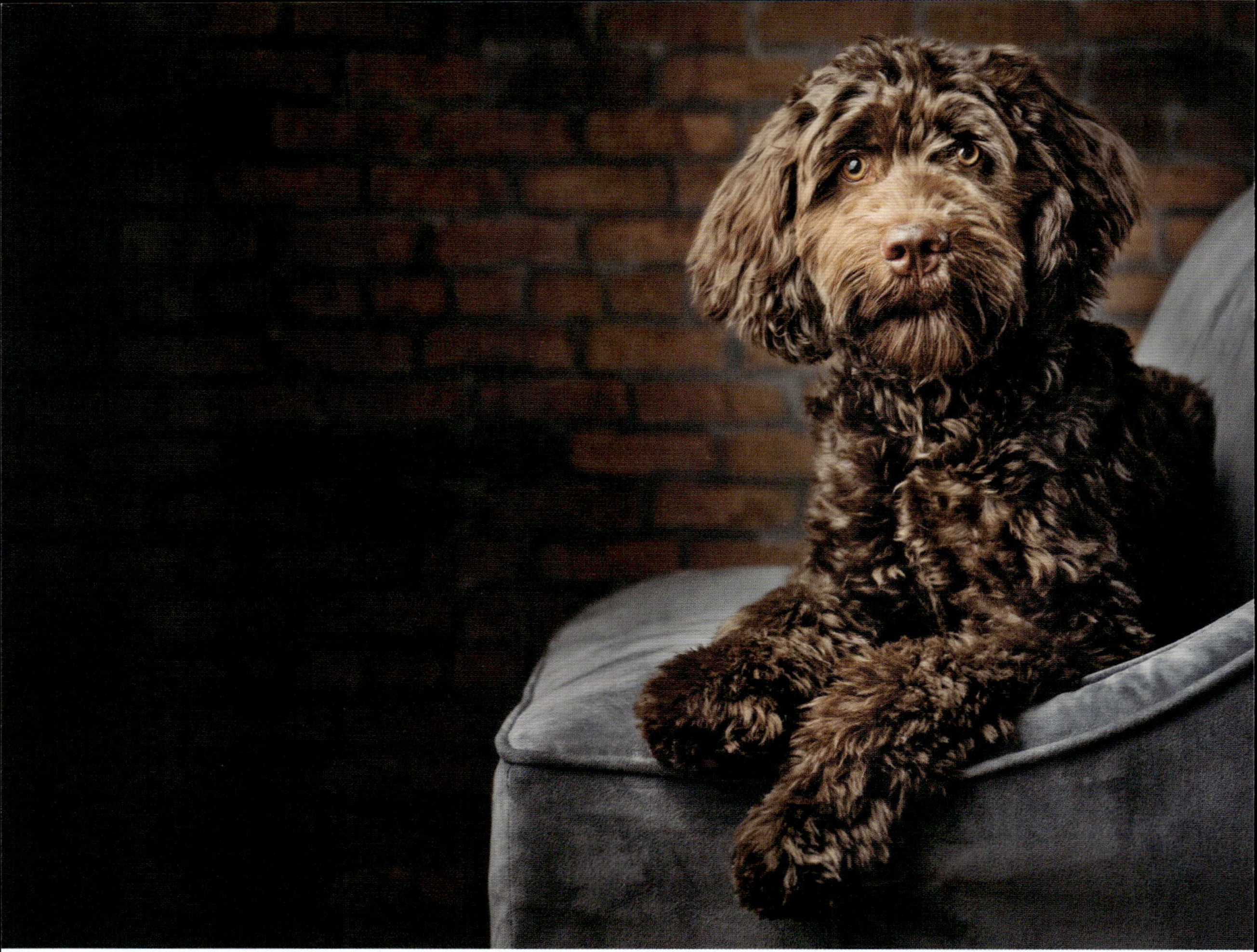

"Place a large reflector opposite your main light to bounce light onto the shadow side of the subject."

We want to make sure that we are giving the side opposite of the main light some love, too. I use a large silver reflector on the shadow side because it gives more punch to the specular highlights, bringing out the natural shine in a dog's fur, than a traditional white reflector does. White reflectors are often used for people portraits because they provide a very soft, forgiving light. A silver reflector will pick up more of the shine and texture in the animal's fur. The "pop" that a silver reflector provides is especially helpful when you have a dog that lacks a shine in their fur, like this cute Labradoodle. You can also use a fill light if you prefer a bit more pop, but that requires a second light—an umbrella or a strip light.

It's a great trick to use a reflector as a hair light, as well. You can position it at an angle behind the subject on the opposite side of your main light to bounce light onto the back of the pet's head.

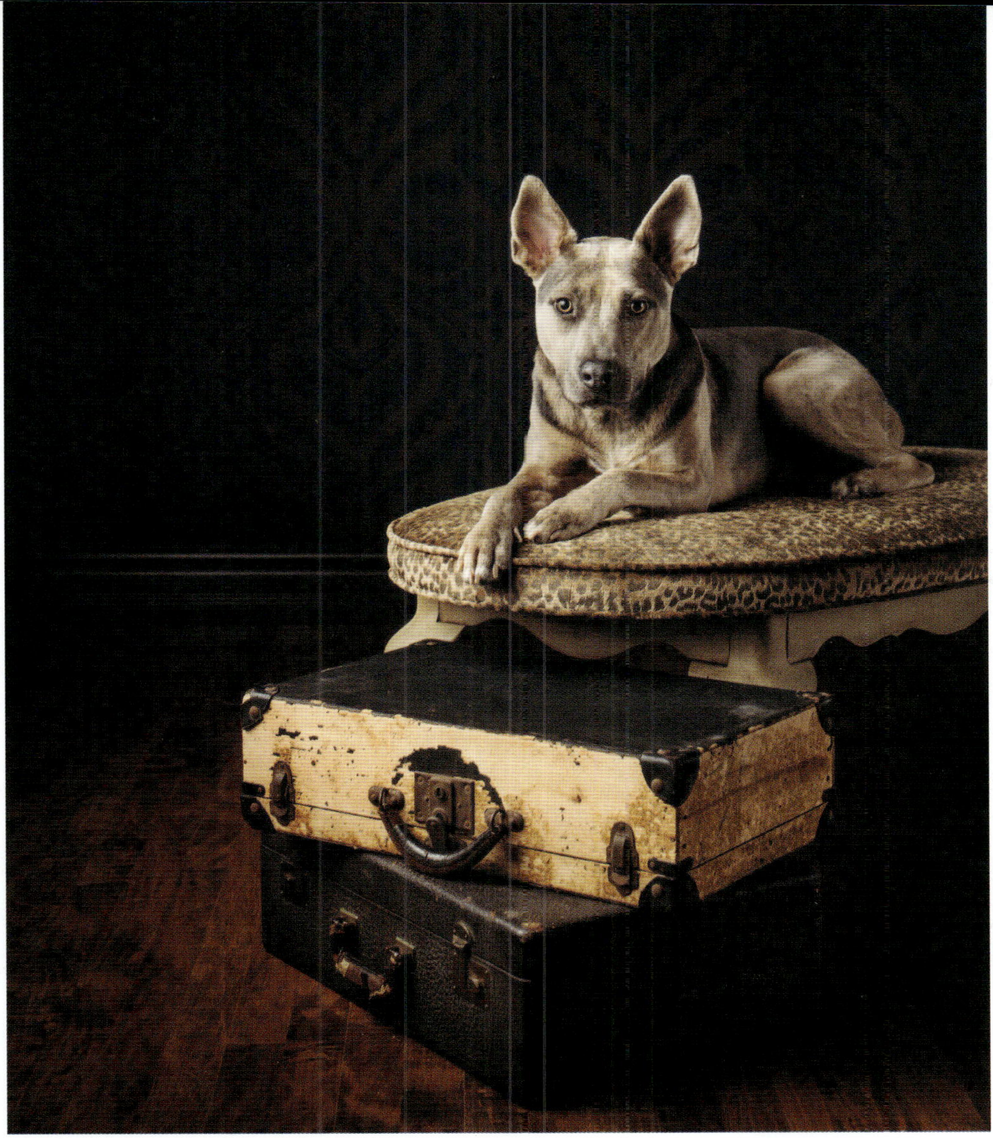

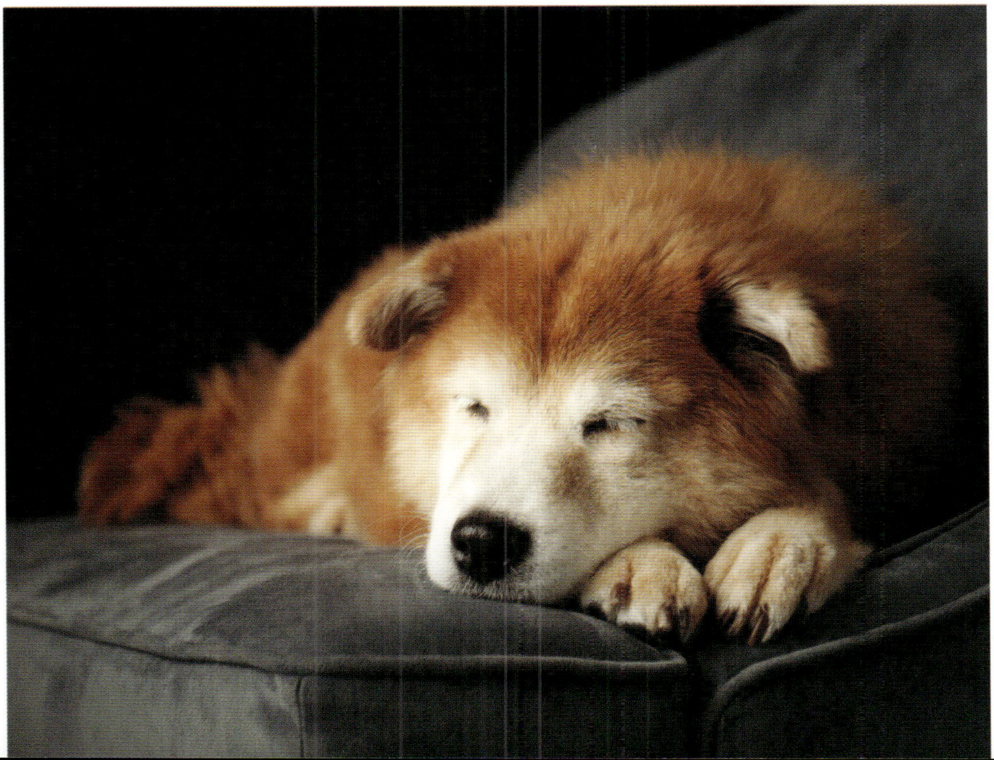

Catchlights

One of the biggest advantages of using artificial lighting as opposed to ambient light only is great catchlights—a reflection of the main light source in the subject's eyes that gives them a sparkle. A portrait without catchlights in the eyes lacks that professional touch. With that little bit of light, you can bring a lot of finesse to your portraits. Take a look at the image of the Boxer on the following page. His eyes draw you in. Without those catchlights, the portrait would not be as effective.

Some dogs have deep-set eyes, and for those subjects, getting good light in the eyes will help to visually draw them out and make for a much more polished result.

"Bring life to all of your pet portraits. Create catchlights."

Moving On

Now that we've gone through the equipment options for working in the studio, it's time to take a look at setting up your lights.

The bottom image on the following page was made with my most-often-used lighting setup, which requires just one light and a reflector. This is also one of my most-requested poses, and Sammy always delivers!

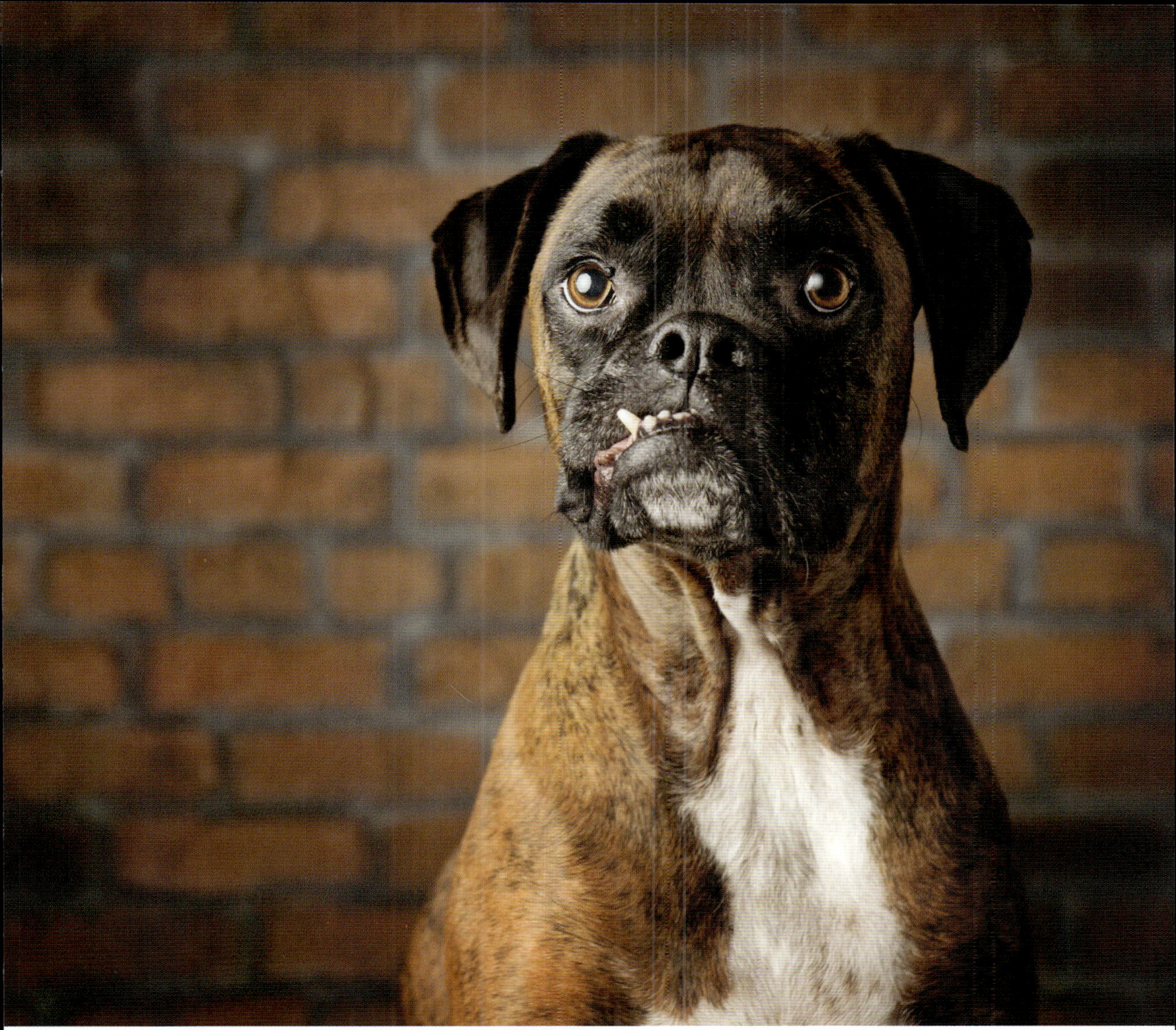

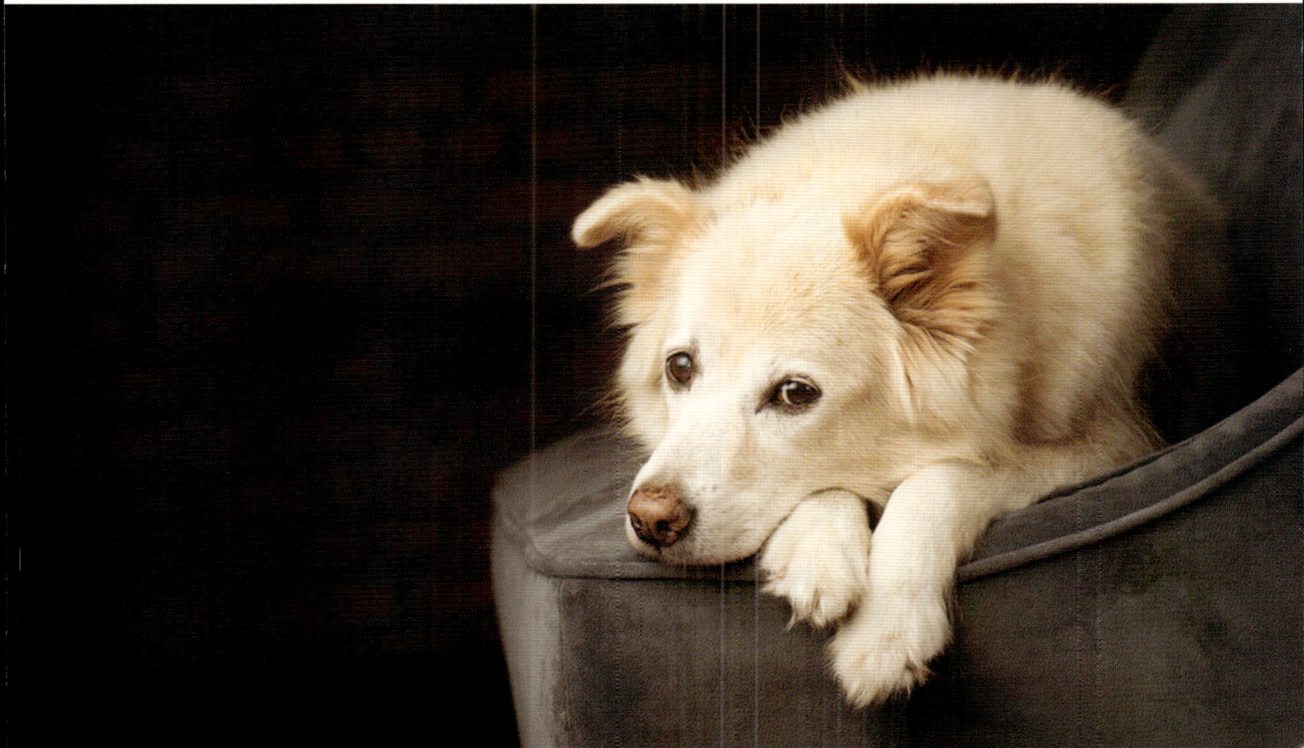

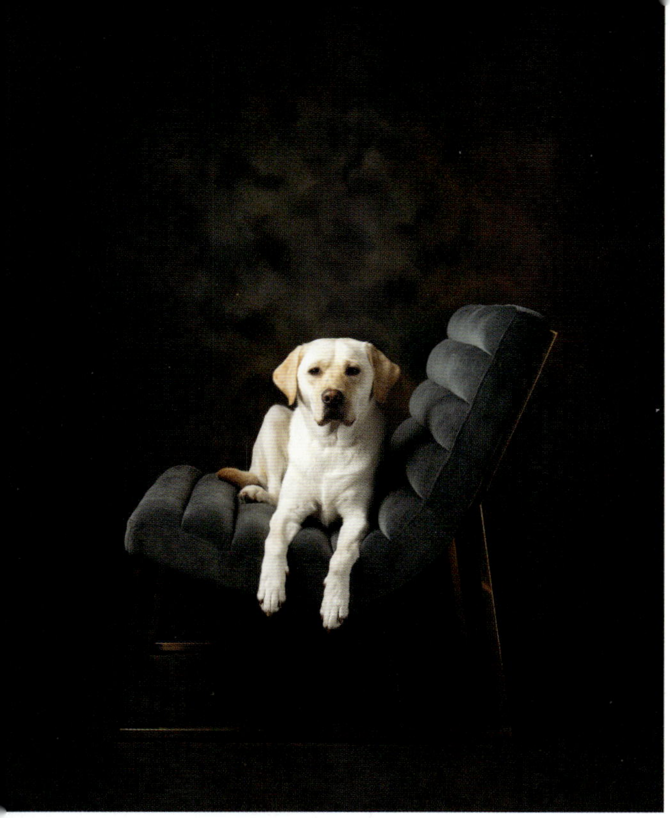

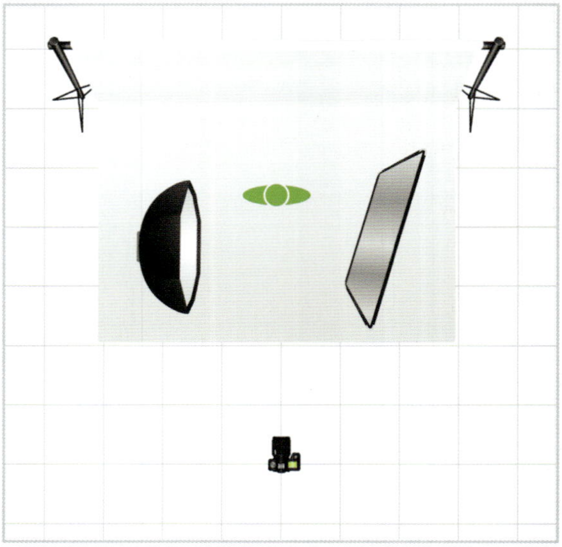

Lighting Single Subjects

Let's take a closer look at my in-studio lighting setup. I want to show you just how I achieved the results in each of these three portraits.

For the first image *(above)* I used my 5-foot octabox and had my model positioned to the very back of the light. This gave me some wiggle room in case she moved. I also had the chair pushed back so that the light would reach both sides of her face and the chair. By placing the light at 90-degree angle to the dog, I got less light on the background, which caused her to be the focus of the image with less distractions.

This image is presented straight out of the camera to show you what you can get from a lighting setup like this. Minimal retouching is needed to finish this image.

You will see this lighting diagram a couple of times, because I want you to note just where the light is positioned in relation to the pet. Again, the subject is at the back edge of the softbox. This allows for enough light on the face, catchlights in the eyes, and detail in the fur. The reflector should not be too far back. The subject is positioned toward the back of it so that light is reflected back on them.

For the second image *(following page),* I used the same setup, but I wanted you to see what happens when the pet is not placed at the back of the softbox. The amount of light on her face is dramatically reduced, there are no catchlights in her eyes, and there is a lot more light on the backdrop. The

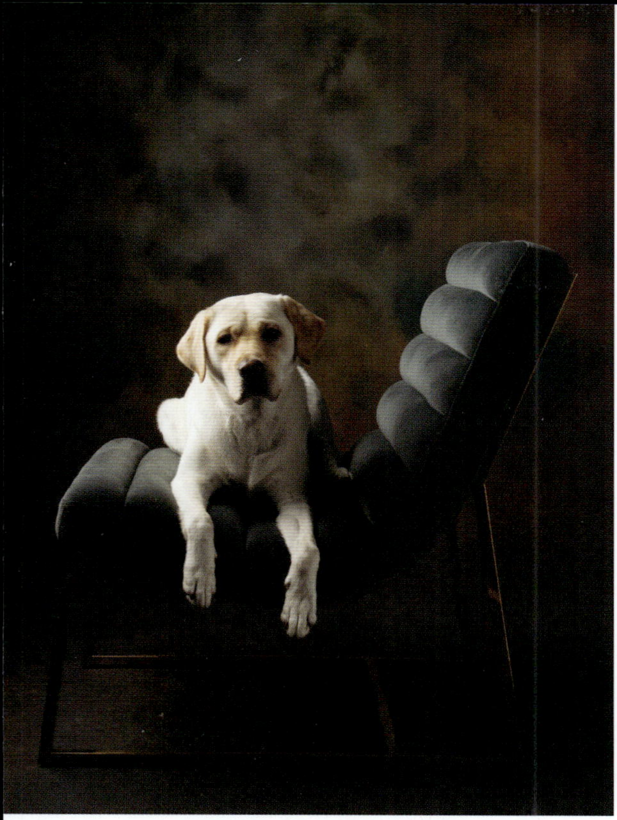 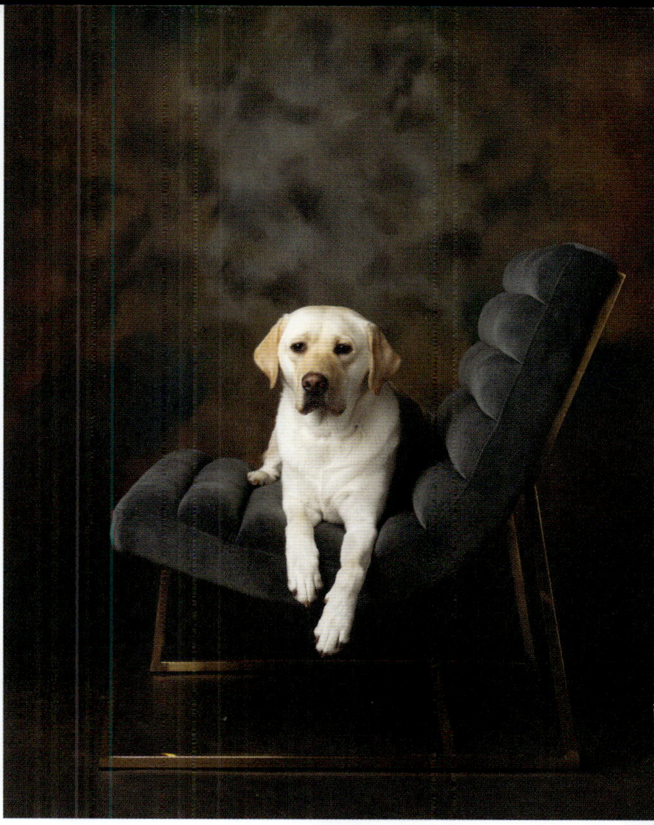

difference between the position of the light in this image and the previous one isn't huge, but the results in the second one are not as good. The second image would require a lot more time in front of the computer to fix the portrait.

Notice what happens when you position the light at a 45-degree angle versus a 90-degree angle. In this third image *(above, right)*, the pose is the same, but there is much more light on the subject's face. There is also more light on the background. The image doesn't pop as much as the image where the light was at 90 degrees, but it is properly lit.

These little tweaks come down to personal preference. If you like a more dramatic look and darker background, you might want to position your light at 90-degree angle to your subject so you can save time retouching a darker background in.

"Position your light at a 90-degree angle to your subject so you can save time retouching a darker background in."

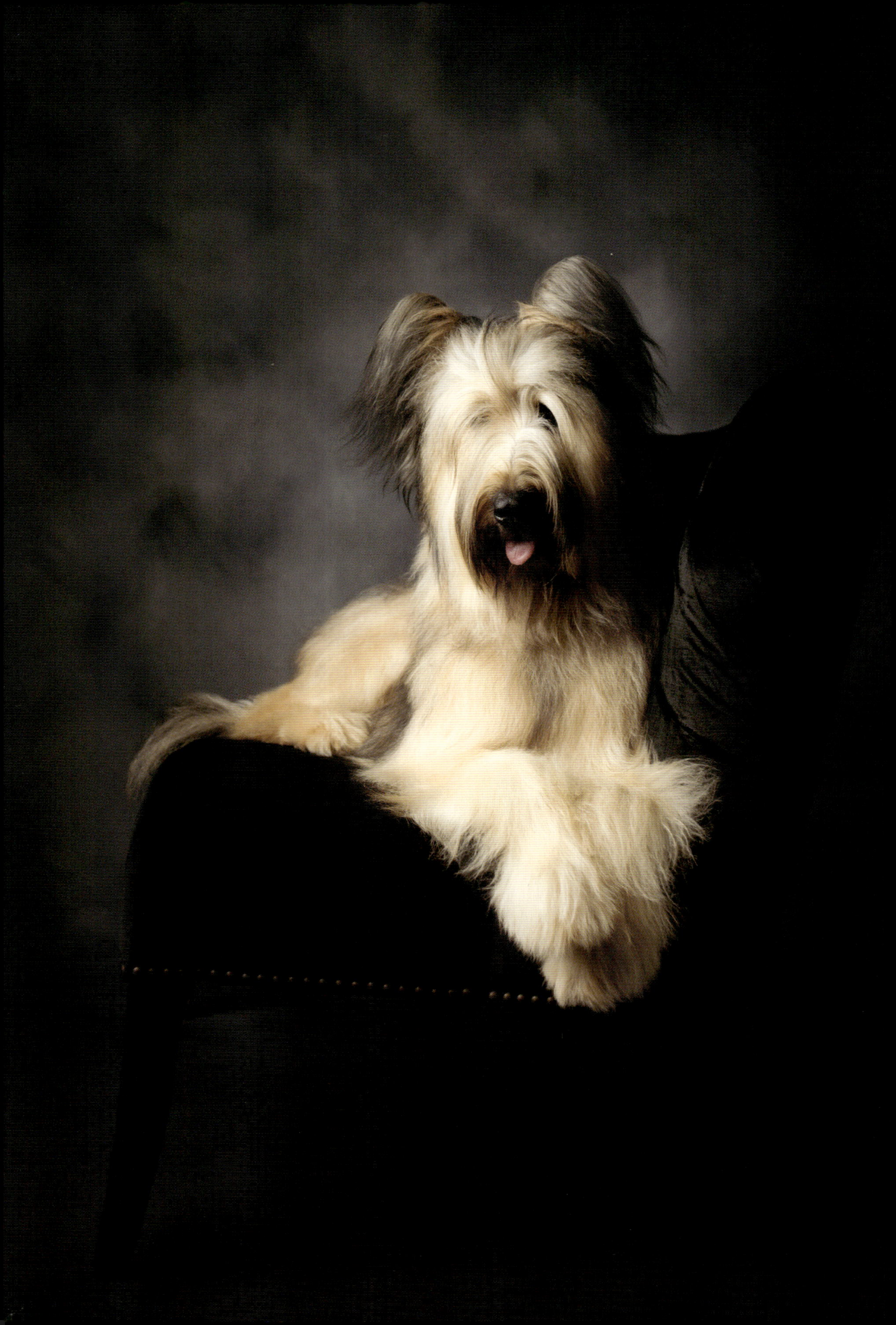

I typically use my 90-degree lighting setup for single subjects to get the most drama and depth possible out of my image in-camera. Again, if you want to dial back the "drama," as I like to call it, you can adjust the angle of your light by moving it more toward the subject from the front.

It's easier to use this setup when you're working with one pet rather than multiple subjects, because you don't have to worry about the light getting to another pet in the image.

On the right, you'll see another portrait made with my typical studio lighting setup. I adore this image of Nellie. I love adding in fun props to set the pet apart from the scene, and a chair like this is also a great tool to keep a pet in one place for a few seconds. Sometimes a few seconds is all you have to get that image!

For this photo, my light was placed on the left side of Nellie, and my silver reflector was positioned on the right.

"Use one light, at a 90-degree angle, for lots of drama in the image."

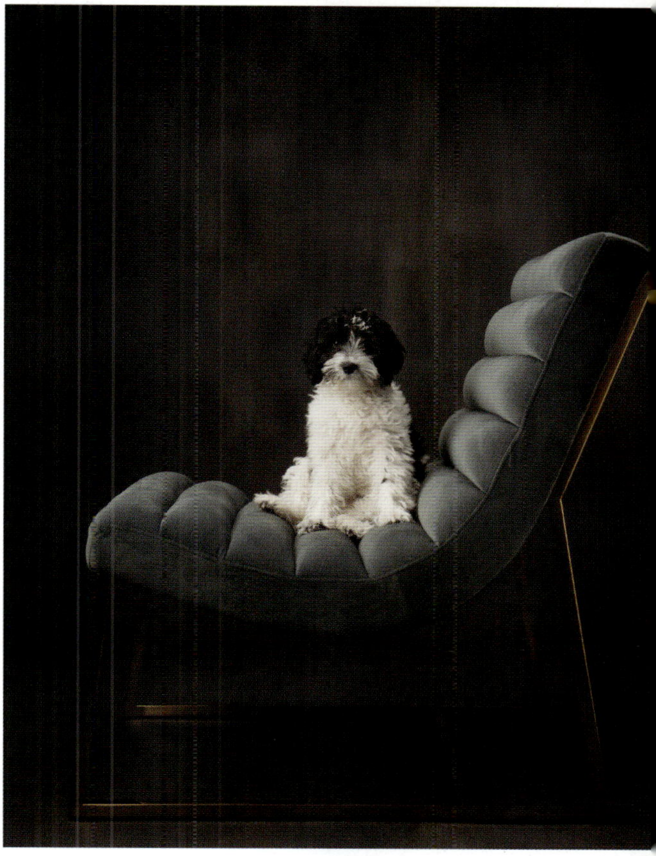

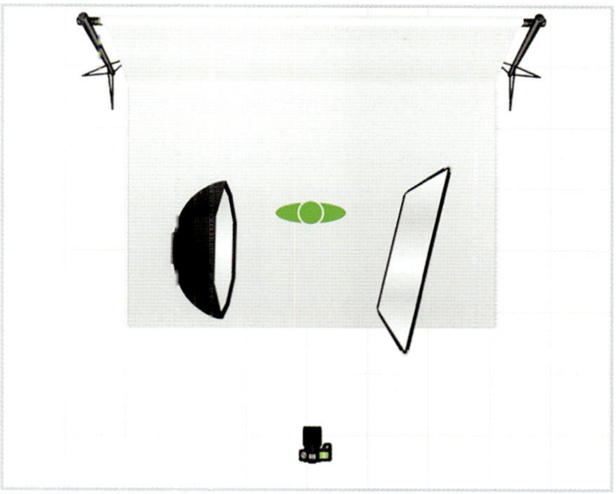

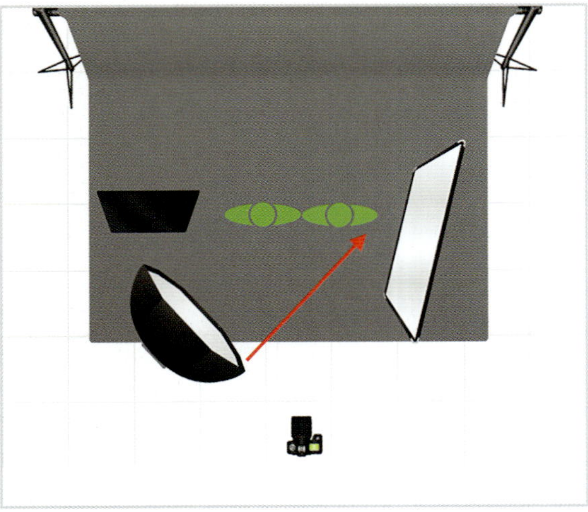

"For more separation between your subject and the background, you can add a strip light or a reflector to pop more light in."

Lighting Multiple Subjects

Lighting for multiple dogs in the same image, or dogs and their people, requires an approach that is slightly different from the one used when you are working with only one subject. When lighting multiple subjects, the key is to angle your softbox so that the front edge of the light reaches the edge of the farthest subject. This will ensure that everyone gets enough light on them. You can see this concept illustrated by looking at the red arrow in the diagram above.

You will get more light on the background when you move the light, but you can always use a gobo to restrict the illumination. If you need a little more separation between your subject and the background, you can add a strip light or a reflector to pop more light in, as I did for this image.

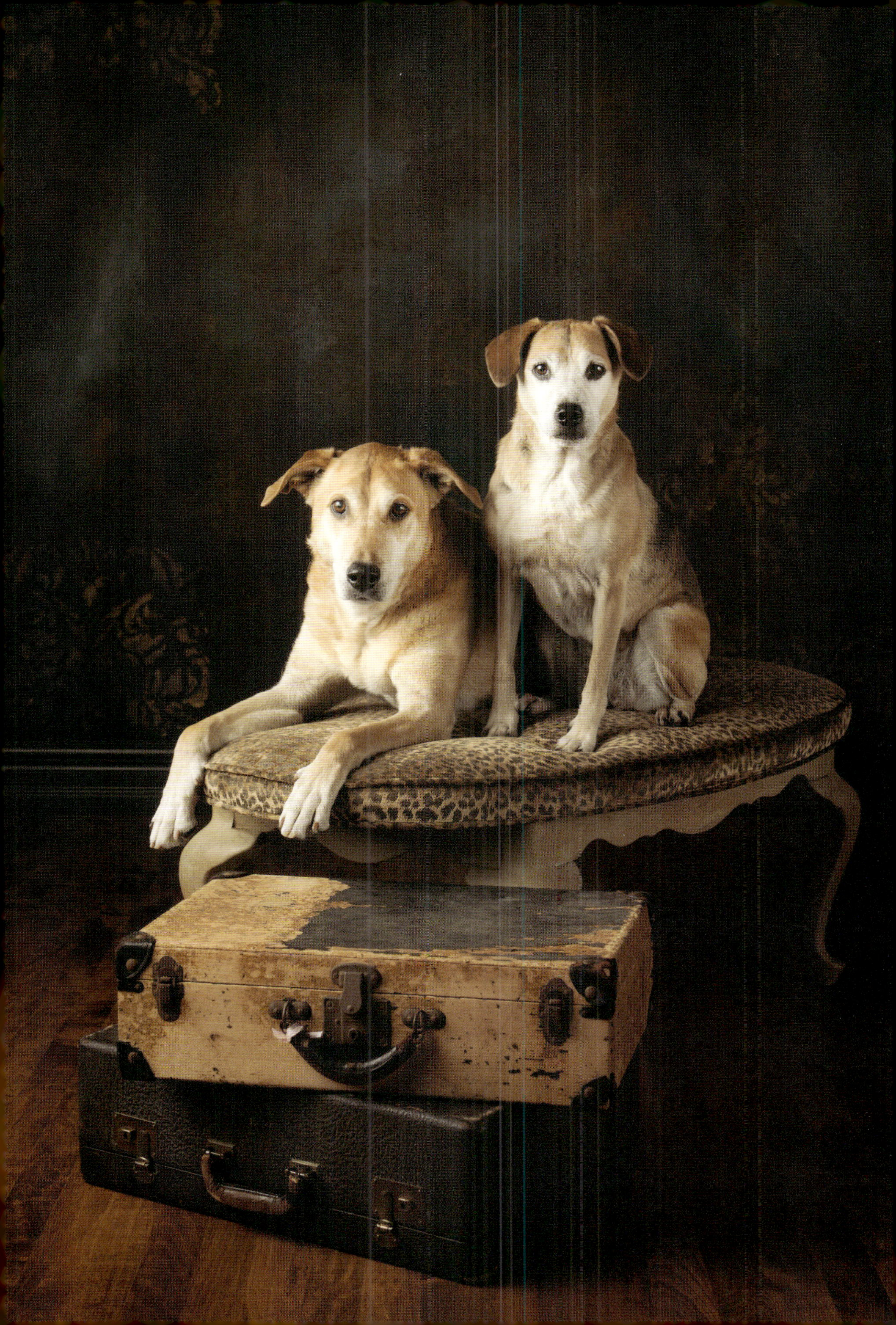

Here you can see a straight-out-of-camera image of lighting two dogs. The photograph below was made with the 90-degree angle lighting that I typically use for one pet. You can still achieve a good photo, but it may require a bit more retouching than if you angle the light a bit more to reach both of the dogs. As you can see, the Golden Retriever's face is pretty dark on the right side, and there are no catchlights in the eyes. I can definitely brighten that up and add a catchlight in postproduction, but that would mean more work for me.

In the straight-out-of-the-camera image on the following page, you can see what happened after I made a slight adjustment to the angle of the light, as described earlier. There is now great light on both of the dogs, catchlights in their eyes, and a lot less work to do in Photoshop.

This is a great trick to use when you have more than one dog, and it works especially well for groups of pets in the same image or for portraits of pets and their people.

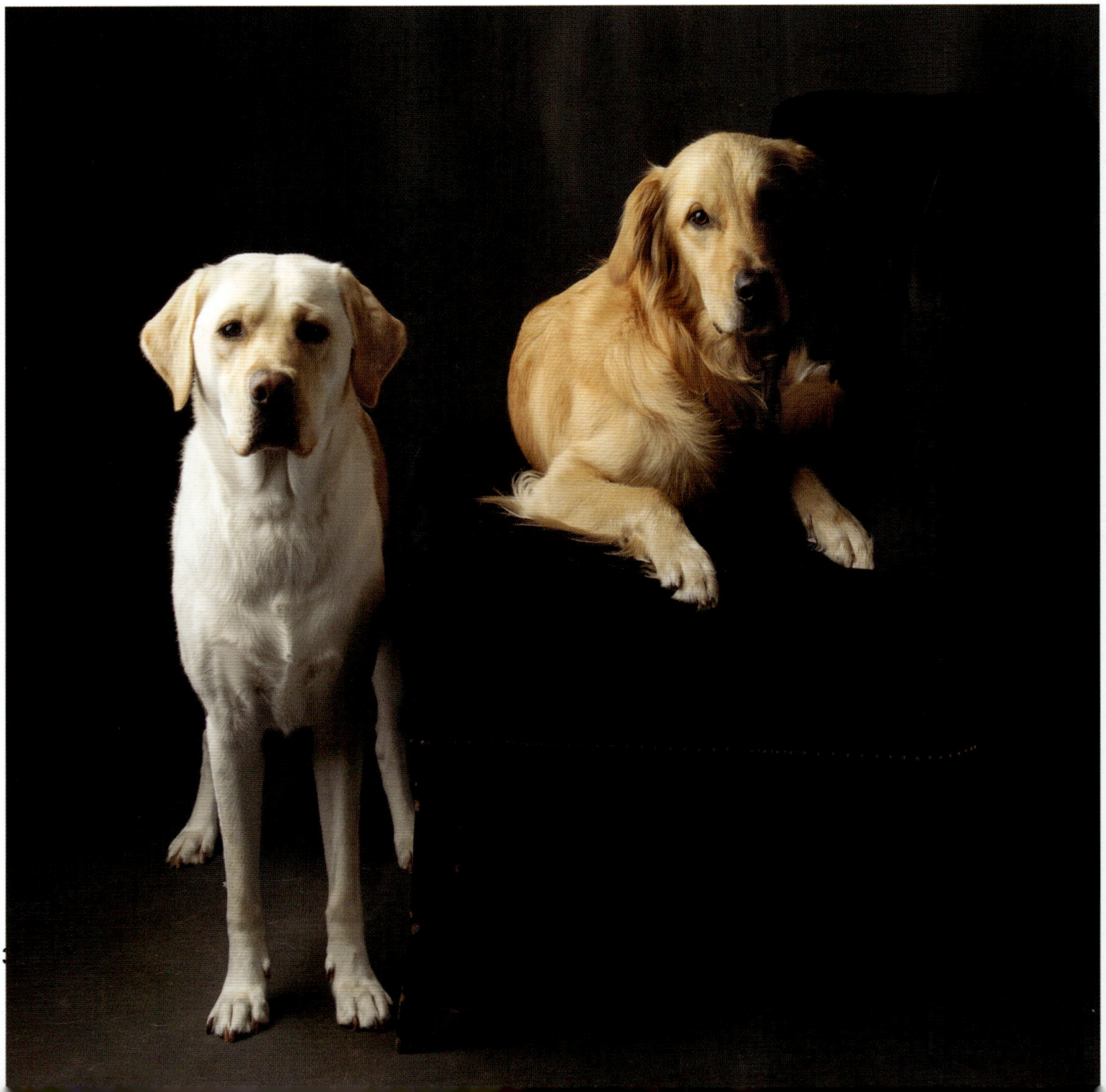

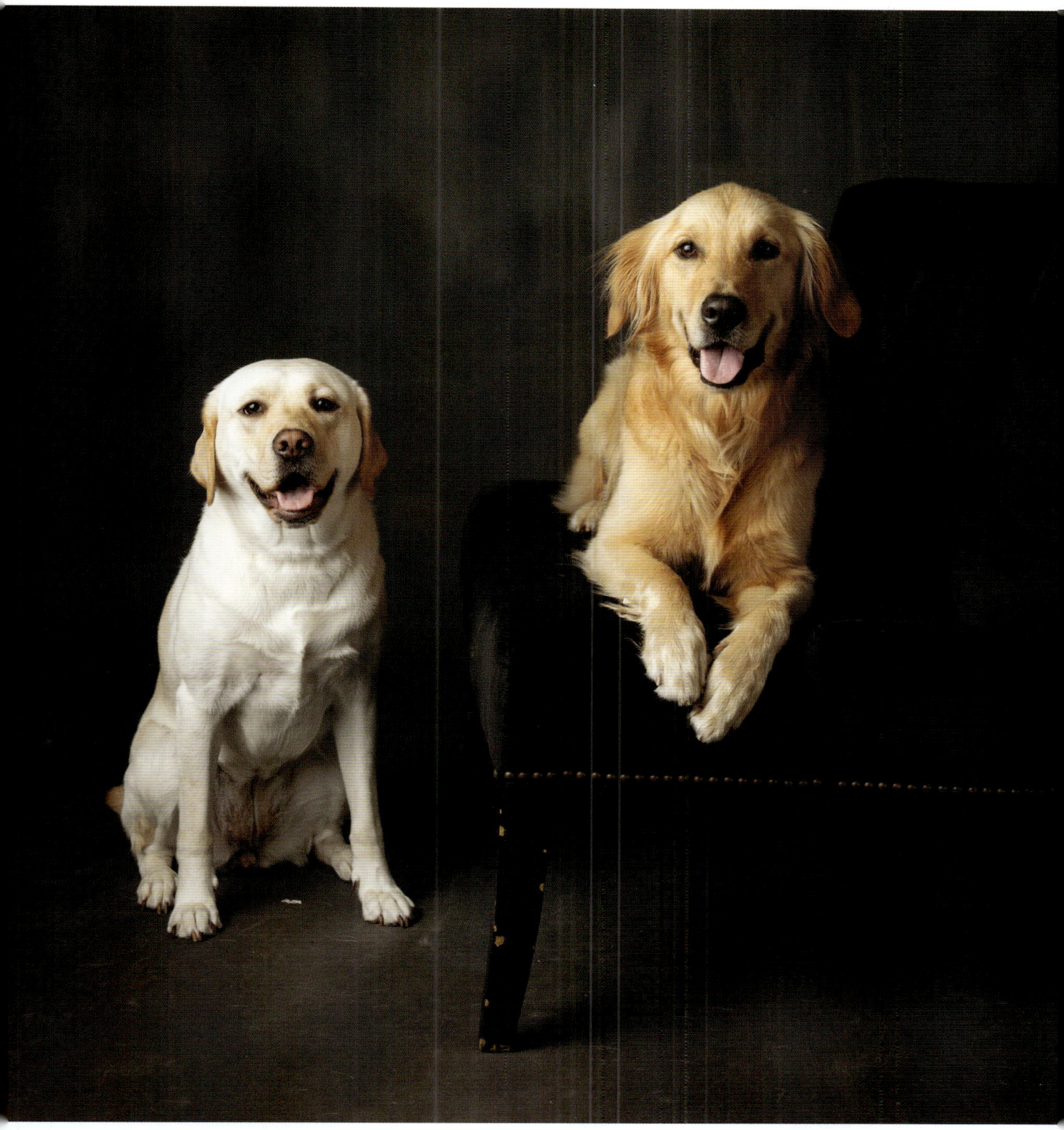

"Get great light on two or more subjects and ensure there are catchlights in the eyes by adjusting the angle of the light."

Here is another example of a dog photographed in the same setting, with the same output and quality of light, and the same modifier. The difference is how the light changes as the angle of the light changes in relation to the dog. In the first image, the light is straight on the dog, making it pretty flat. You can see the fur, but it kind of melds together.

This second image shows you how the image changes when the light is at a 45-degree angle to the dog. The lighting is better, you have a bit more dimension in the fur, but the background is heavily lit, and it doesn't do much to really highlight how beautiful this dog is in real life.

This final image was made with the light at a 90-degree angle to the dog. You're able to see so much more depth

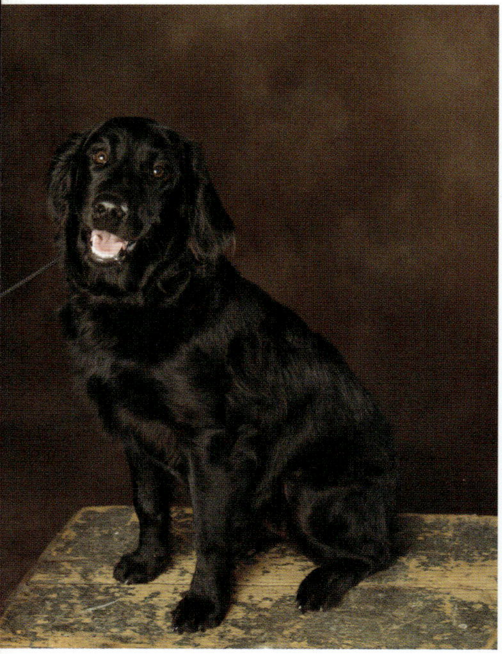

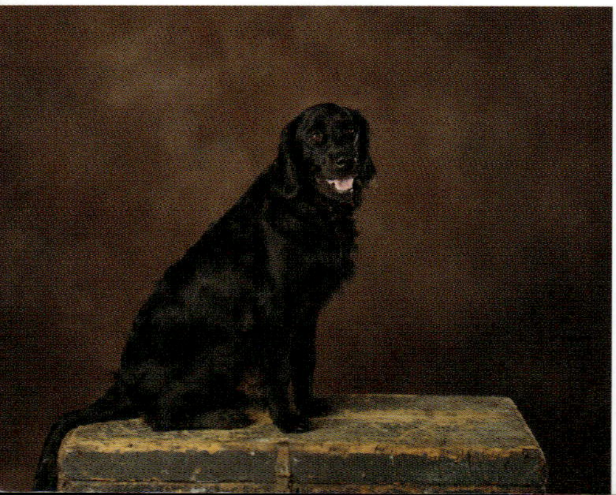

and texture in the gorgeous black fur. The face is highlighted beautifully, as are the back paws. You can also see that the background is less lit than before, making it less of a focal point. There's more drama, texture, and interest after one simple move of the light. Keep in mind that it is always easier to move yourself or your light than your subject. If the pet is in place, don't move them if you don't have to.

"Move the light, not the dog, when possible."

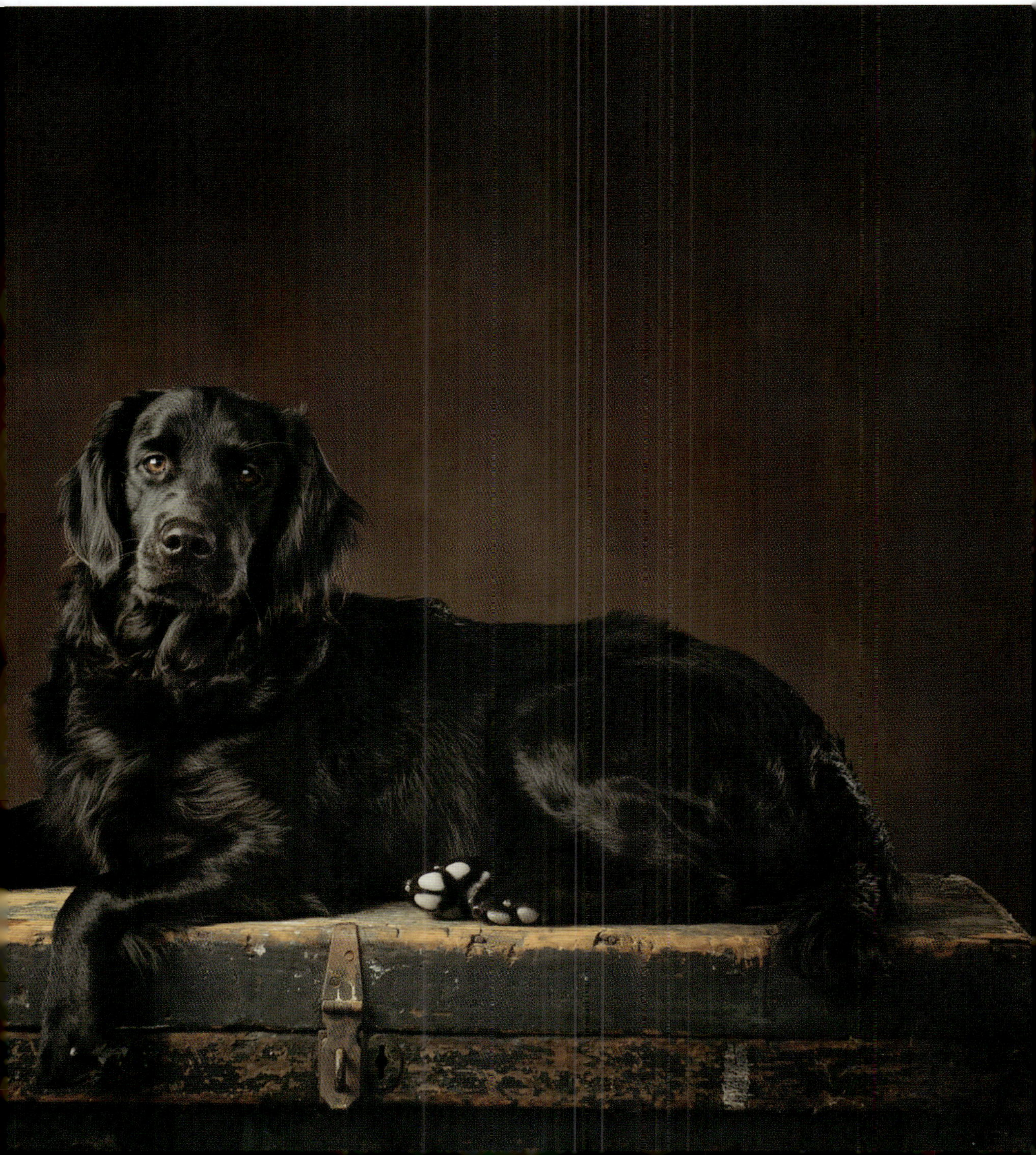

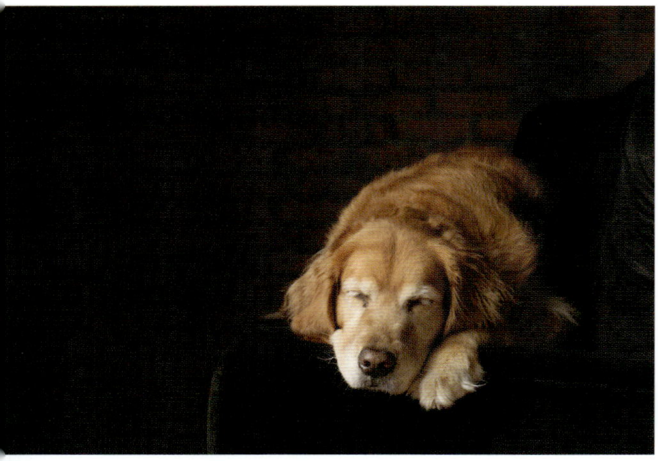

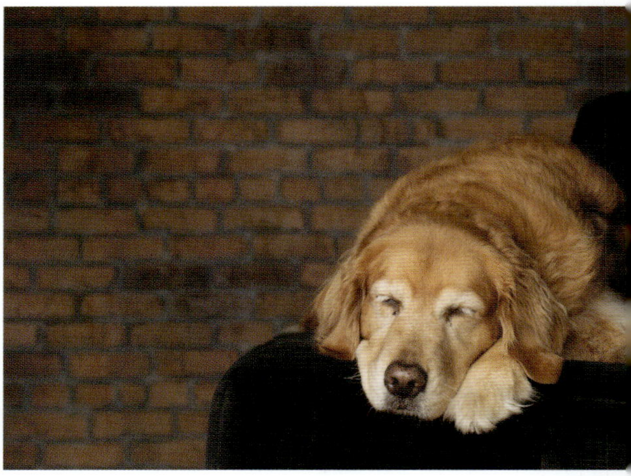

Here's another example of how different the light looks at different angles to the subject. The top-left image (previous page) was taken with the light at 90-degree angle to this gorgeous Golden, and the top-right one was made from 45 degrees. The difference in the final result is pretty incredible. The one with the light at 90 degrees has so much depth and dimension to it, plus getting rid of the distracting background really highlights the dog.

The final image, made with 90-degree light, with minimal retouching, is shown below. All I had to do was remove the sleep from her eyes.

"Use careful lighting to reduce your postproduction work."

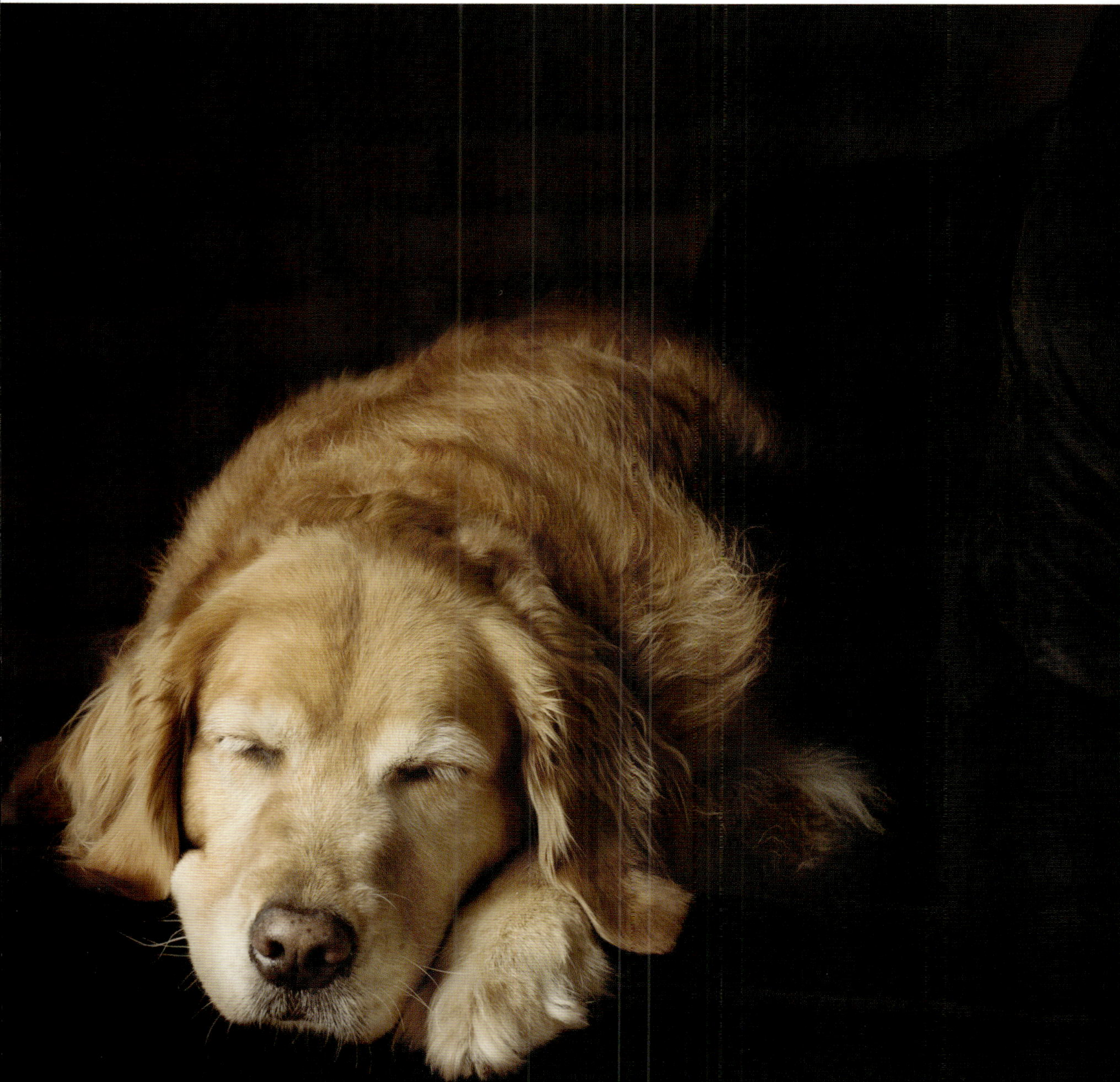

Positioning Pets

You can see how the angle of the light to the pets makes a big difference, but how you position pets in relation to the light also play a huge part in your final image. Most people have more than one pet in their homes, and they don't all look the same, either. So, how do we make sure we light them all properly? The key is to position darker animals closer to the light versus the lighter ones, as pictured in the image below. I specifically position the dogs with the darkest colors in their fur closest to the light because their fur is going to soak up that light. If I were to put the French Bulldog closest to the light, her fur would have been overexposed, and the Dachshund's fur would have been underexposed.

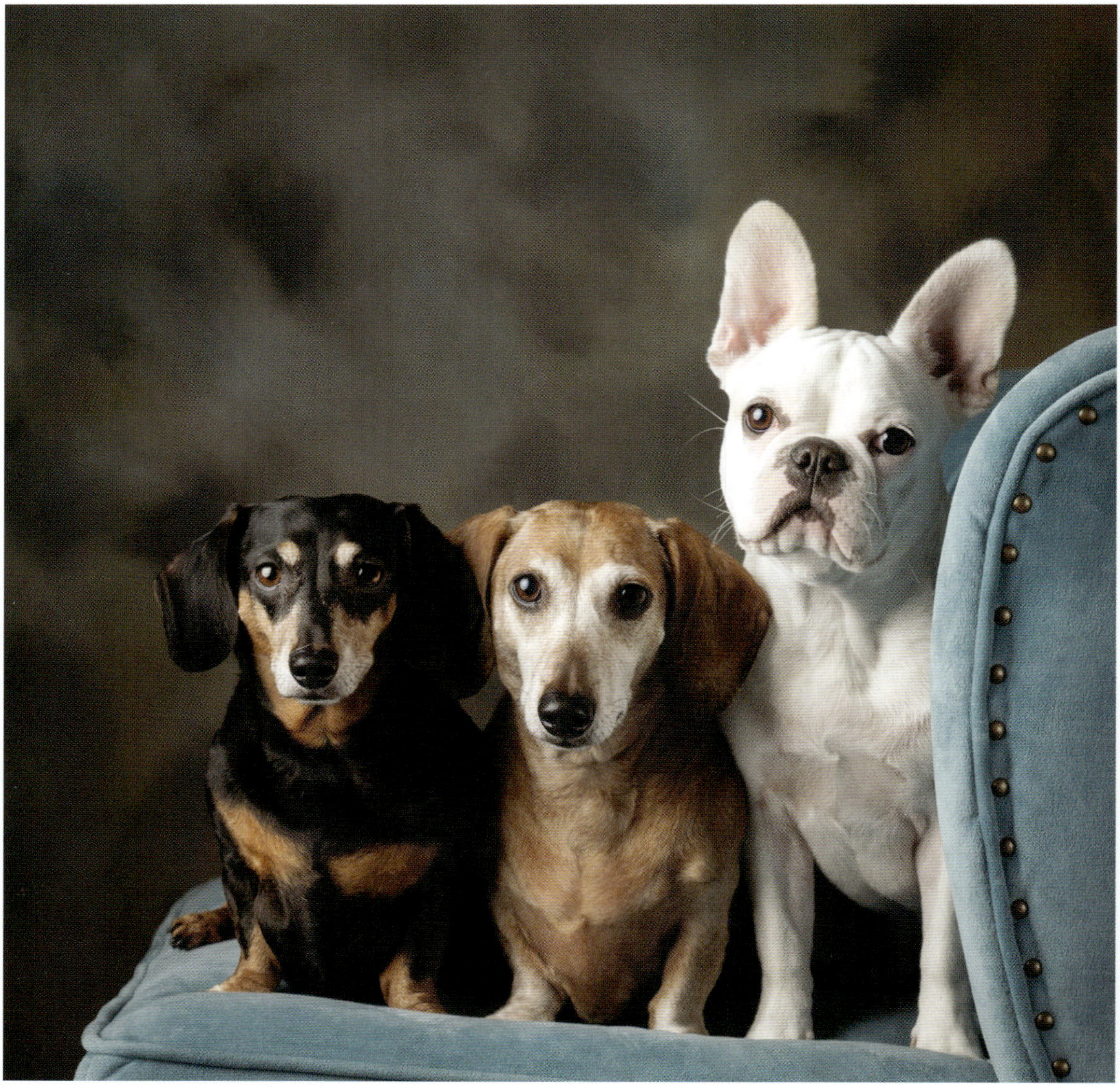

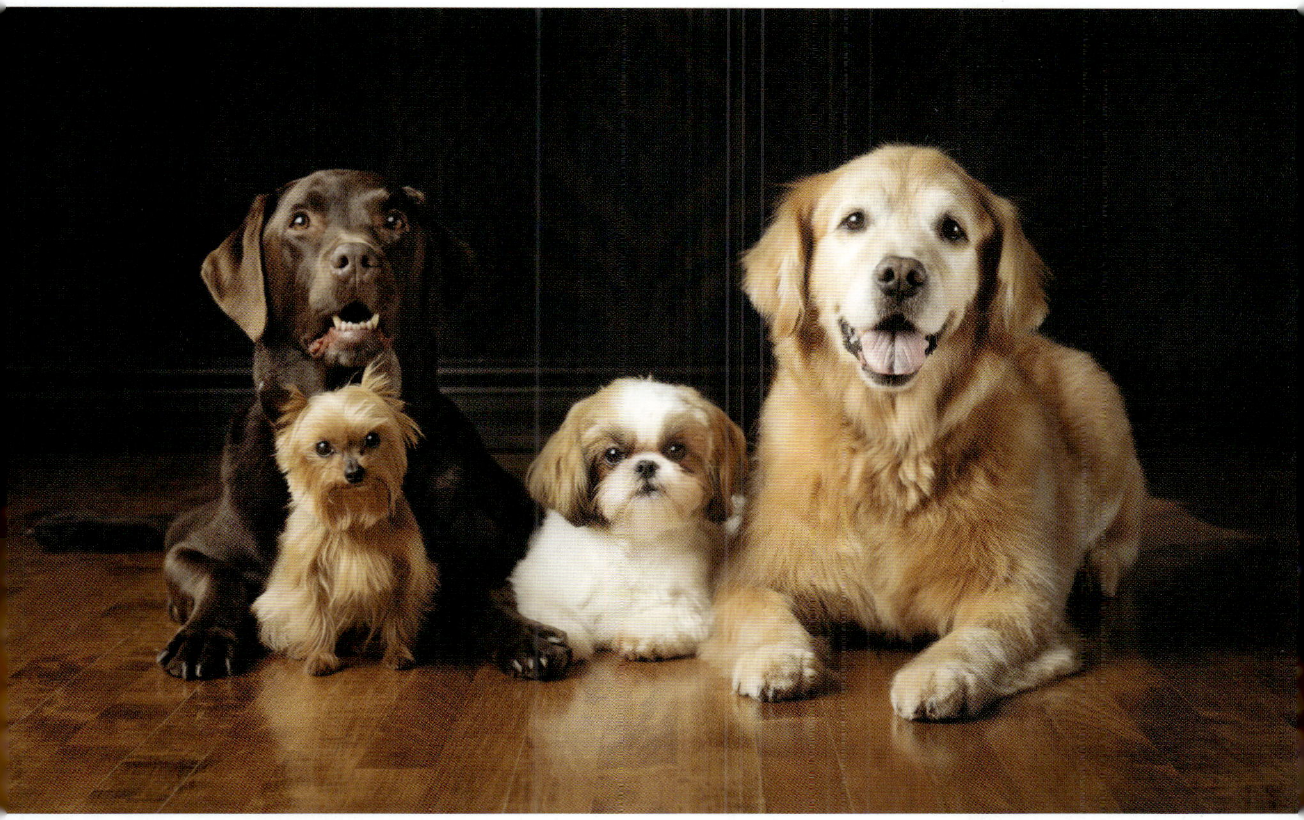

Here is another example of how to pose pets based on fur color. I posed these dogs very strategically. I wanted the Chocolate Lab to get the most light on his fur, and then I placed them on down the line based on fur color. The Shih Tzu is lighter than the Golden, but I placed him where he is because he is smaller than the Lab, and some of the light was being blocked by the Lab. The Lab acted like a gobo between the Shih Tzu and the light, which is why the fur on the smaller dog is not blown out.

"Position subjects with dark coats closer to the light and lighter-toned dogs farther from the light source."

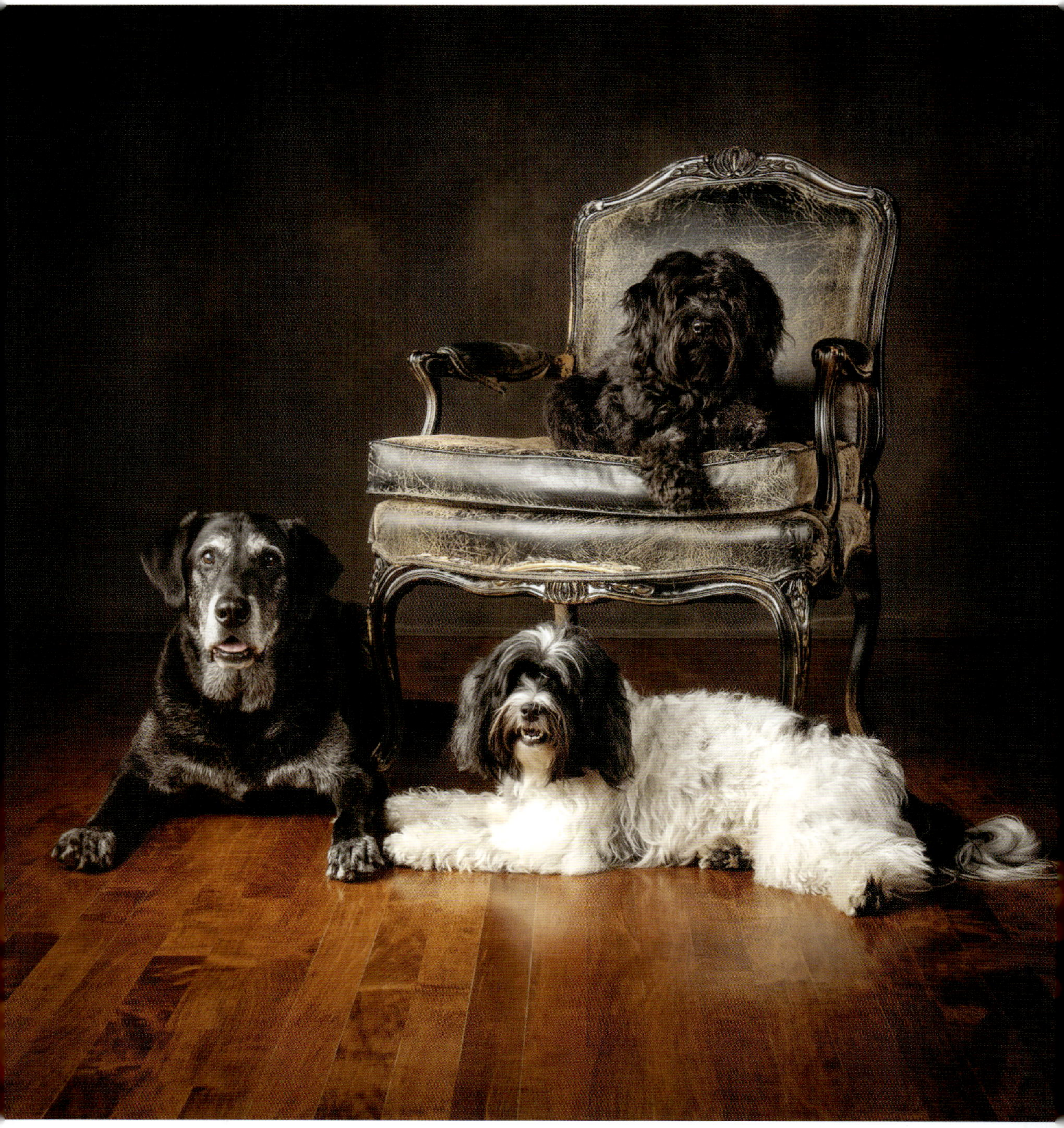

This family had two black dogs and a white dog. The key here was to again position the darker dogs closer to the main light, but I also placed my reflector on the black dog in the chair rather than on the dog on the floor. The white dog was getting plenty of light, but the darker-coated dog on the chair needed a little help from the light bounced by the reflector.

Here is another example of positioning pets with different fur colors. Again, the darker-colored dog was positioned closer to the light. He served as a gobo and limited the amount of light that illuminated the lighter-colored dog. All three are beautifully lit.

"Mix up your poses for greater variety."

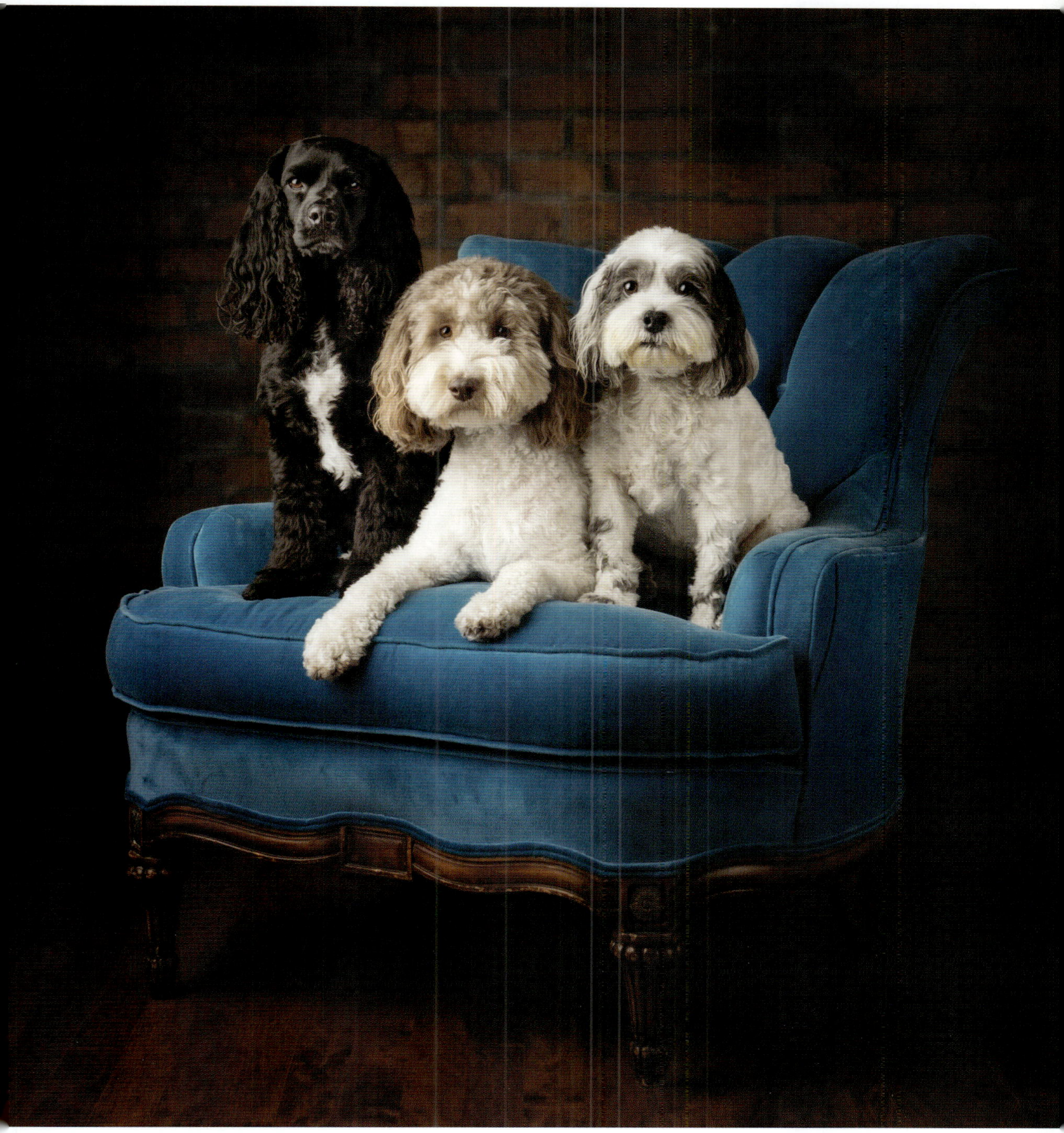

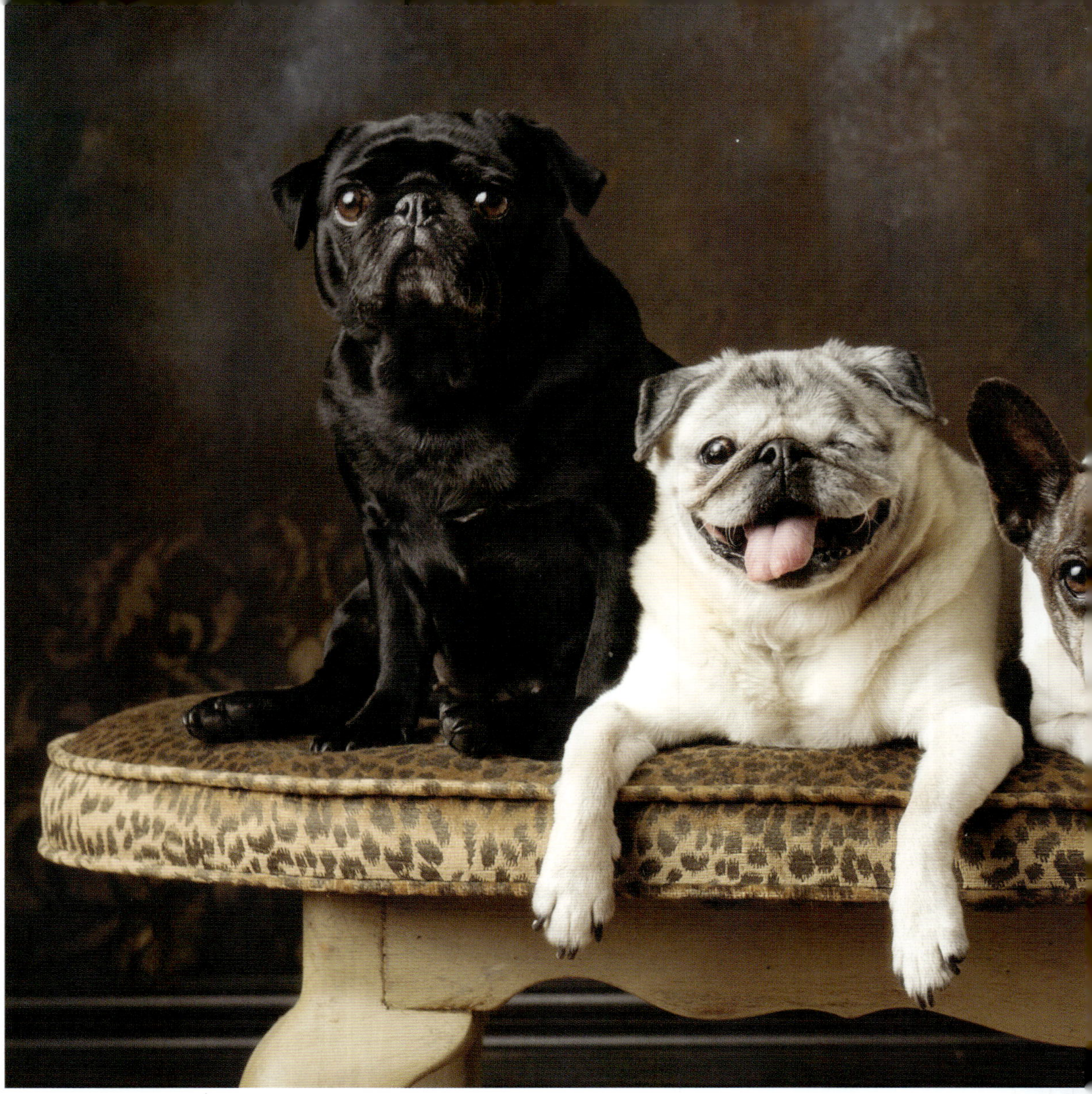

Above is another example of placing pets based on their fur. However, you see the dog that looks like she's having the best time? She is pretty light, and I probably would have swapped her with the Frenchie to her right, but that Frenchie was not going to be moved. So, I had the black dog seated, rather than lying down so he would block a bit more light on her. Sometimes, a dog will not move, so you have to work with what you have. It's smart to get at least one image "in the bag" and *then* try for perfection!

In the photo example on the bottom of the following page, I would have preferred both dogs with black-and-white fur to be closest to the light, but the little guy on the right had different ideas!

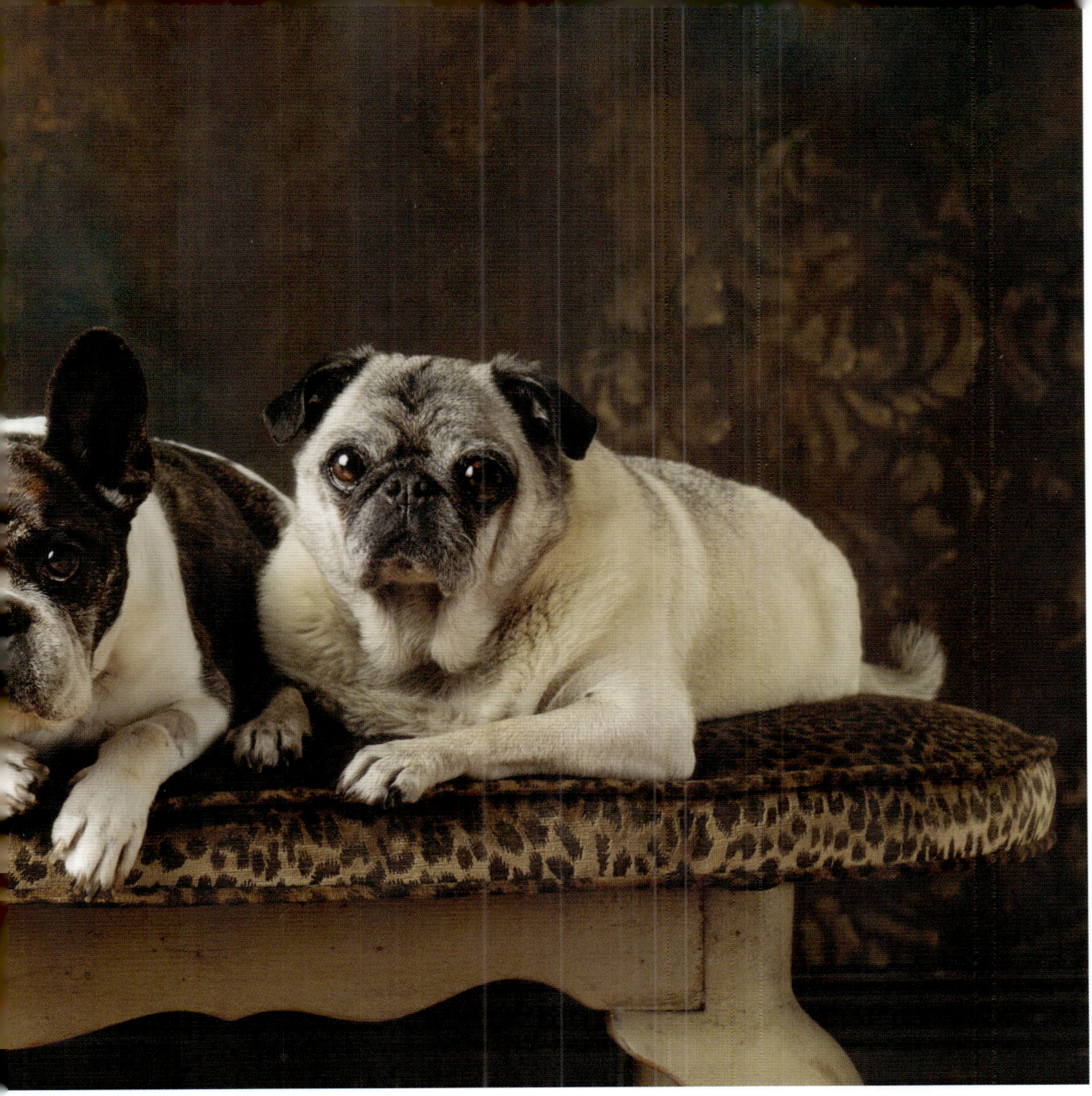

"Get one shot 'in the bag' before trying to finesse the posing to perfection."

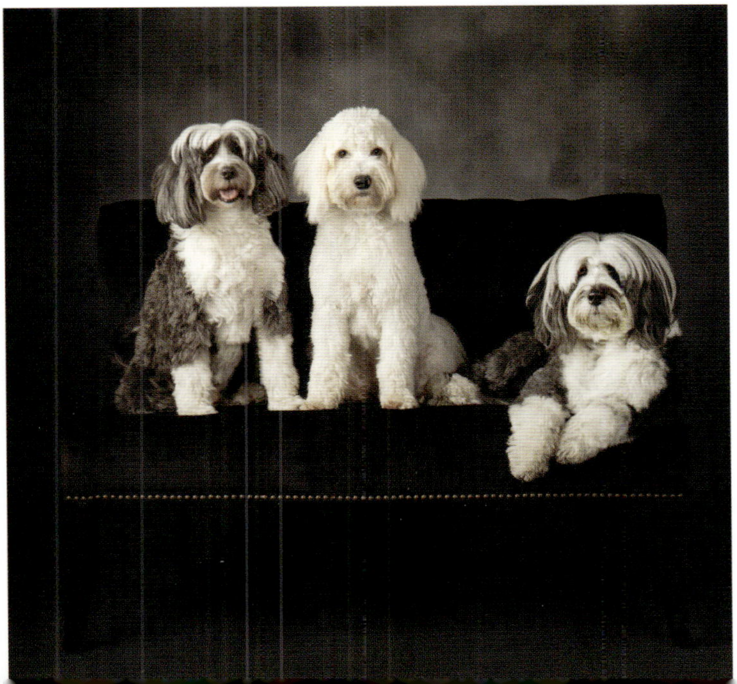

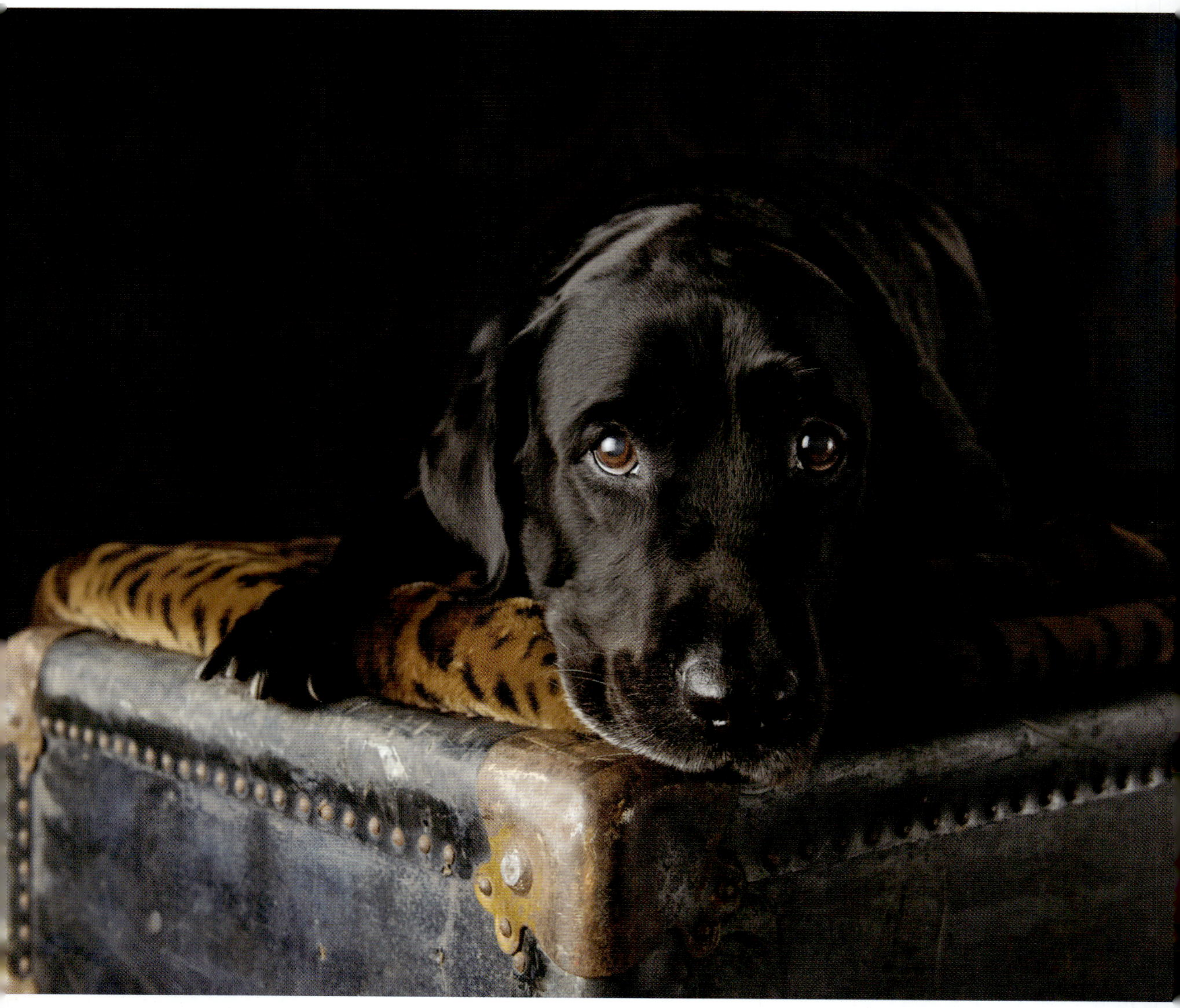

Photographing black dogs may seem like a daunting task, but this is something that your clients typically can't do at home—and it *can* be done! The key to success is to keep as much detail in the fur as possible. The easiest way to achieve this is to photograph in manual mode on your camera so that you can really control the exposure on the fur. Also, you *must* make sure that you have separation between your subject and the background so that the subject stands out and their head and ears can be easily seen against the background.

"Make sure there is separation between a black dog and a dark background."

To create separation between a dark-colored dog and the background, and ensure that the texture of the fur is on point, use a hair light, reflector, or a light-colored background. I love to photograph black dogs against a black background. It's not that difficult to do. I light a black dog the same way I do a lighter-colored dog, but I always use a hair light with a softbox angled behind the dog and a reflector so I don't lose detail in the face.

This diagram shows where the main light, strip light, and reflector were placed for optimal results.

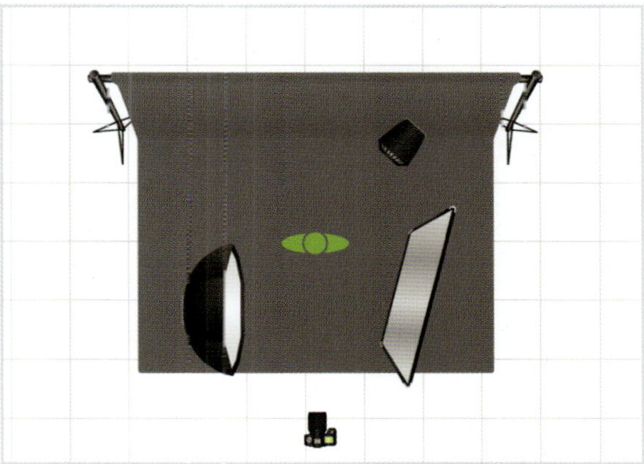

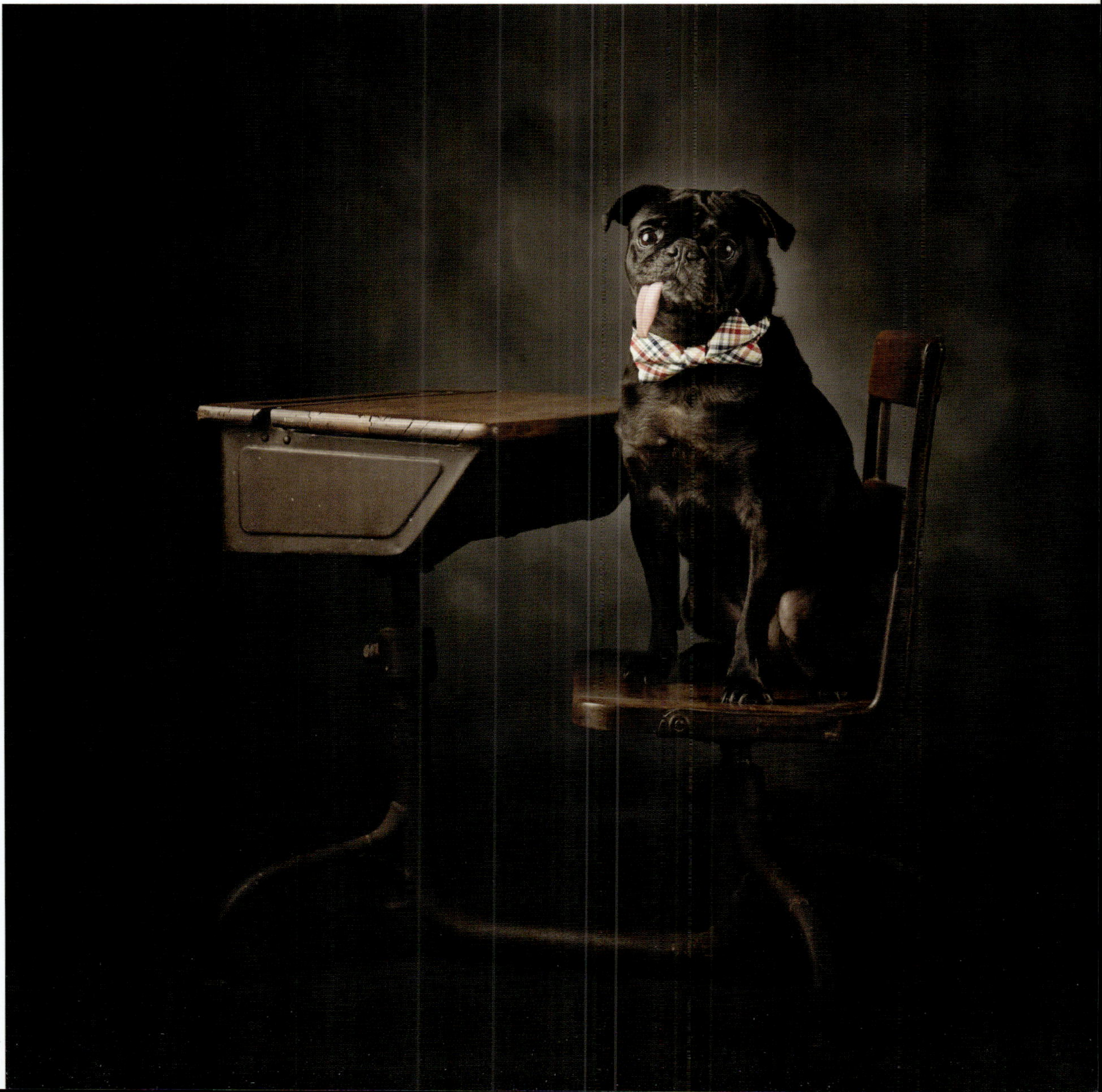

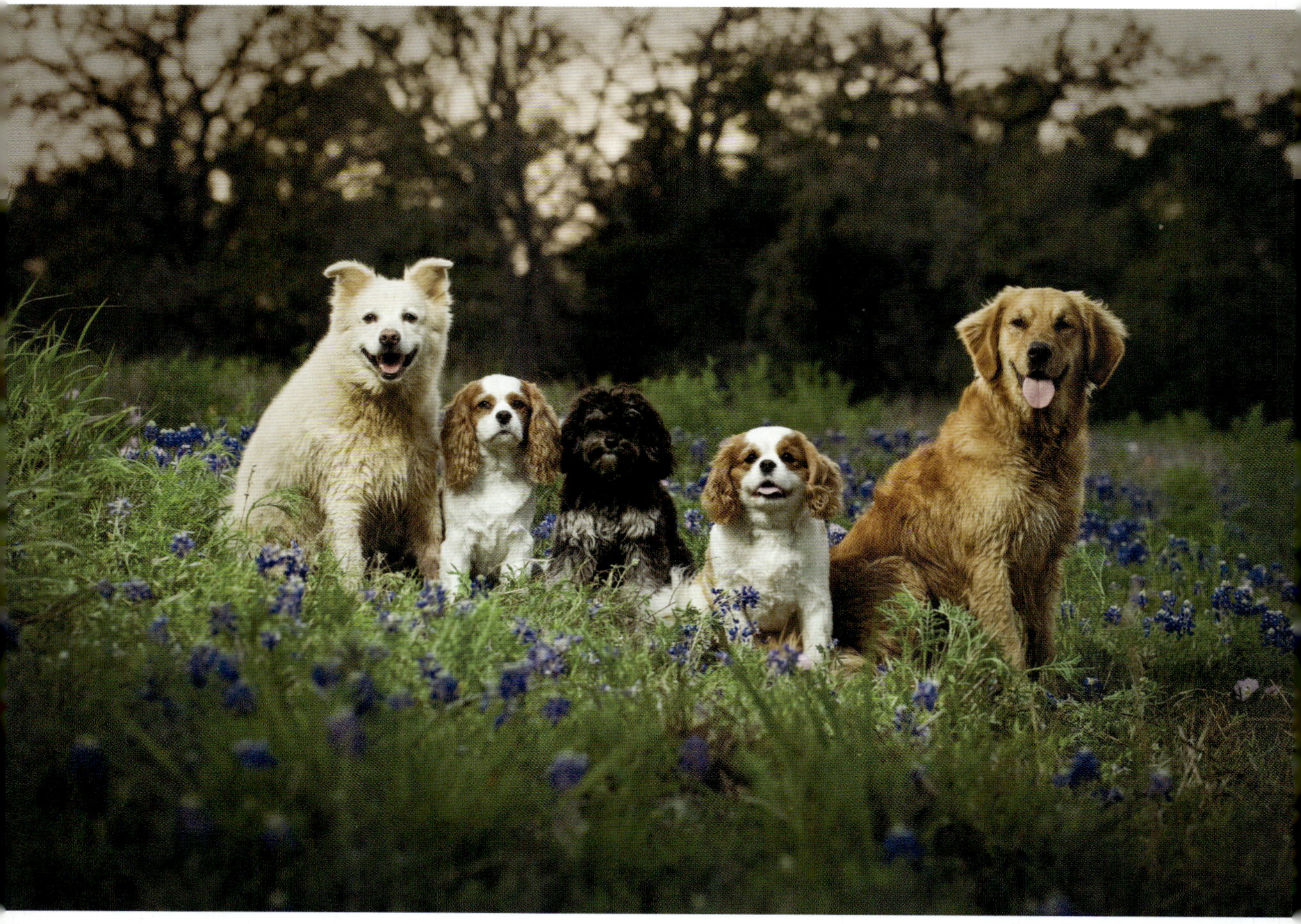

It can be very challenging when you're photographing a black dog with other light-colored dogs or a family because you will most likely need more light on that dog than you do in the rest of the photo. The best way to achieve this is to use a snoot pointed directly at the darkest dog. Again, you always want to position the darkest dog closest to the light. Sometimes that's not possible, though, so you may need to adapt to the situation.

You can try for a slight silhouette image, as well, as long as you keep some of those details in the dog's fur and face highlighted.

This is a good time to talk about the possibility of photographing an animal who is afraid of the studio strobes, because it does happen. The Lab in the next image *(following page),* for instance, was terrified of my lights. This was literally the only image we got of her in studio because she was so scared.

"Use a snoot to direct light onto the darkest dog in a group."

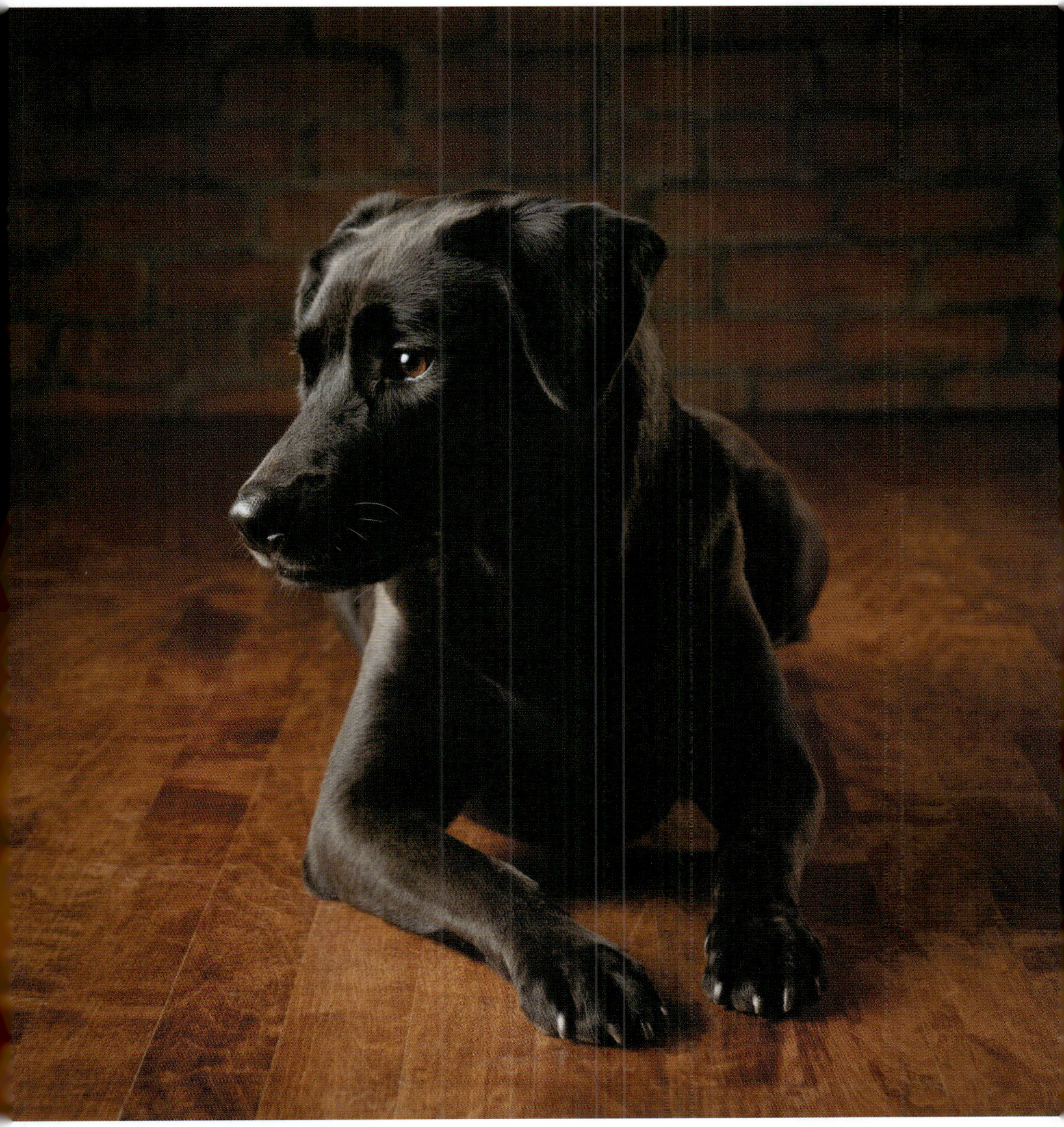

If that's the case, you can try positive reinforcement by giving a treat when you flash the lights. If that doesn't work, you can consider using continuous lights, but they don't have the same punch as strobes. Lastly, you can reschedule and do an on-location shoot, which is what I wound up doing for this lovely girl.

CHAPTER THREE

Selecting Great Props

Great light is key when creating an effective portrait, but I want you to be able to complete your image with fun props, effective posing, and a great expression. If you can't finish an image, it doesn't matter much how well it is lit. So, let's turn our attention to choosing the right props.

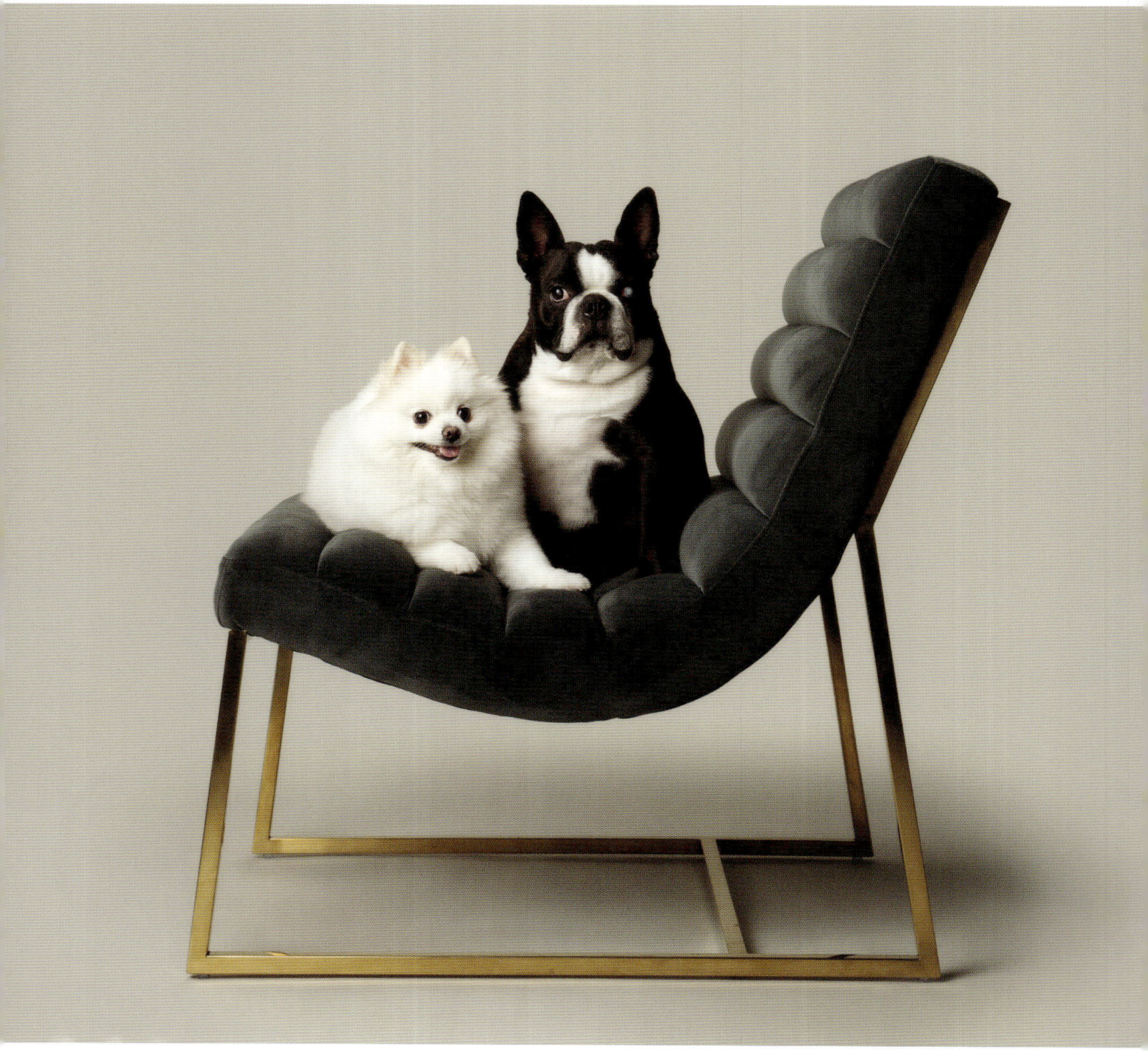

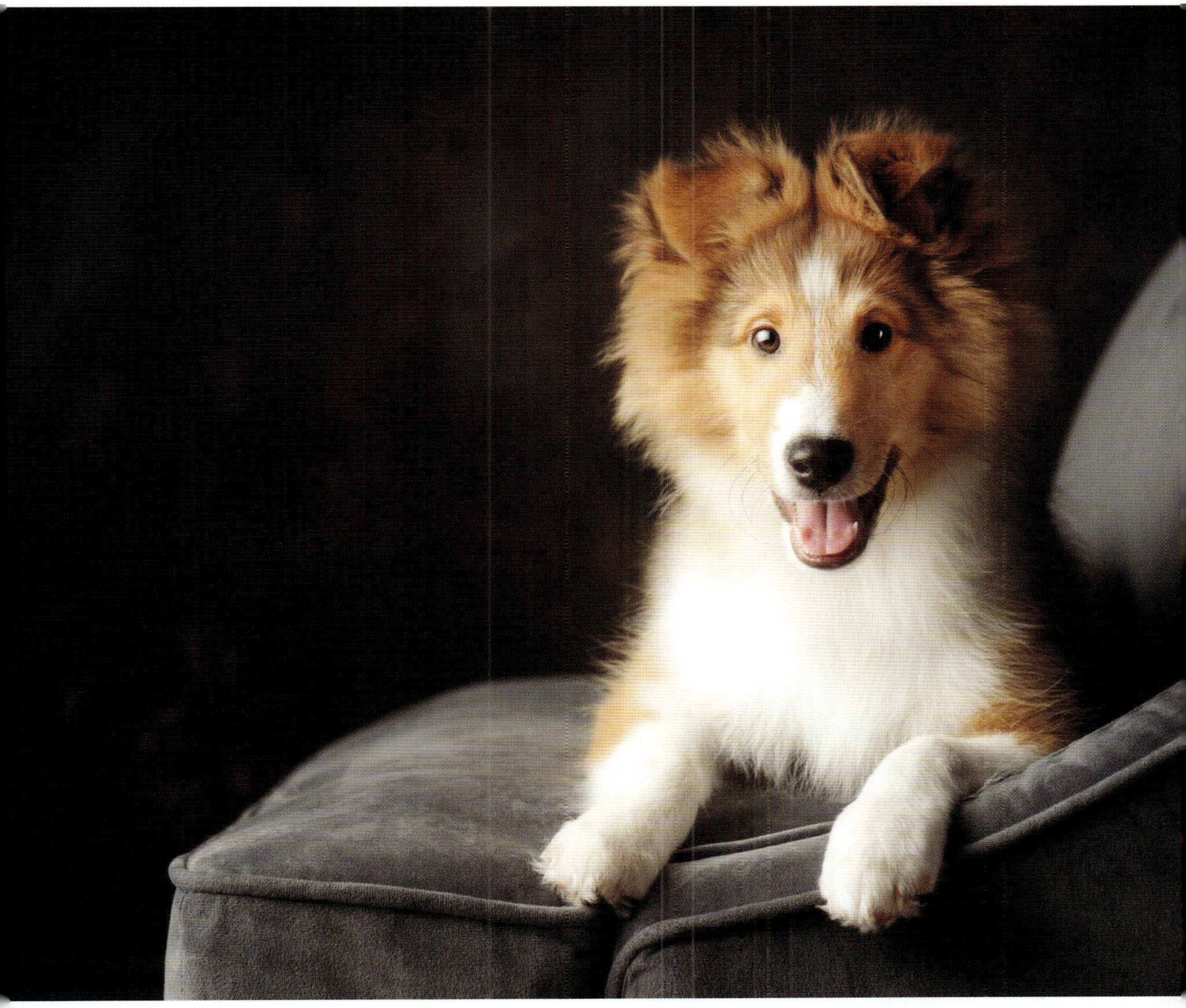

When choosing props for pet portraits, there are several things to consider. First, the backdrop is very important. It's hard to use fabrics or muslin backgrounds because the backdrop may bunch up when the pets move around, which becomes a Photoshop nightmare. You will want to stick to seamless papers you can tape down, or a hand-painted canvas (my personal favorite), like you see here. Hand-painted canvases are a great choice because they are heavy, don't move around, and add a bit of interest to your background without being distracting.

"Use a paper backdrop or hand-painted canvas for your dog portraits."

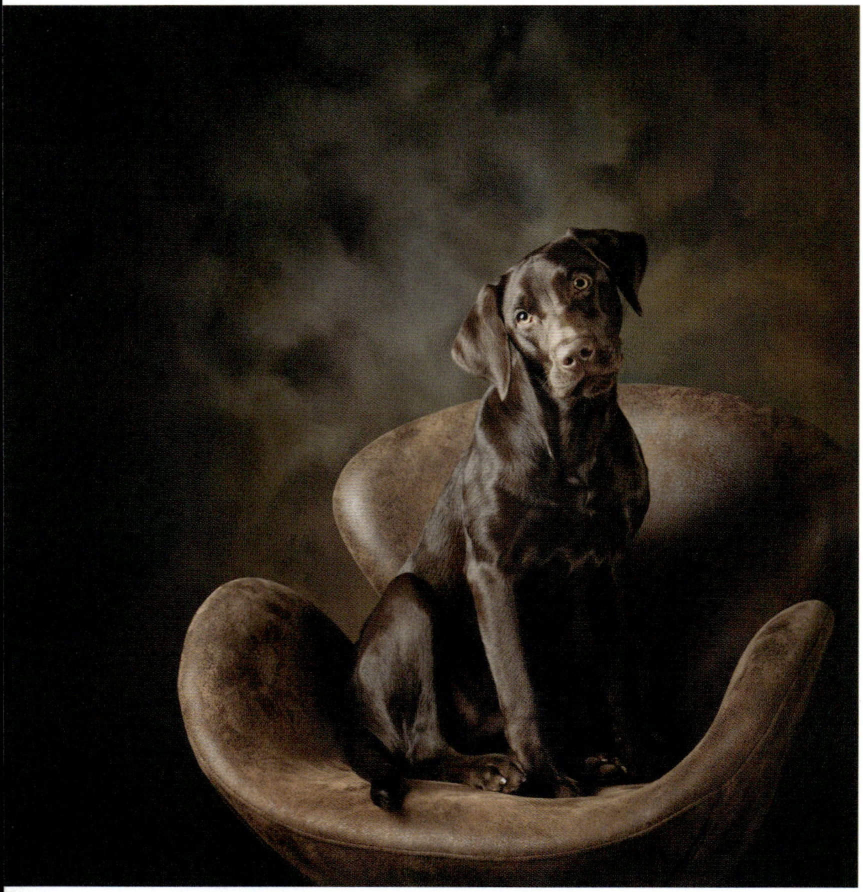

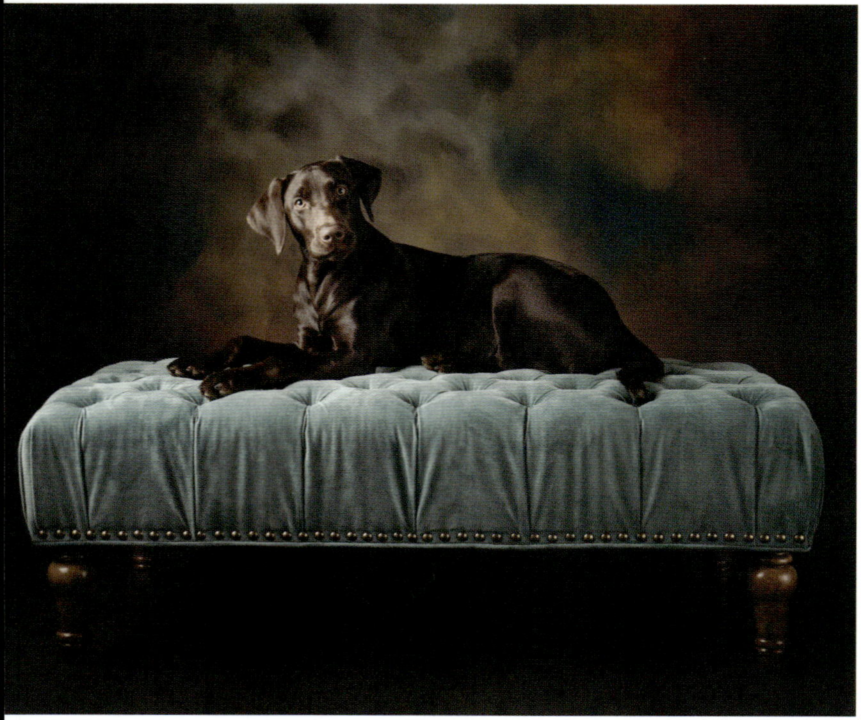

Choosing actual props can be a bit more challenging for pets because we are limited in how we can pose them, which we discuss in more detail in the next chapter. If we use sofas and arm chairs, we may lose some of the details in their bodies, so it's best to look for comfortable furniture that is armless, or something like this ottoman, with four sides you can photograph from. An armless sofa or chair will also lead to a lot more flexibility in getting the most out of your props. If you're like me, you're limited on storage space, so it's not possible to have tons of props. Using options like the furniture in these images allows me to provide variety in my sessions.

You also want to make sure that your props are in line with your photographic style. It's okay to go out on a limb and try new things, but you don't want to use things that just don't fit in with your current style. If you're working with tricky props, like this tricycle here, you have to keep in mind that you can only do what the pet will allow you to. Don't force anything to happen because that is the easiest way to stress out the pet and/or the pet parent, and bring your session to an abrupt end. You can always revisit one of your props if you want to try again later.

"Do not stress the dog or owner by forcing an idea that is tough to implement with that subject."

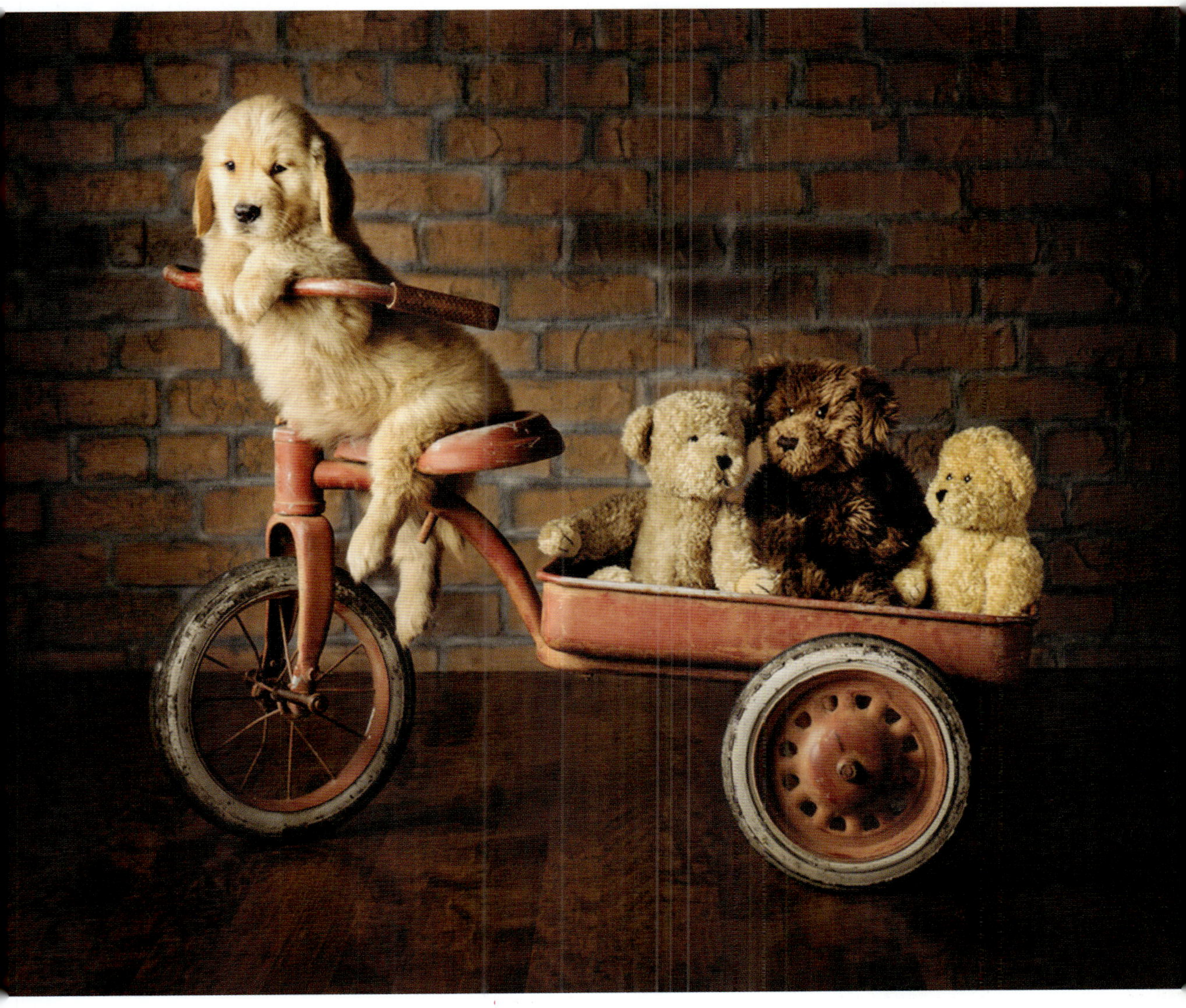

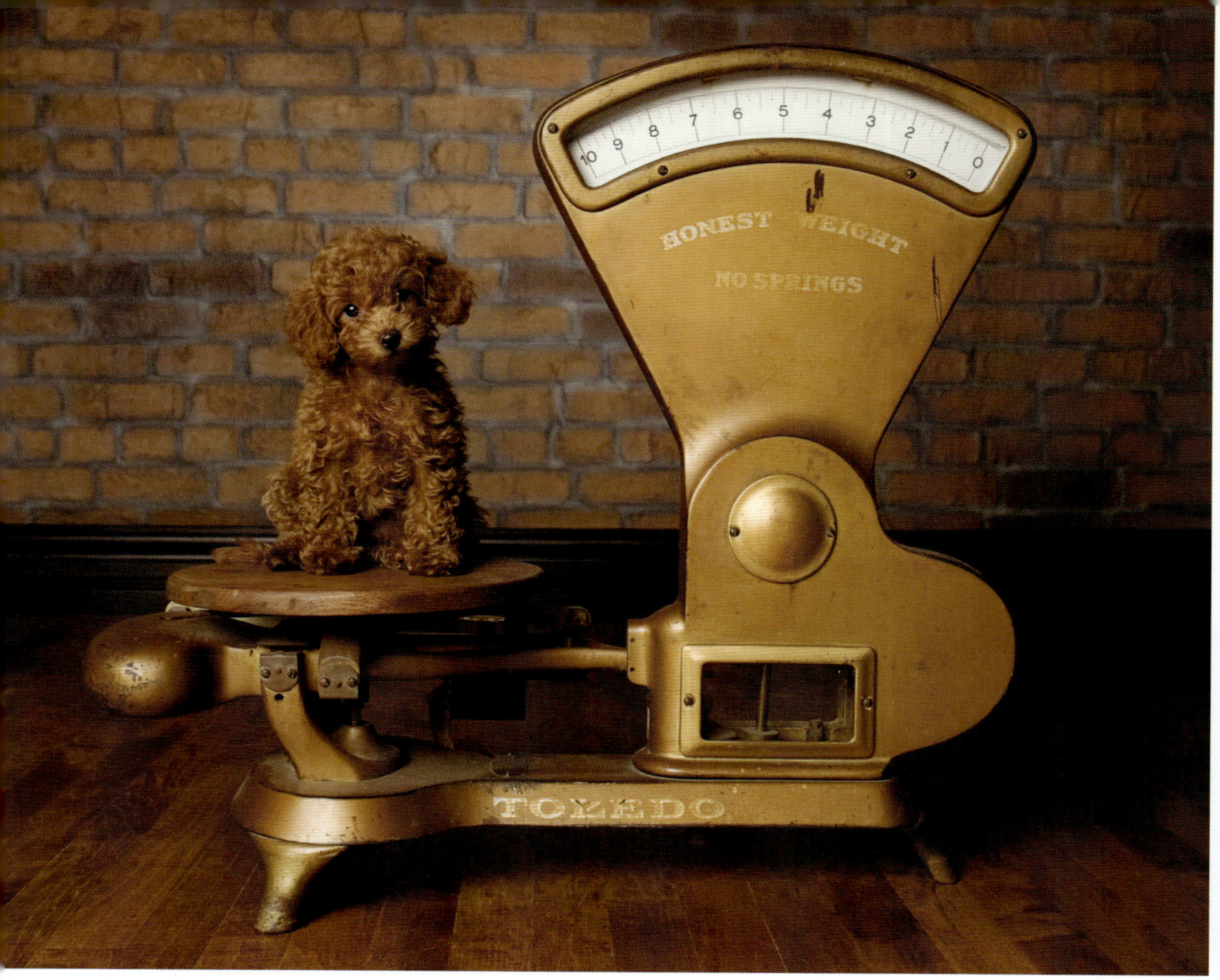

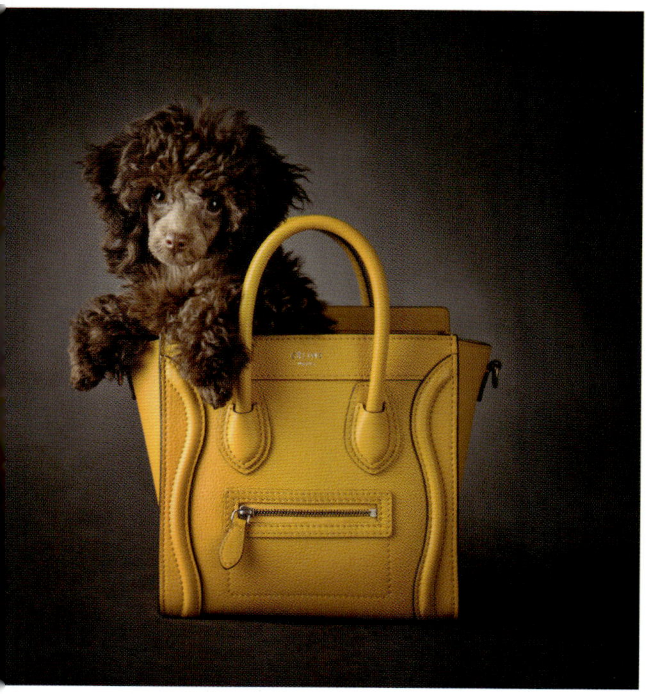

I love being able to show just how small an animal is by using a prop. You can establish a sense of scale (no pun intended!), like I did in this image of an adorable little Maltipoo.

You can also use props to tell a story and add a pop of color. In this case, this little Chocolate Poodle has a personal stylist for a mom, so the purse was a very appropriate prop for the image. Not to mention, it just makes for a fun image and a way to get a tiny, four-pound dog to stand up and out more in the frame.

"Choose a prop that tells a story about the dog or owner."

Don't be afraid to ask the pet parents if they want to include anything fun in their photographs to make them more personal.

I had an owner come in for her shoot and she had the most beautiful purse and a tiny little Yorkie, so I asked if we could use her bag in the images. We had to put a few blankets in the bottom to prop the dog up a bit, but we were able to get some great images in the purse. Ultimately, this is the image the client chose to display on her wall.

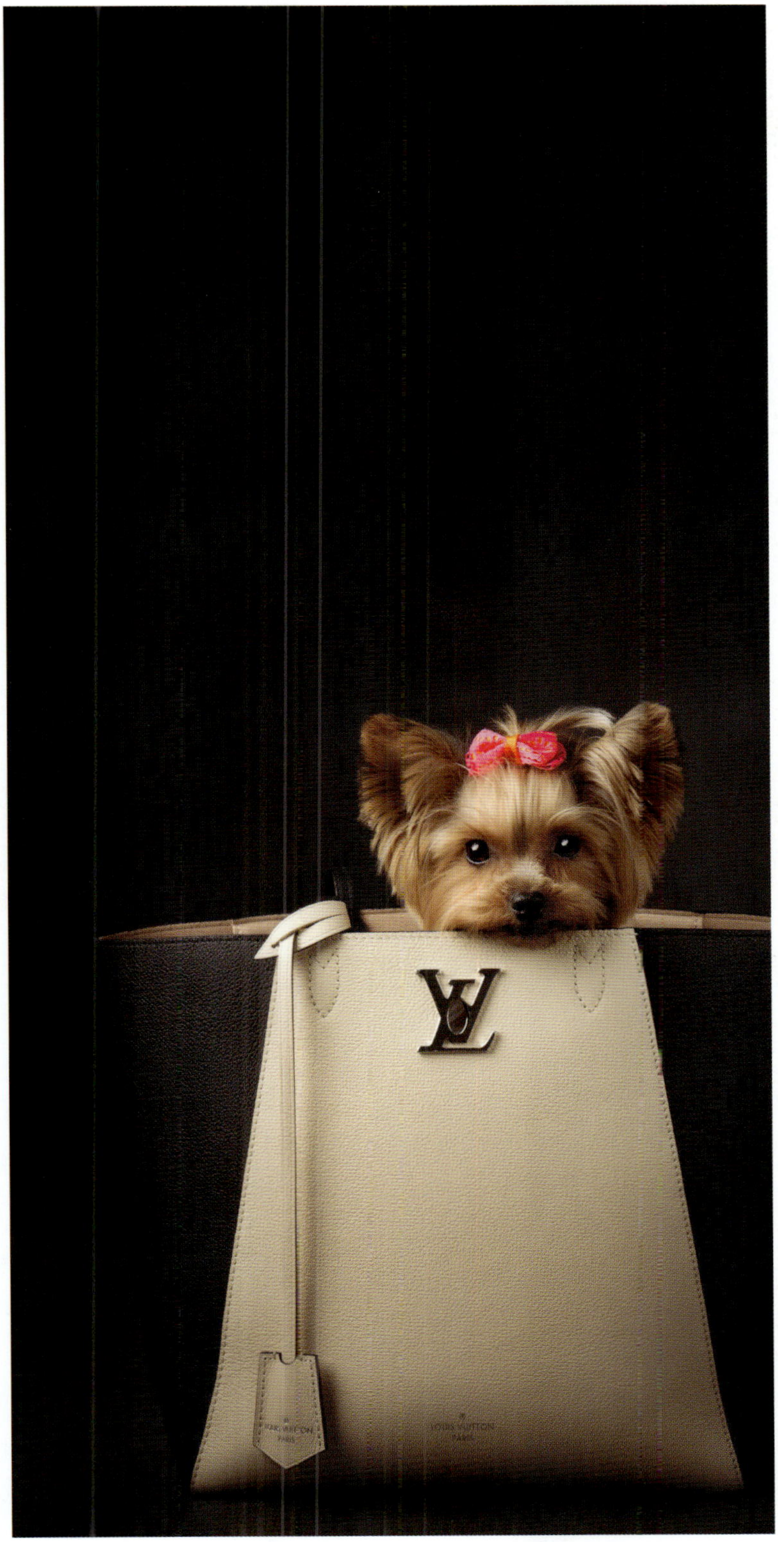

Getting the most out of your props is so important for creating variety in your images. Here are some examples of how you can create a different look in the same session with the same props. In these images, the light output, modifier, and position stayed the same. The only difference is the pose.

You get a completely different image just by angling the sofa to get a photo

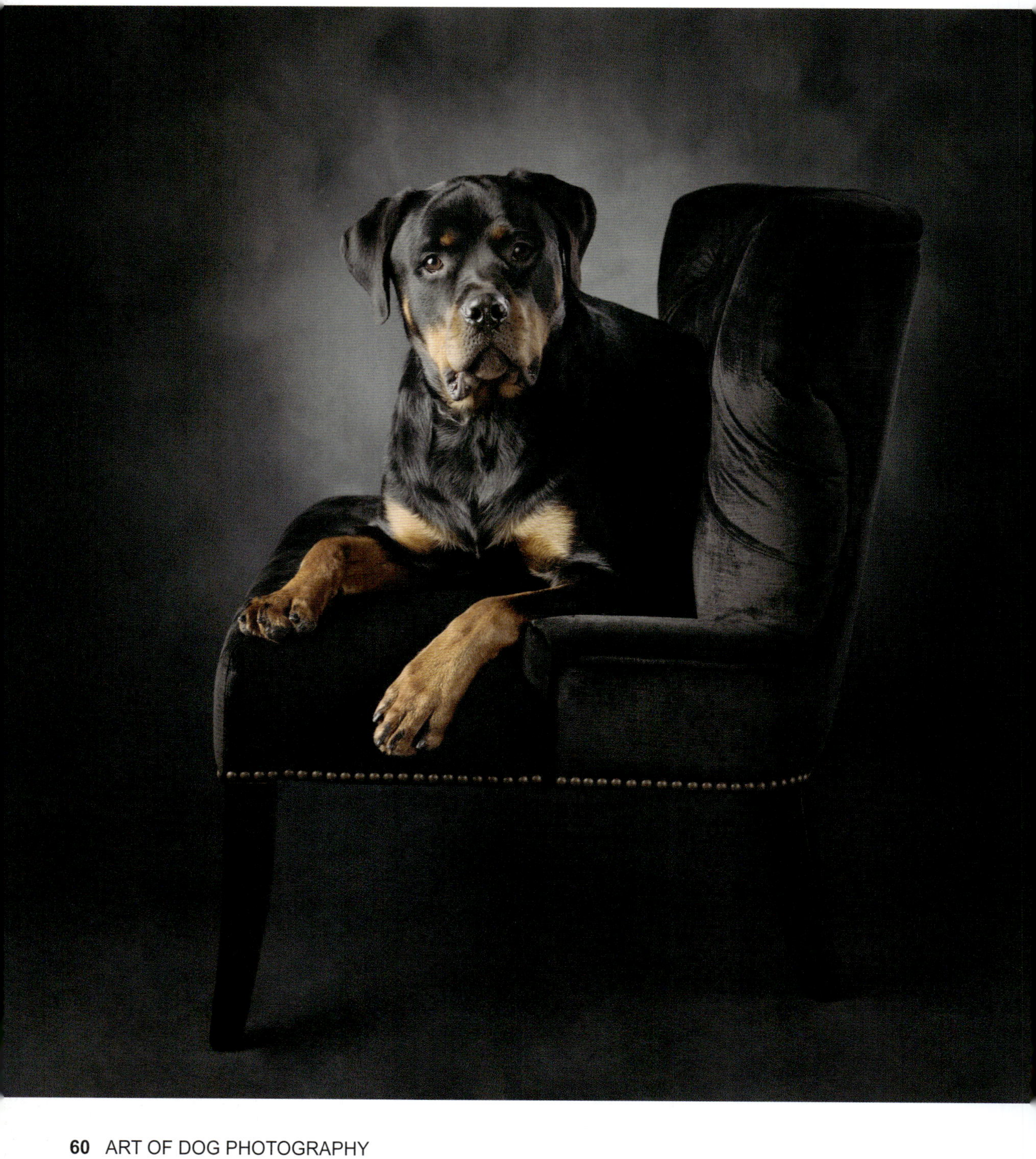

with the face as the main focus, or showcase the entire body. It is important to get different body positions on the pet where you can see all of the body and then some of it. We are limited to stand, sit, and down with a lot of pets, so you have to be open to how you show those different poses.

"Change the pose and shooting angle to produce a series of images with different looks."

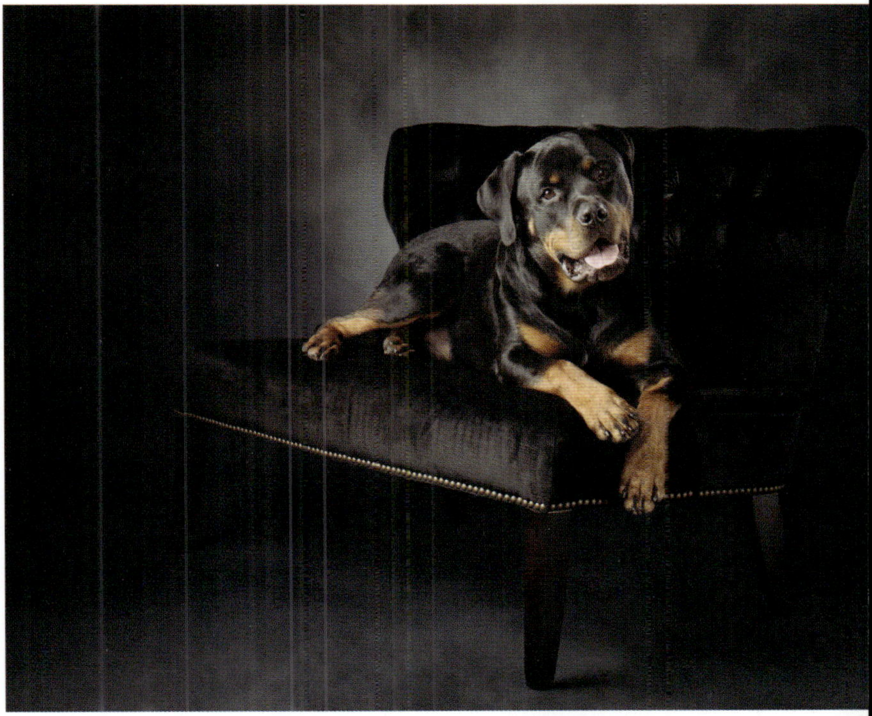

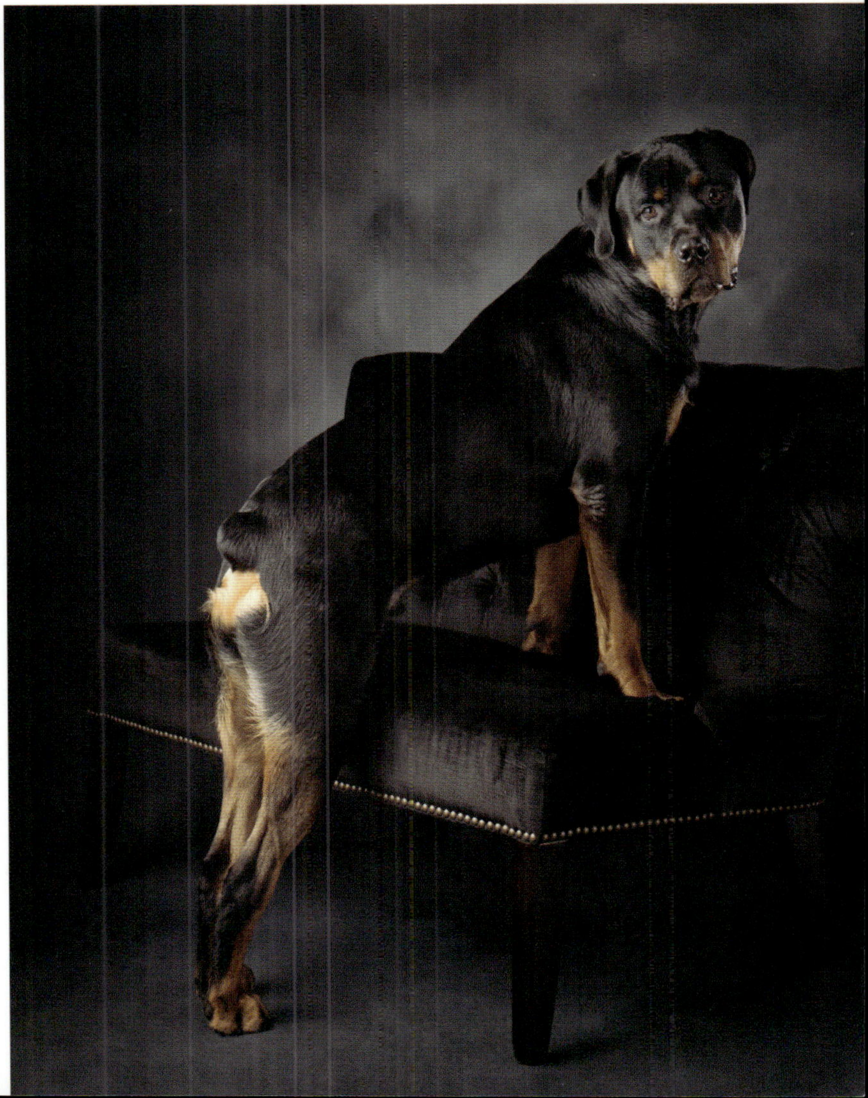

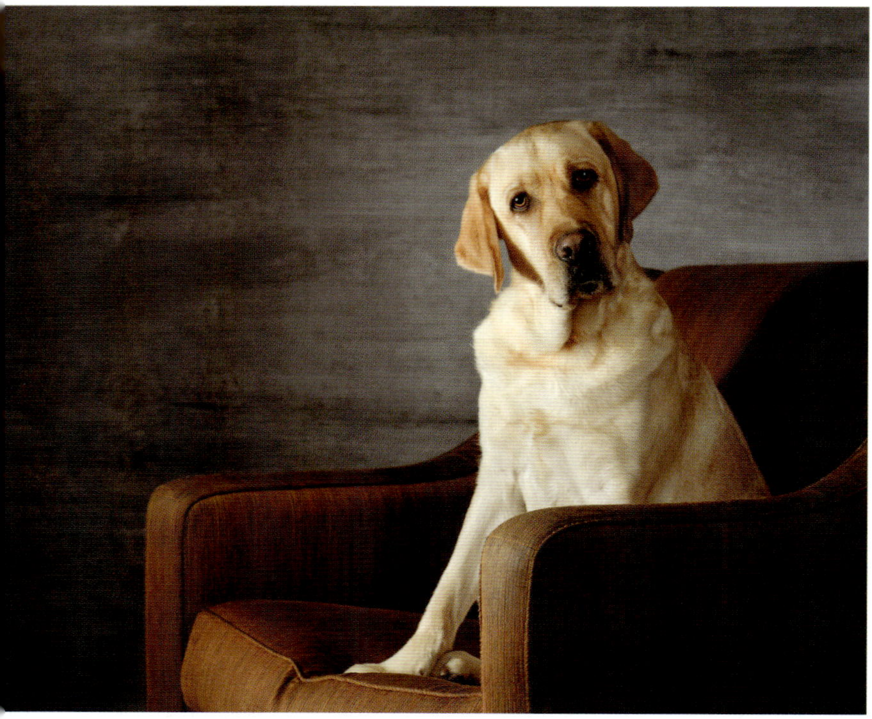

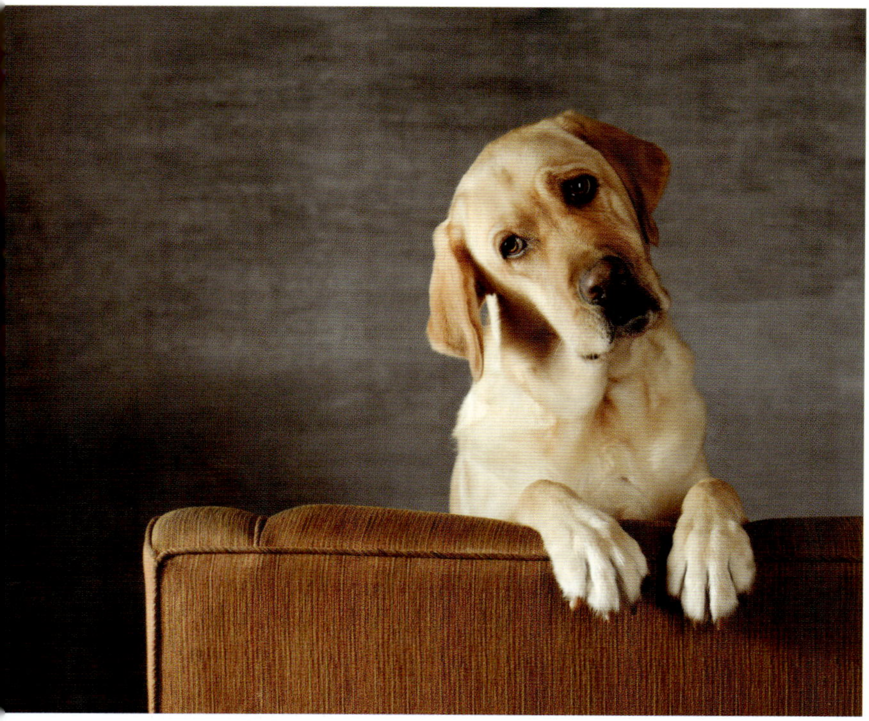

Here are a few more examples showing an adorable dog I photographed while speaking at a convention. I had never met this pup before, and I didn't get my choice of props. But, sometimes you have to make it work, like when you photograph in a client's home and don't have a lot of options to work with. See how I was able to get a variety of images just by changing the angle of the chair? You have to be flexible and ready to adapt on the fly as needed. It's amazing how many poses you can get out of one prop if you try.

I ended up using a hotel chair that had arms and was not a great color, but I was able to get lots of variety with different sits and downs. Also, the dog's expression changed based on the different ways I got his attention. That's why having an array of noisemakers is key to getting wonderful, varied, expressions. If you can get head tilts and ears perked and spot-on lighting, you'll have a winning image!

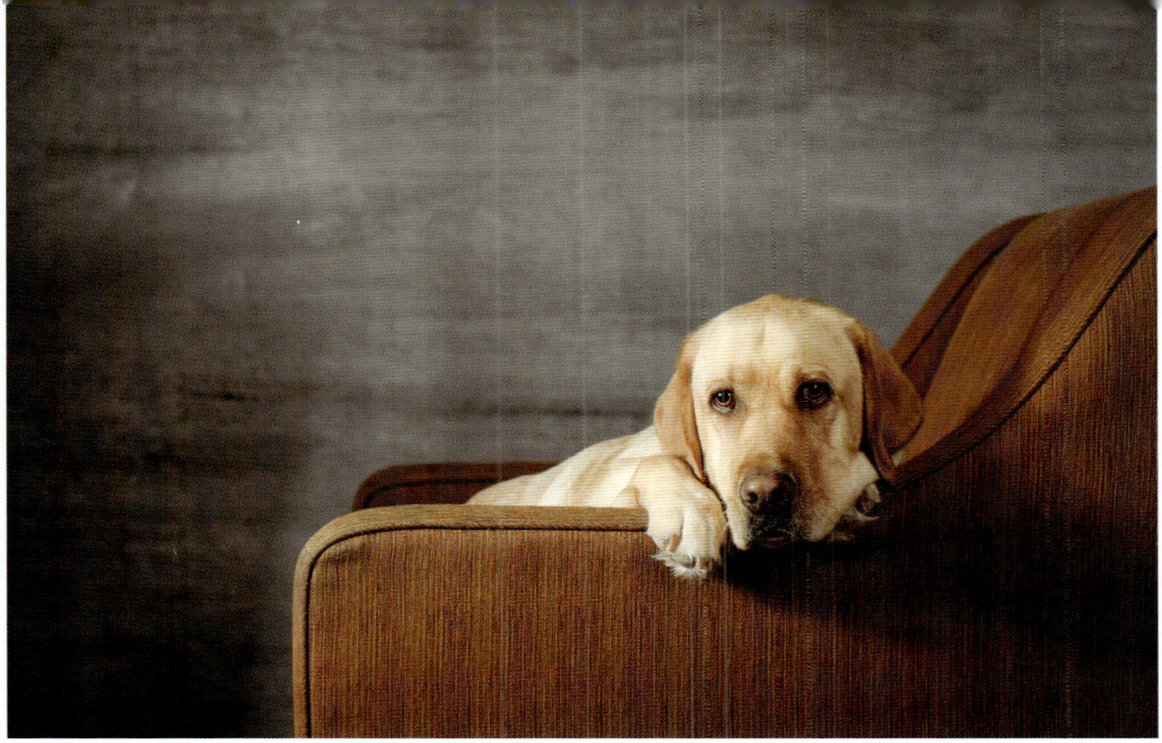

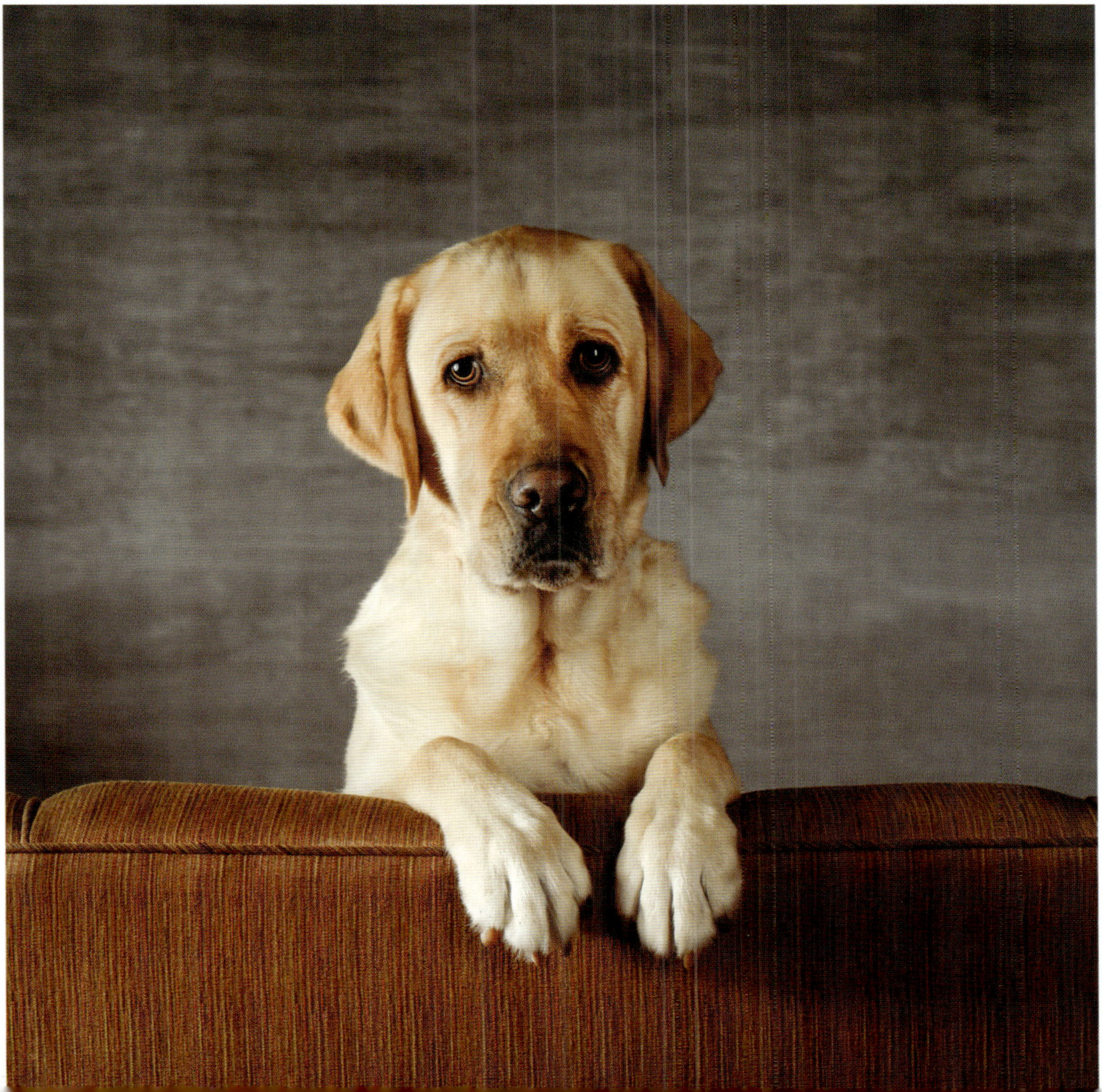

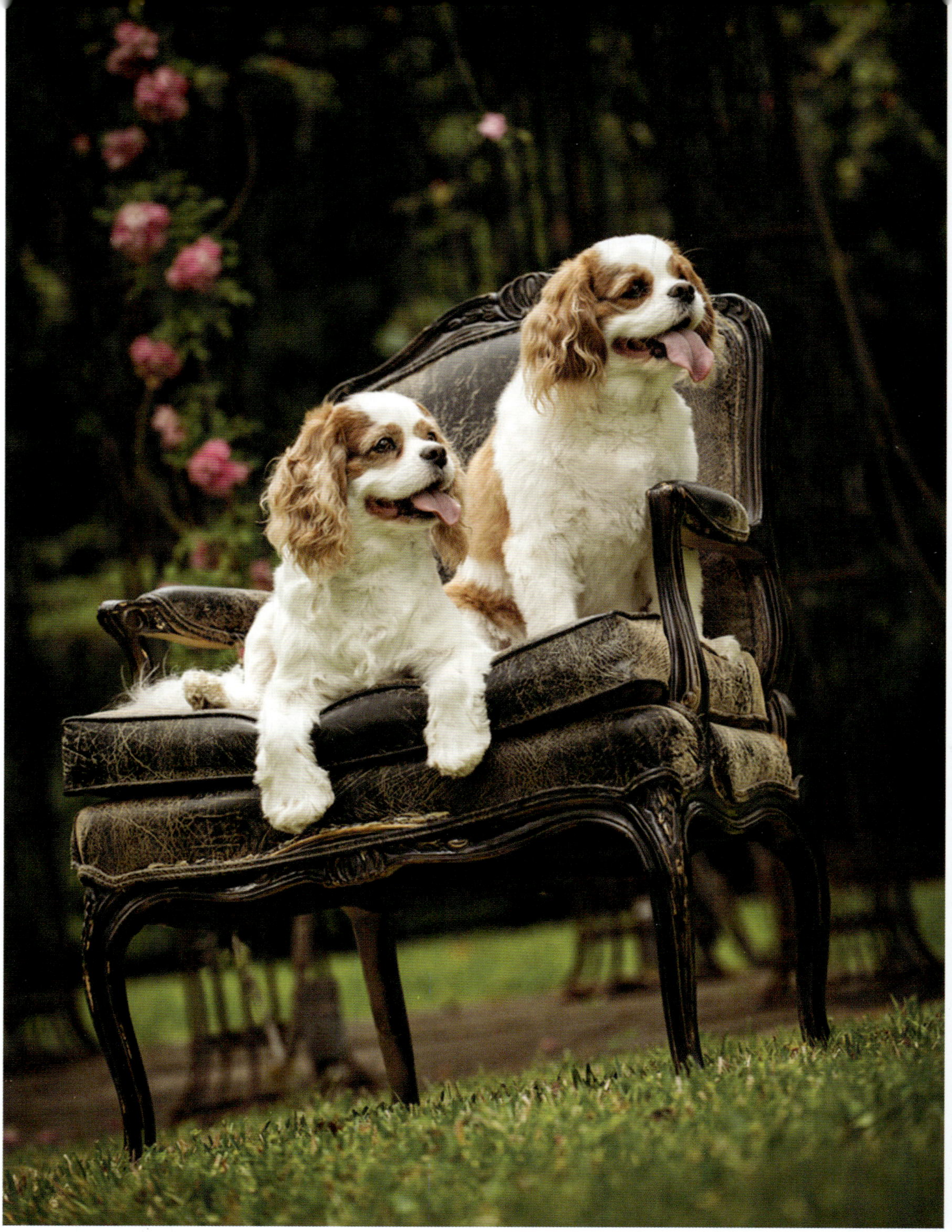

"On location, consider using benches, stairs, or other features that can be used to raise a pet off of the ground."

Props on Location

When you're on location using props is still an option. You can bring your own with you, like I did with this chair, or find out what's readily available on site. I do recommend scouting the location prior to your shoot so you have some kind of idea of what is there and what you can use before you arrive with your client. Props don't have to be chairs, sofas, etc., either. When you're on location, look for benches, stairs, retaining walls, or anything that might add interest and get that pet off the ground.

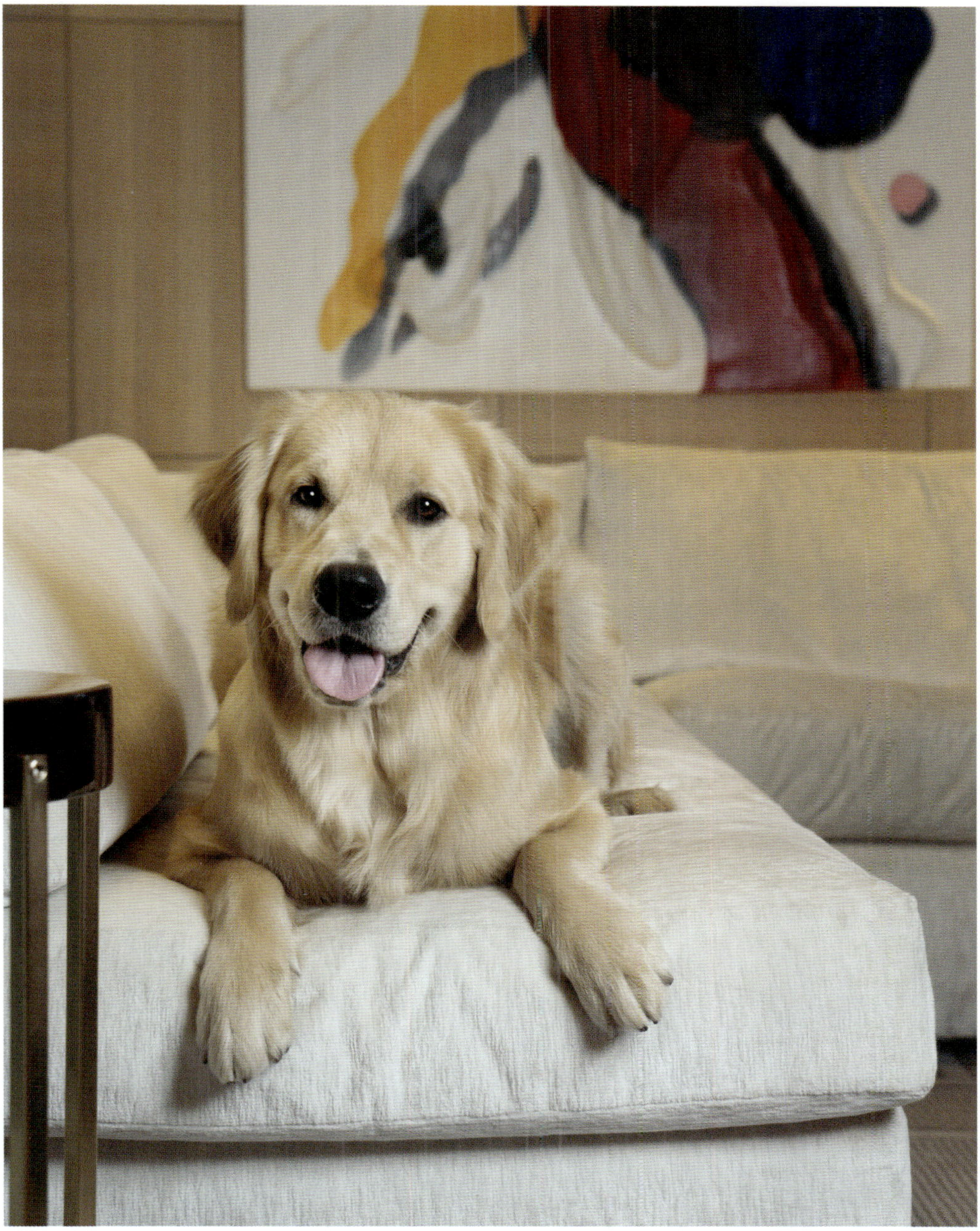

It is important to scout a location prior to shooting at it. If you're meeting a client on location and show up without previewing the locale, you might be in for a surprise. All it takes is going to the planned location on a day prior to the shoot at the same time of day to see what options you have for locations and lighting. It will make a difference in your images as well as your professionalism because you will know where you are shooting next.

This image below was taken for me by a client, as the location was out of town. She photographed it at the same time of day as our shoot to give me an idea of what I was in for.

That scouted image may not look that appealing, but I was able to look around it for other options. Look for interesting lines, concrete, brick pavers, or shapes in the space for you to work around.

I was photographing this adorable Nova Scotia Duck Tolling retriever *(following page),* and her fur color was very similar to the brick siding at this location. Here *(top)* is one of the images we got during her shoot. I love this shot because it shows the bond between the dog and the parents. The focus is on the pup's face, but you can feel the bond in the rest of the image. The second image *(bottom)* is another pose shot in the same location.

"Scout the location prior to the session, at the same time of day, to get a feel for the scene and lighting."

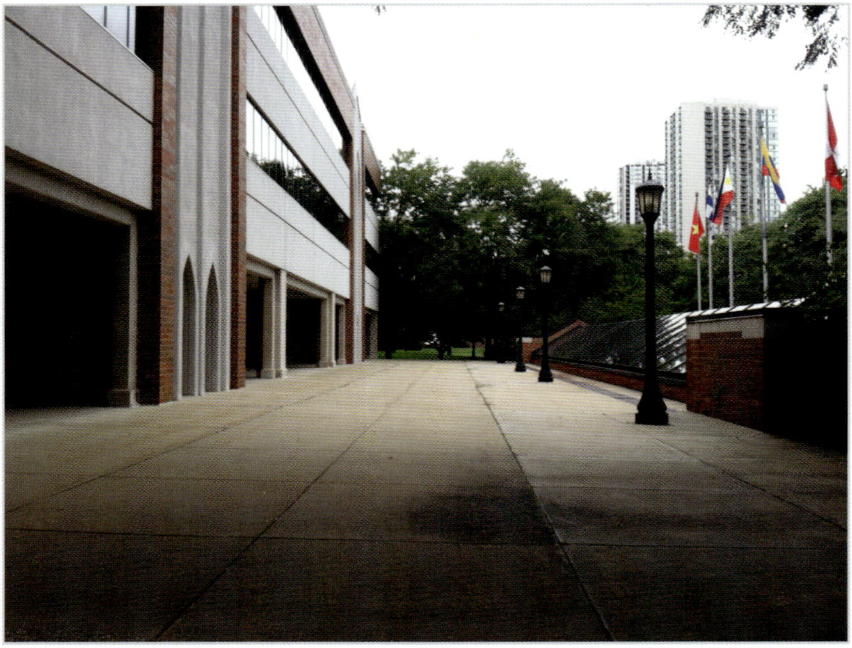

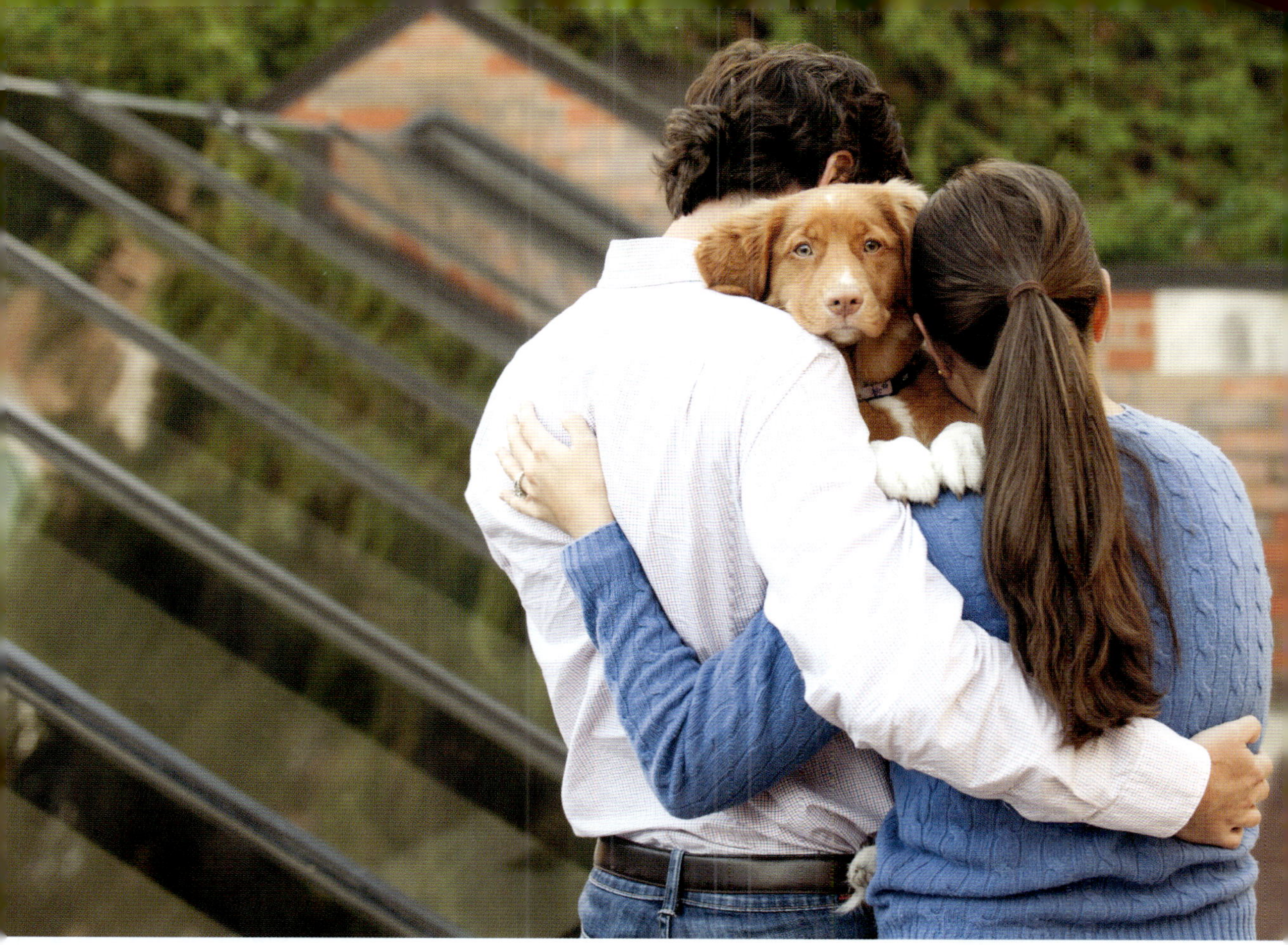

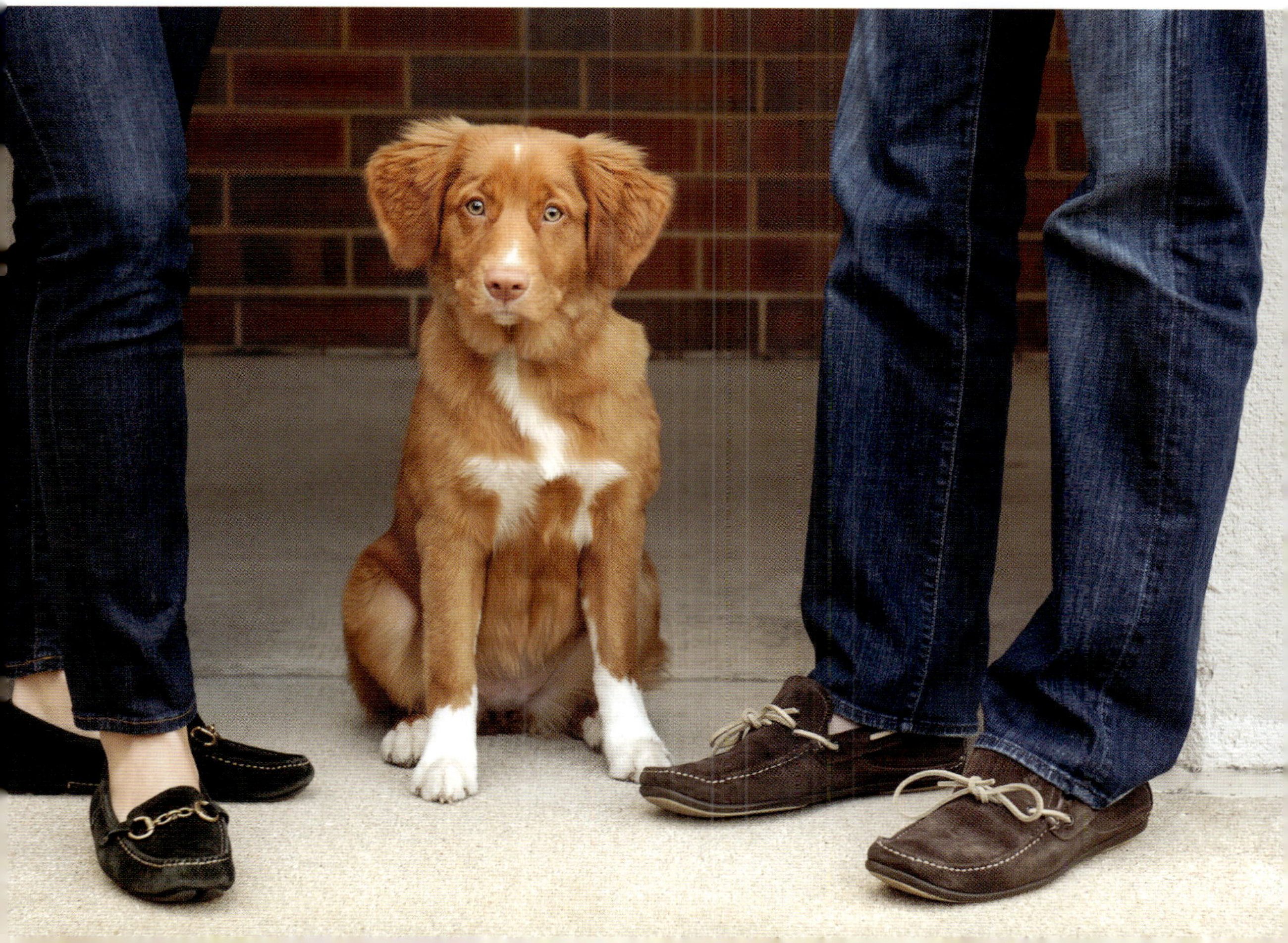

I have my favorite vendors when shopping for new props, and I'm happy to share them with you! One of my favorite places is Cost Plus World Market. They offer a wide variety of armless chairs, ottomans, and loveseats in fun colors, and they are lightweight and easy to move around. Other places to check out are Ikea, Home Goods/TJ Maxx, Marshalls, and antique fairs (I love to go antiquing!).

Also, don't hesitate to ask your clients if they have anything meaningful that might serve as a unique prop. They may have something at home that is amazing to photograph, and if you don't ask, you won't know.

"Look to boutiques, thrift stores, and import stores for unique props."

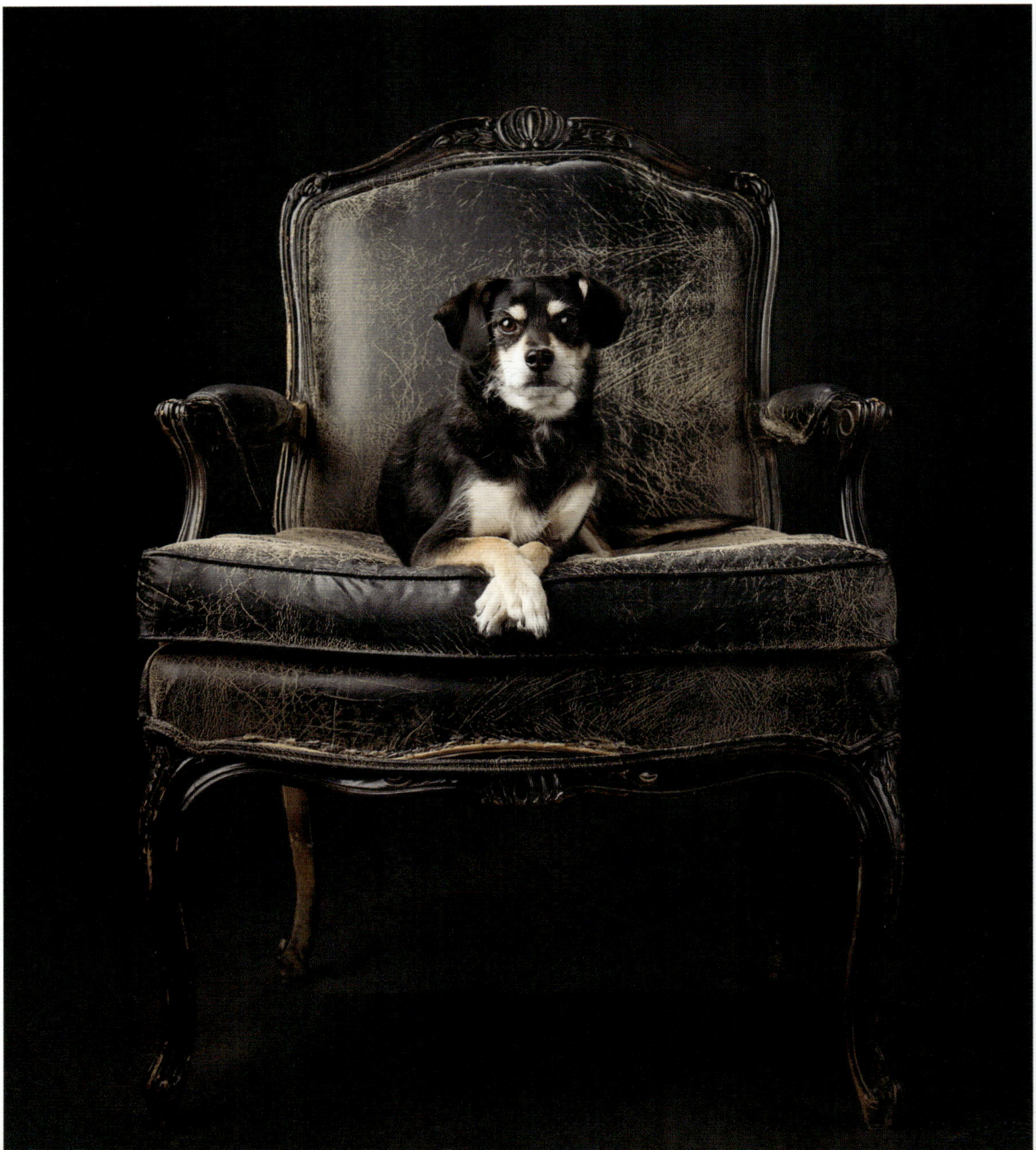

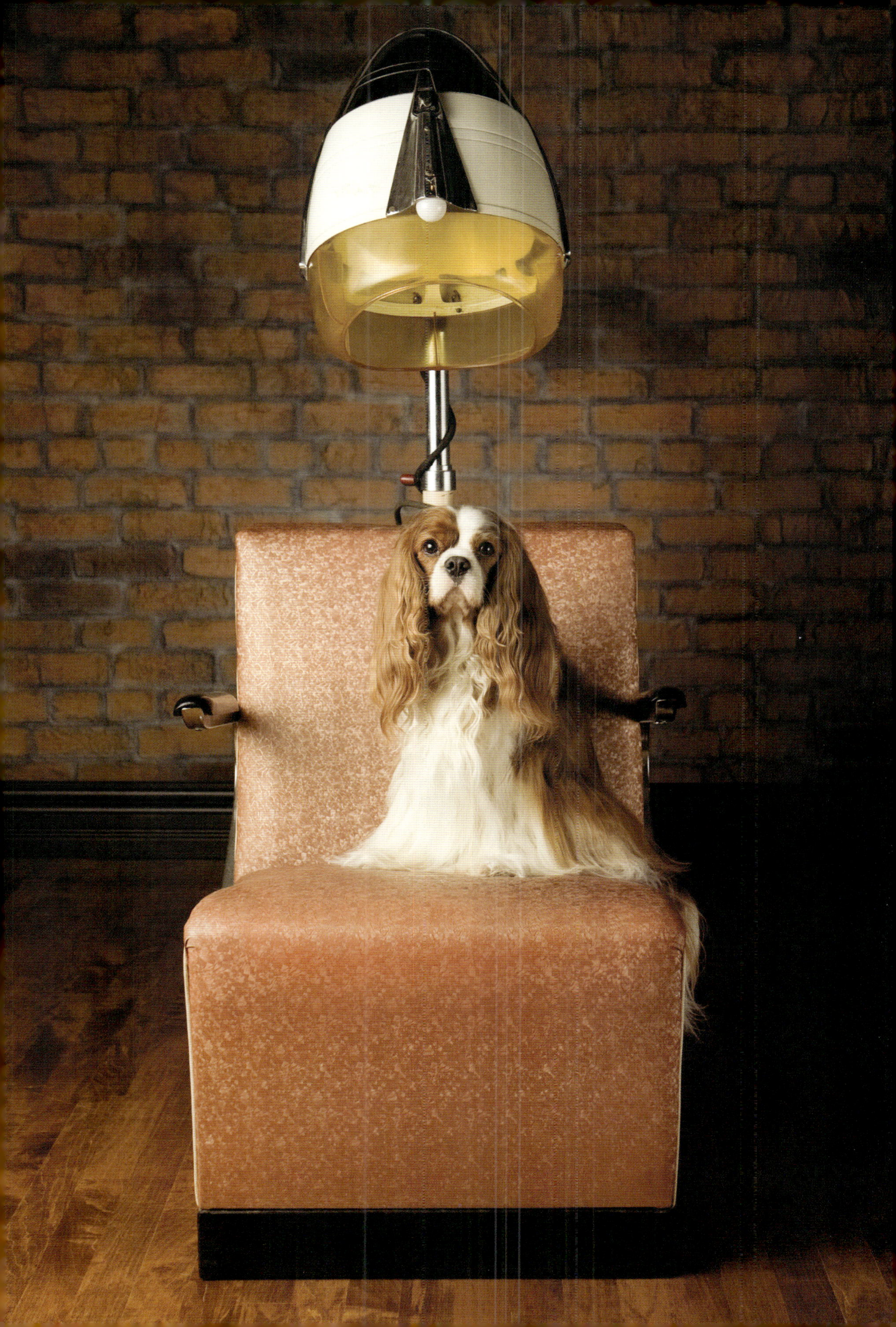

CHAPTER FOUR

Posing Dogs

Posing dogs is not like posing people. With people, you have a lot of options in how you place and pose, but you also have to worry about slimming them and getting their best angle. With pets, you have to worry about other things, like not photographing a dog full frontal, if you know what I mean! We also don't have a ton of options other than sit, down, stand, and hopefully stay. So, how do you get a variety of looks if you're working with just one pup, like the cutie pie in the image below? The key is to make creative use of props and to adjust the angles from which you capture each pose.

With pets, posing depends on the obedience level and what they will allow you to do. If you can get a dog to sit and stay, you have some options. If you can get a dog to down and stay, you have even more poses at your fingertips. The key is to change things up. Don't pose the pet exactly the same way on the props. Let's look at a couple of examples.

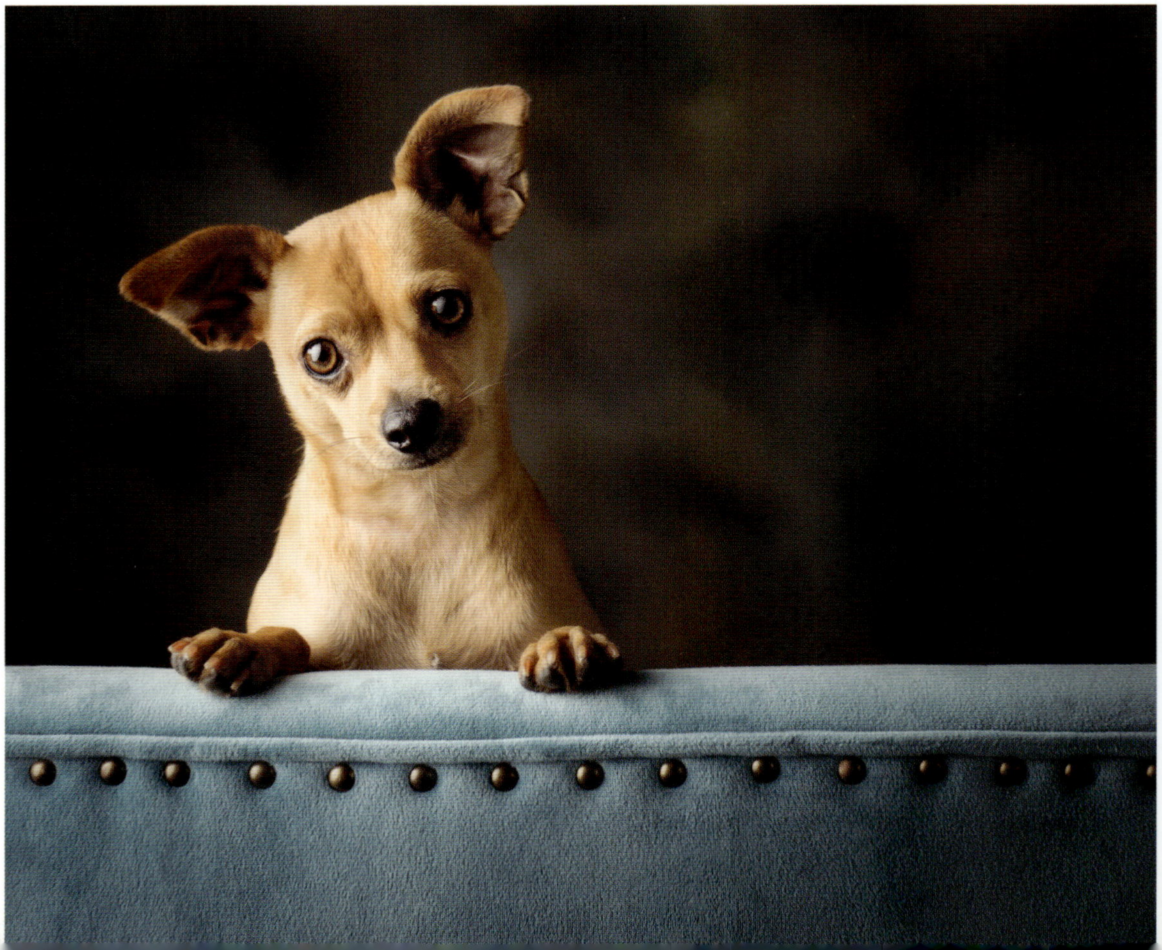

The first image *(top)* showcases the dog's face, not the whole body. Even though he is lying down, I can still get a completely different image by adjusting the sofa and the dog to get an image of his full body.

The second image *(bottom)* is a variation on a typical sit pose, and it is definitely a little trickier than a typical sit because you're asking the dog to look back at you. But, if the dog has a good stay, this is a fun pose to try. Another trick to getting a pet to stay in place long enough to nail a pose and get great expressions is to use a show lead.

"Try this pose if the dog is obedient when you ask him to stay."

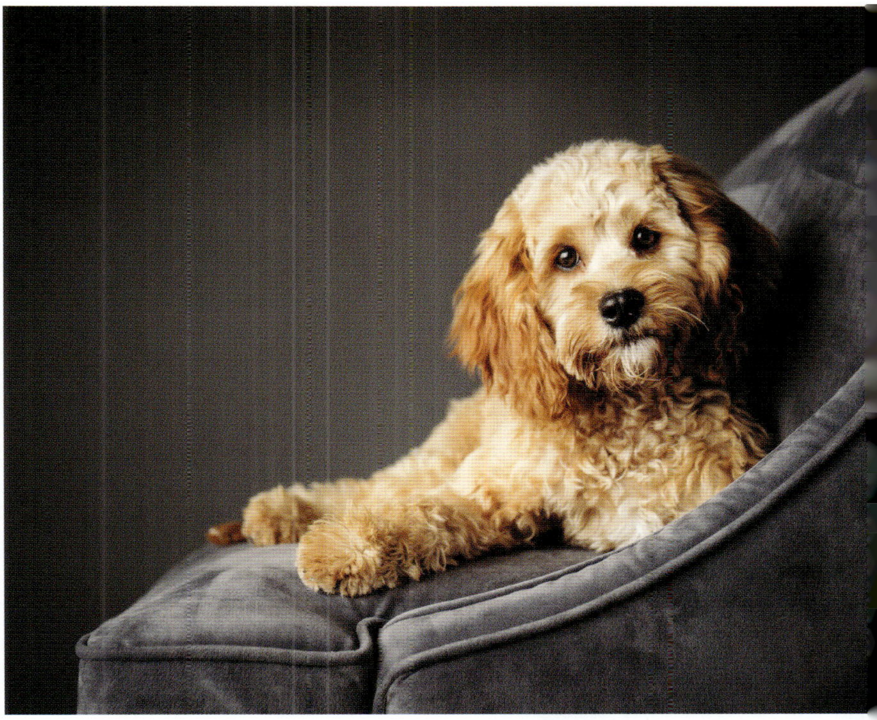

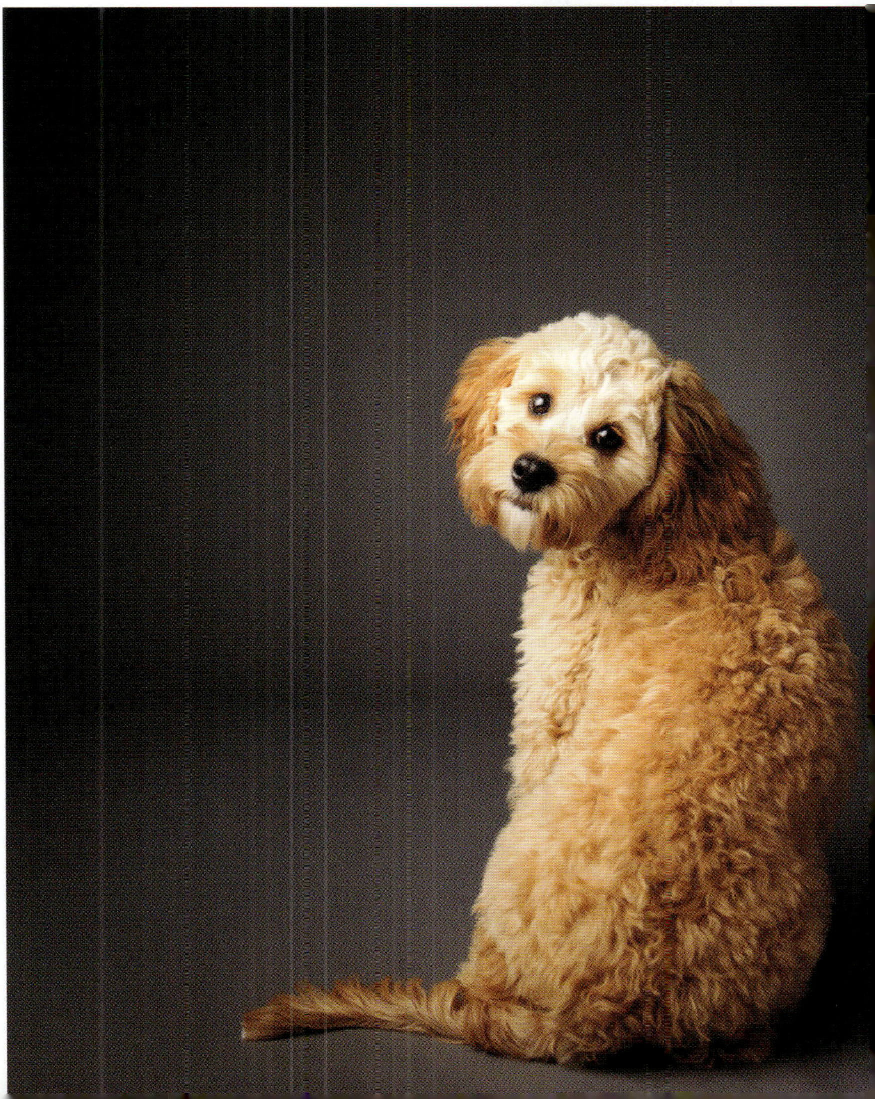

Here are a couple more examples. The little Pug in the next two images couldn't keep his tongue in his mouth, and I love how it translated in the images. He was so cute! Notice here how the chair has not moved, but the angle and image are quite different because of the crop and zoom. You can get several images out of one pose if you do a full shot, medium, and close-up shot.

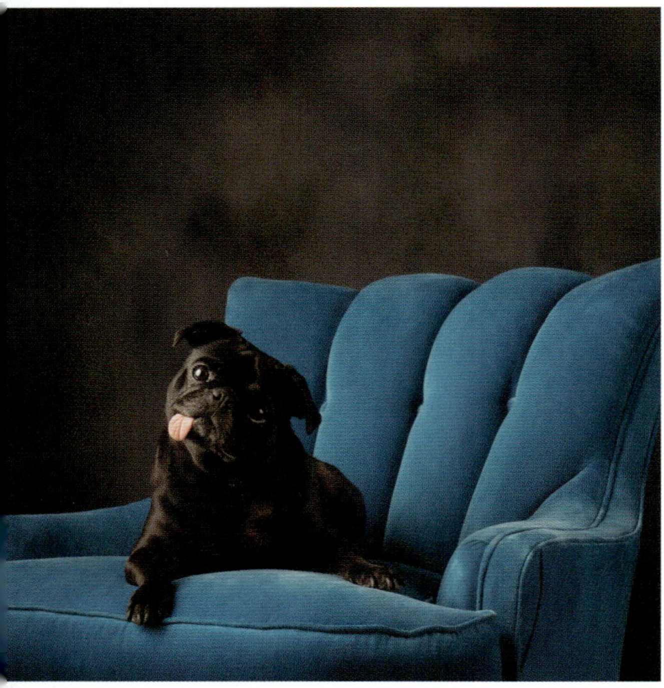

Here are two more posing ideas. For the first image *(facing page, top),* I used the chair in a conventional way. I cropped the image into a panoramic shape for an artful look. For the second image *(bottom),* I used a sofa turned backwards, with the pup peeking over the back. I love this pose because it fully utilizes the prop, and it's fun, too. Some pets are not comfortable in this pose. Read the pet's body language. If they don't want to do it, don't force them. That's a sure way to stress them out and end your session.

You can also try to use a leash to keep them in place long enough to get the shot.

"Try a full shot, take a medium one, and then photograph a close-up."

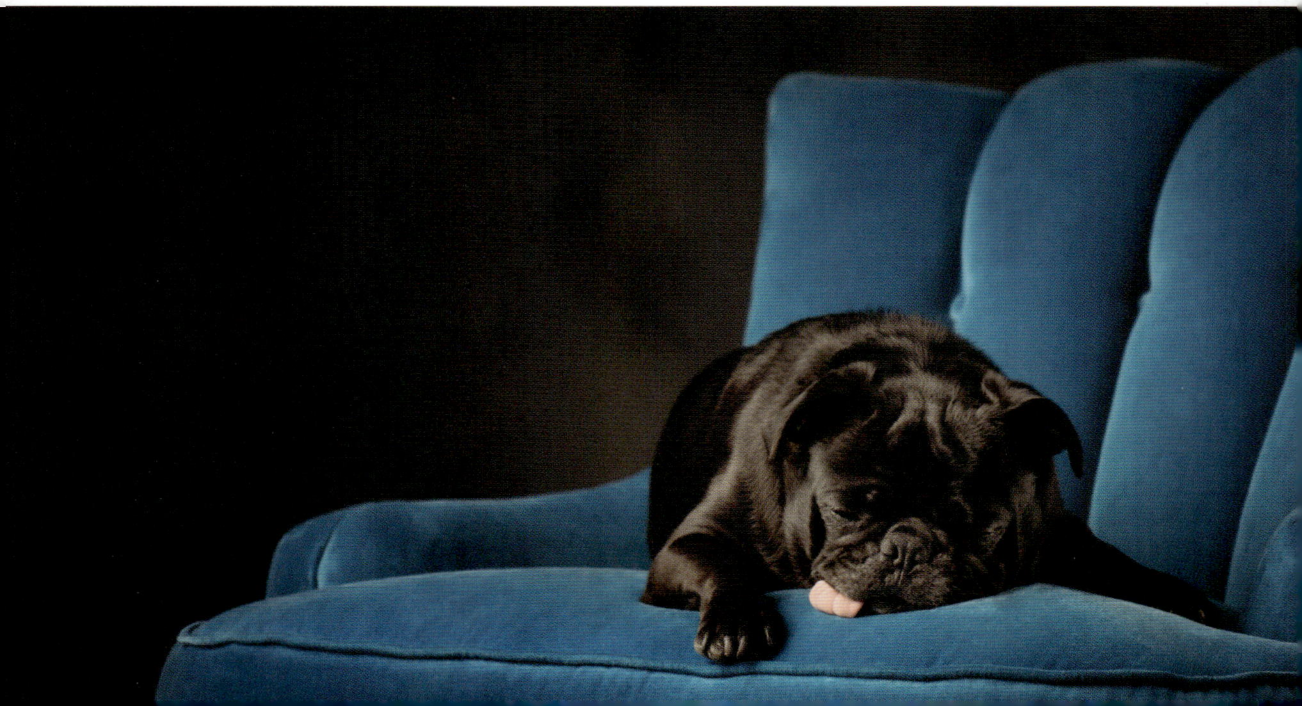

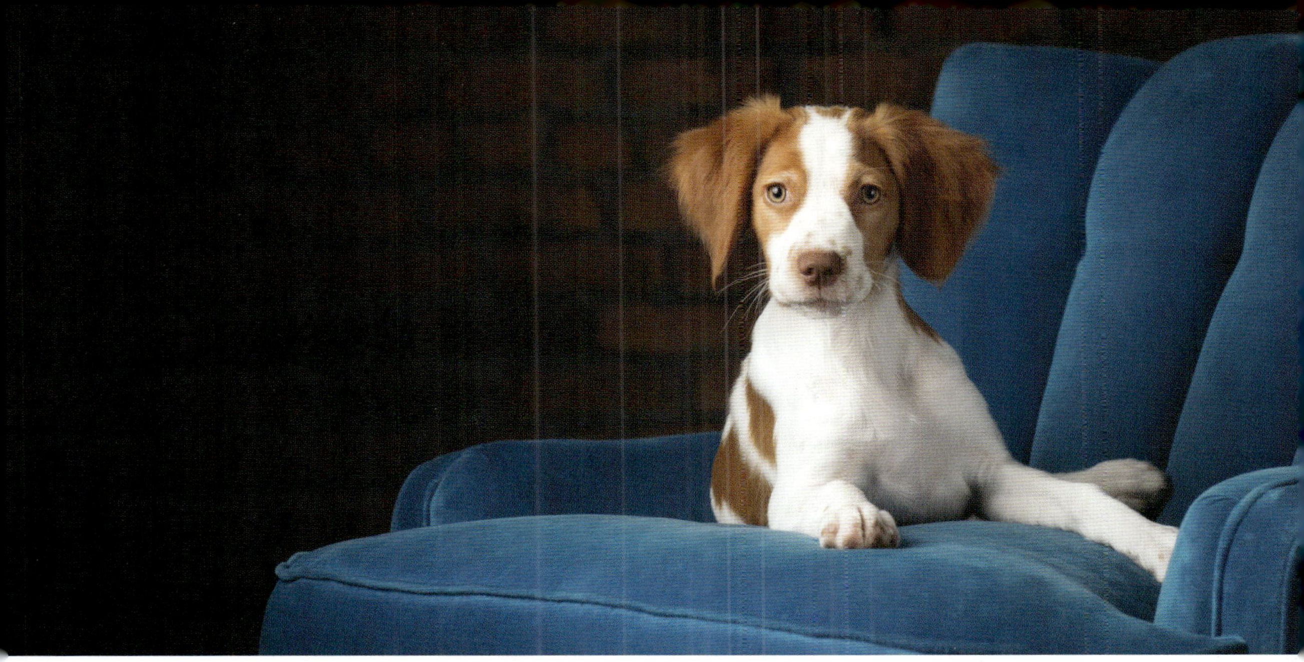

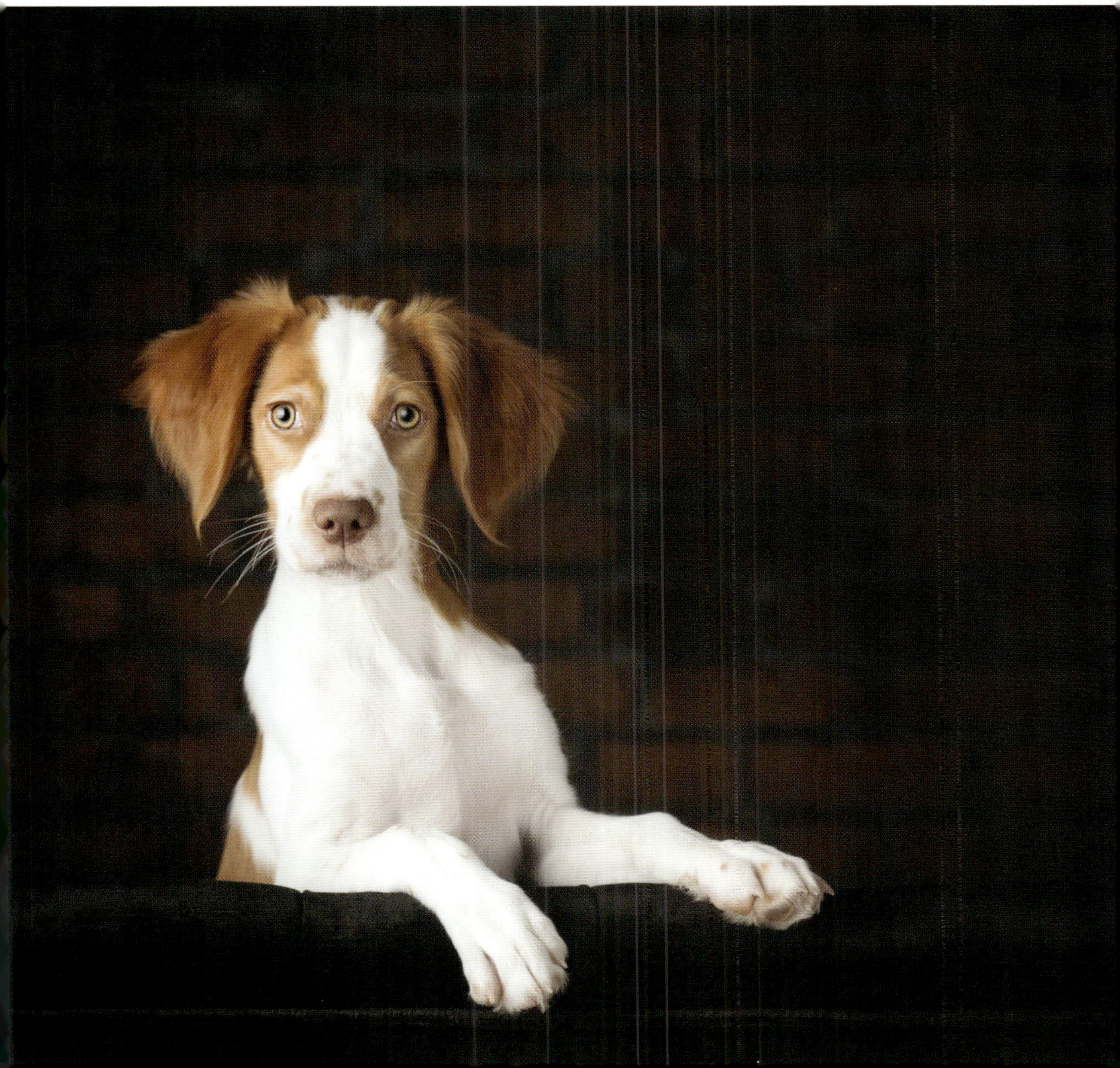

These next two images show one of my most-requested poses—the lying pose with the head down. It's not an easy one to get, and the best time to try for it is at the end of the session. By the end of the shoot, the pet will most likely be pretty tired. Put them into position and then ignore them until they get bored and put their head down.

This is not a shot you want to promise a client that you can get, because there is no guarantee you can make the pose happen. I have been known to spend 30-plus minutes laying on the floor trying to get it!

"This is a very popular pose, but don't promise you can get it, because it can be tricky to achieve it."

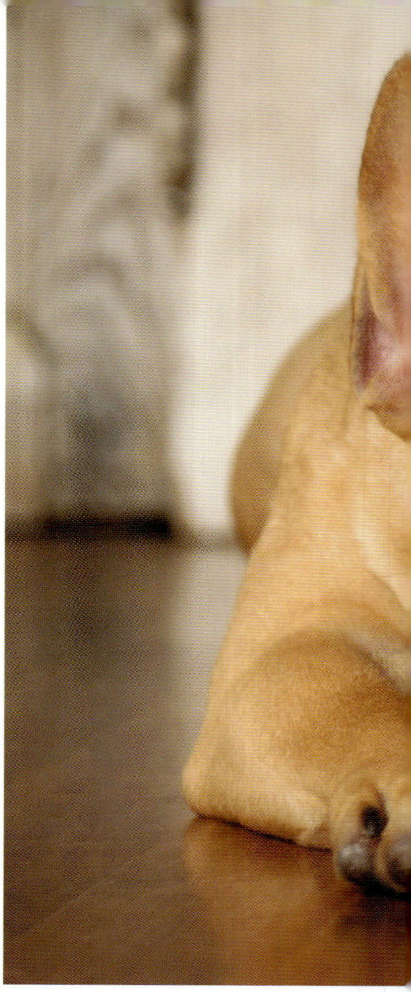

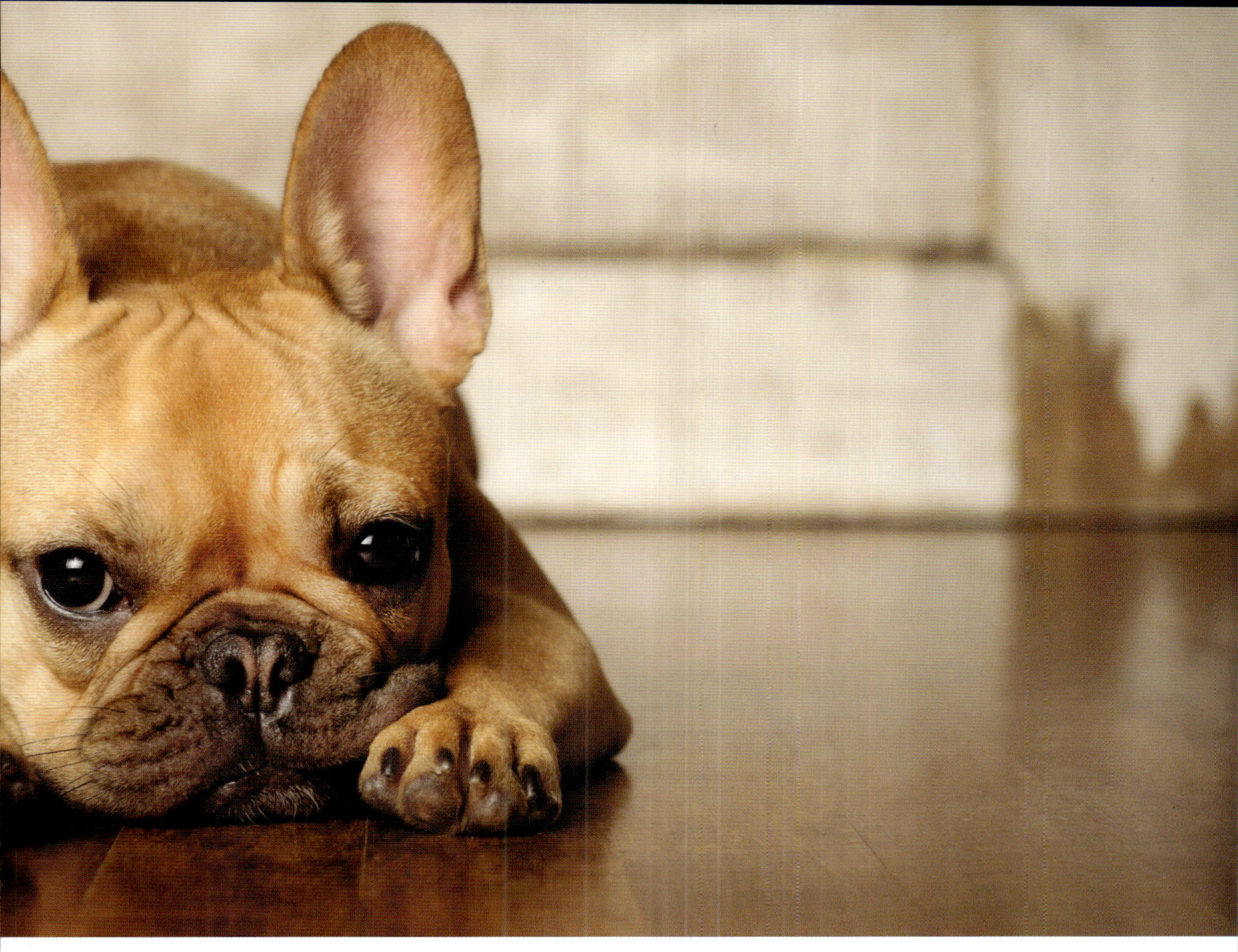
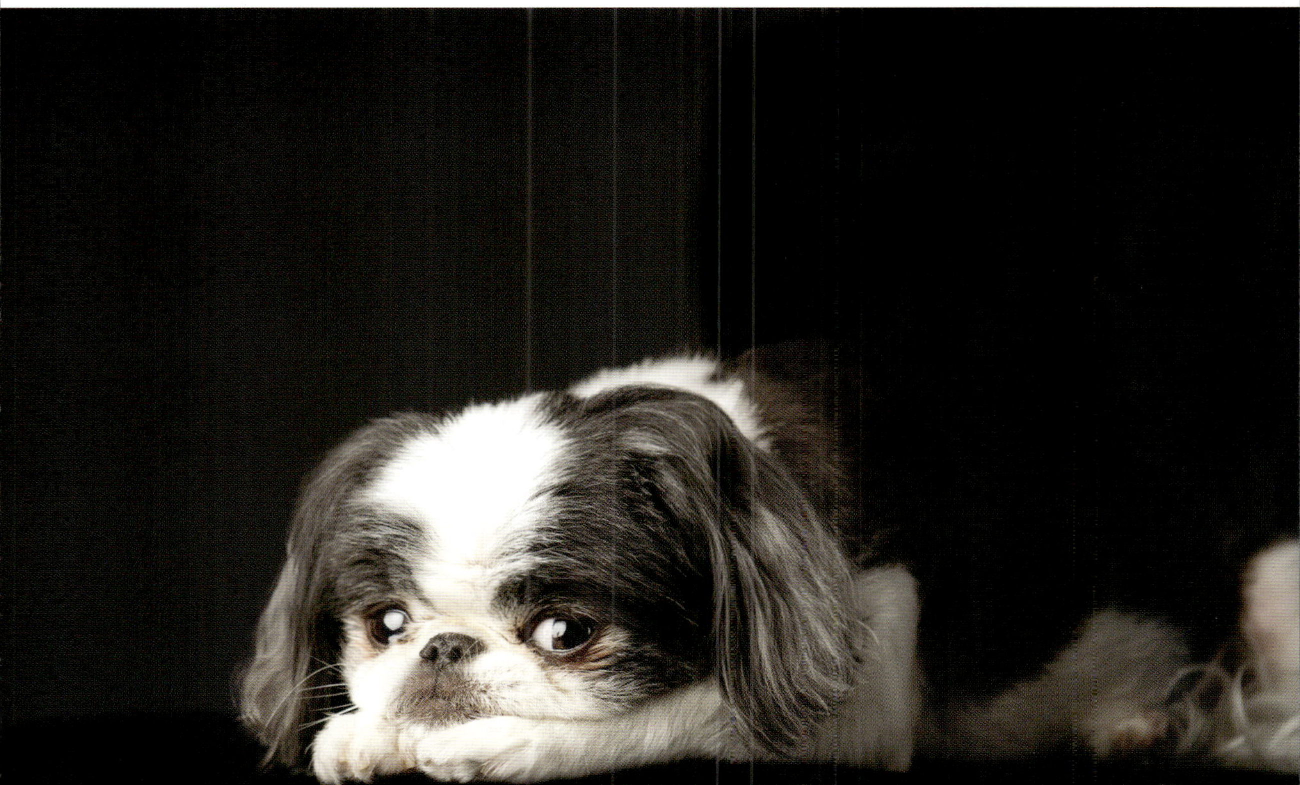

Posing Multiple Pets

Posing multiple pets is not as hard as it looks. I get asked all the time if this image was Photoshopped. It wasn't. This shot is right out of the camera, no head swaps or other postproduction work.

The key to success for an image like this is to have a plan in mind and an extra set of hands. I knew where I wanted each of these dogs to go in this image, and I relayed that information to the owner, who was assisting me. It took several tries to get everyone in place, but when they were ready, I used my noisemaker and took the image. You can't wait around when working with animals. They will get distracted pretty quick, and if you're not ready, you will miss your opportunity to get the image.

"Pre-plan. Be prepared to click the shutter before your subjects get distracted."

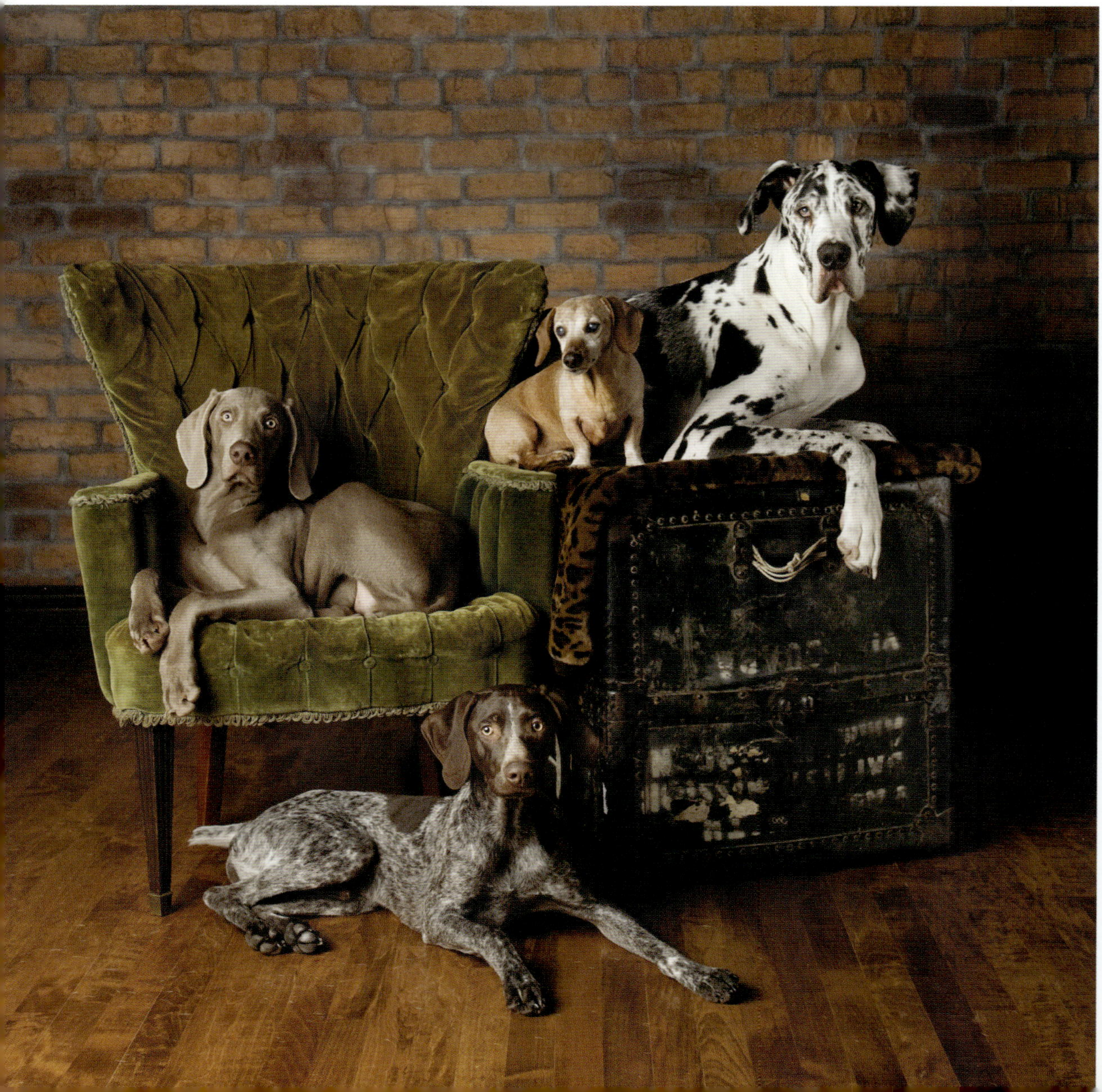

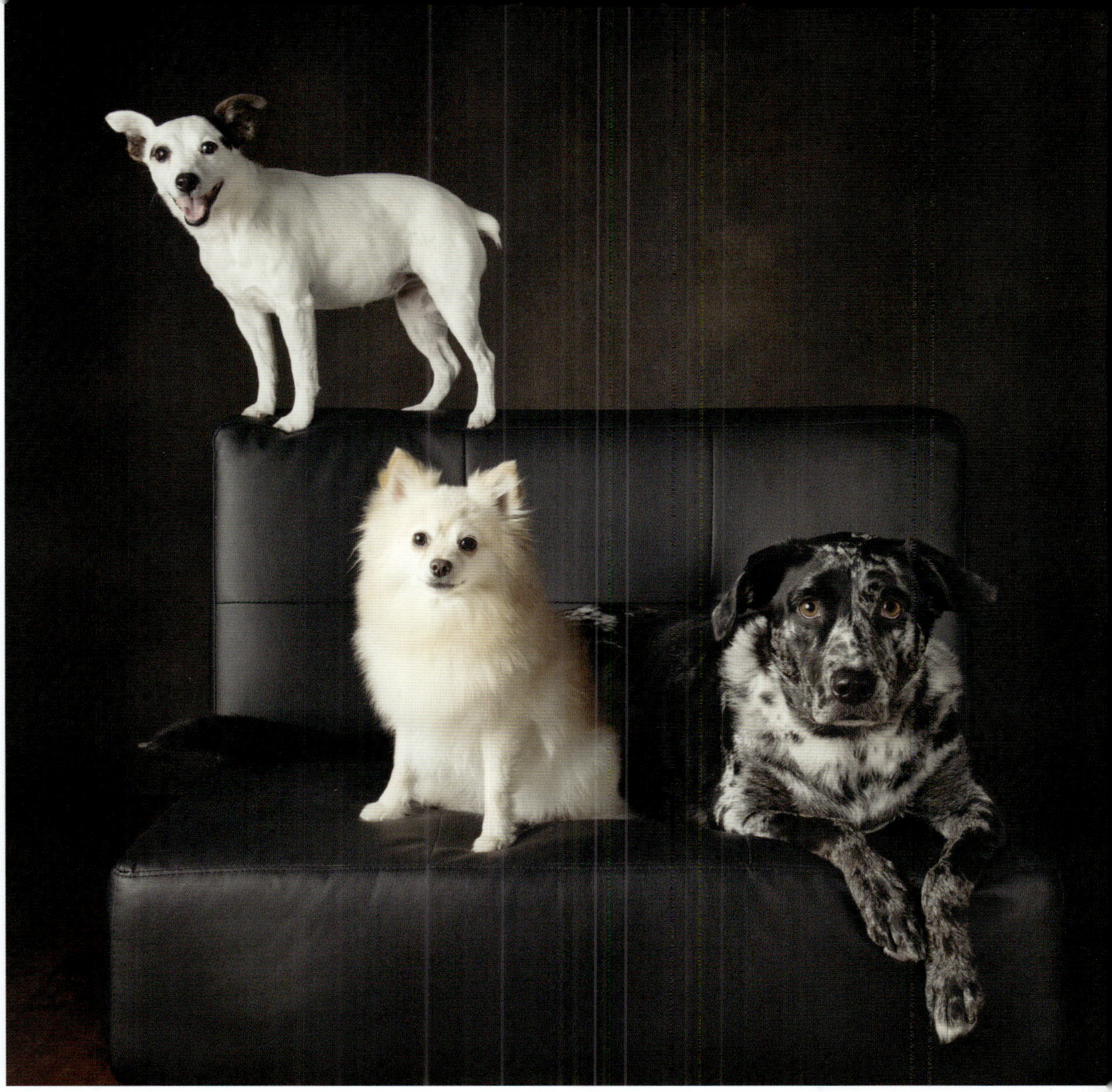

When posing multiple dogs, the head levels should be different, and you want to look for triangles. It's important to pose animals on separate planes to add interest. Here, as you can see in the bottom image, the dogs' heads form a triangle, and each of the heads is on a different level. If the pups are similar in size, you can use a prop to get one on a different level, like I did in this image.

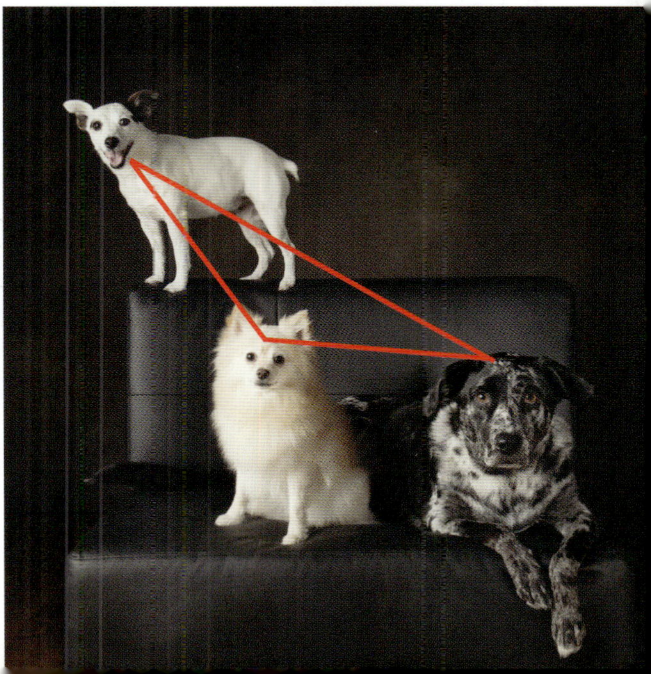

If you can have an assistant who can help you when you are photographing a multi-pet session, it will make your life a lot easier. I don't have any assistants on staff, so I have learned to ask the pet parents lend a hand. The key is to let them know up front that you will be needing their help so that they expect to help you out during the session.

For added control during the shoot, you may also find it helpful to use a leash. I use show leads in my studio all of the time because they are easy to retouch out in editing, and they help keep a pet in place long enough to allow me to capture the desired image.

"Ask an owner to help you to get the pets in the right position or get the dogs' attention."

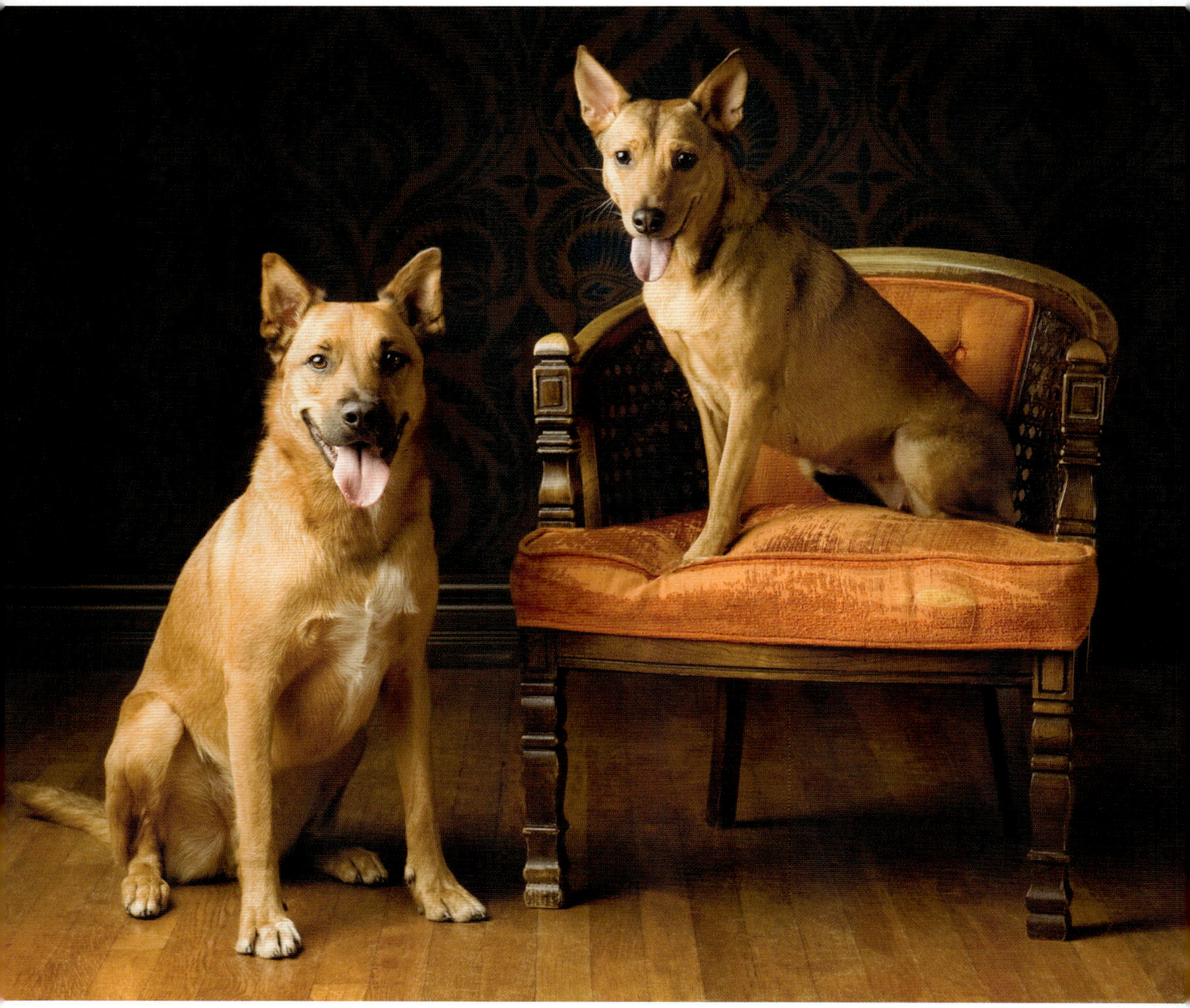

For this image of a German Short-Haired Pointer and Toy Poodle, I wanted to position the Poodle on the hind legs of the GSP, but I wasn't sure she would stay there. I decided to use a show lead to keep her in place long enough to get the image.

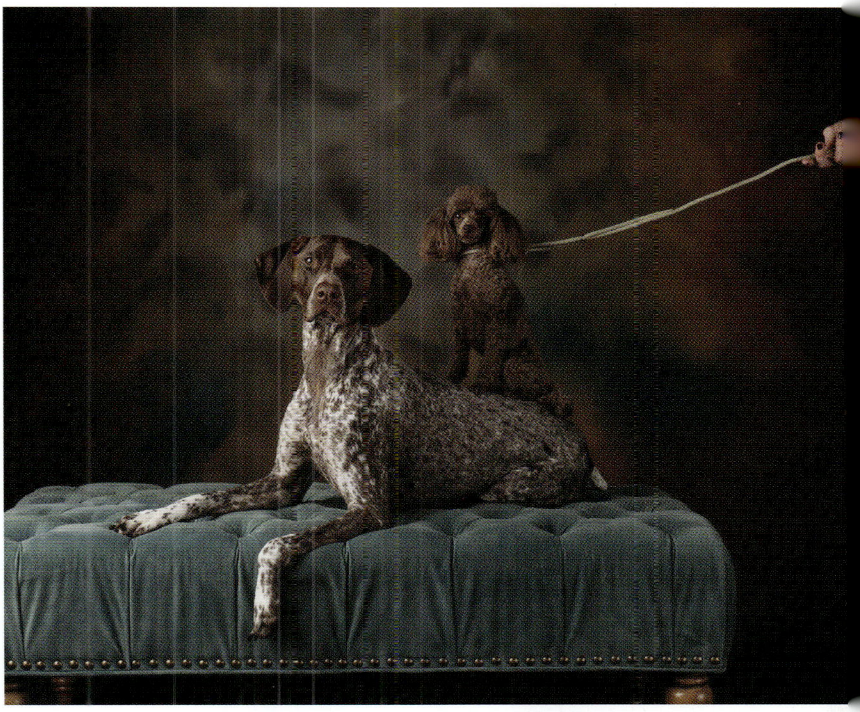

As you can see, in the final, retouched portrait, there is no sign of the lead.

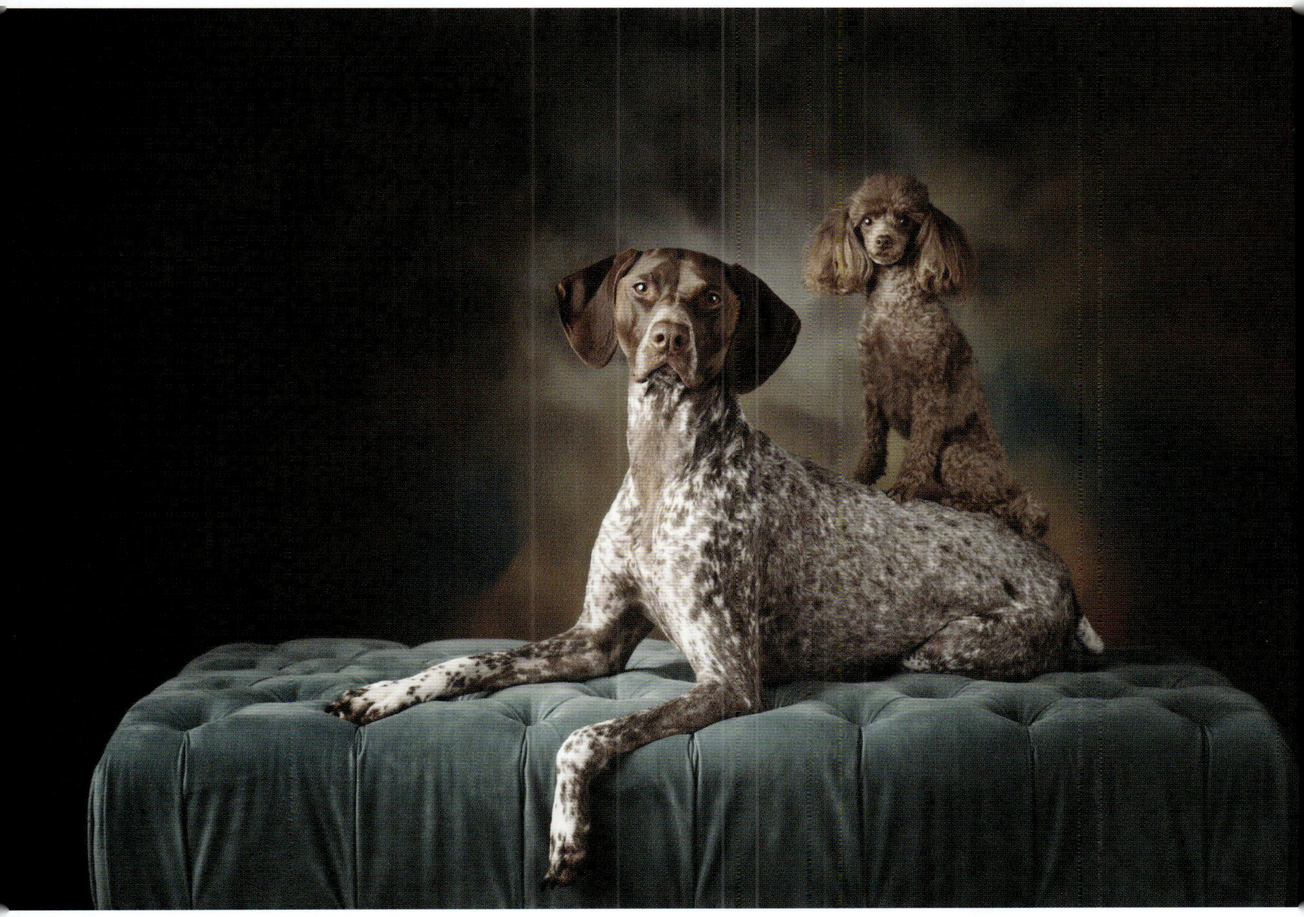

Here is another fun way to pose three dogs in the same image.

I knew what I was hoping to achieve in the image before I started putting the dogs in place. I positioned the three subjects in a triangle formation and made sure their heads were on separate, discrete planes, to add interest in the portrait. The viewer's gaze is drawn to each of the three faces.

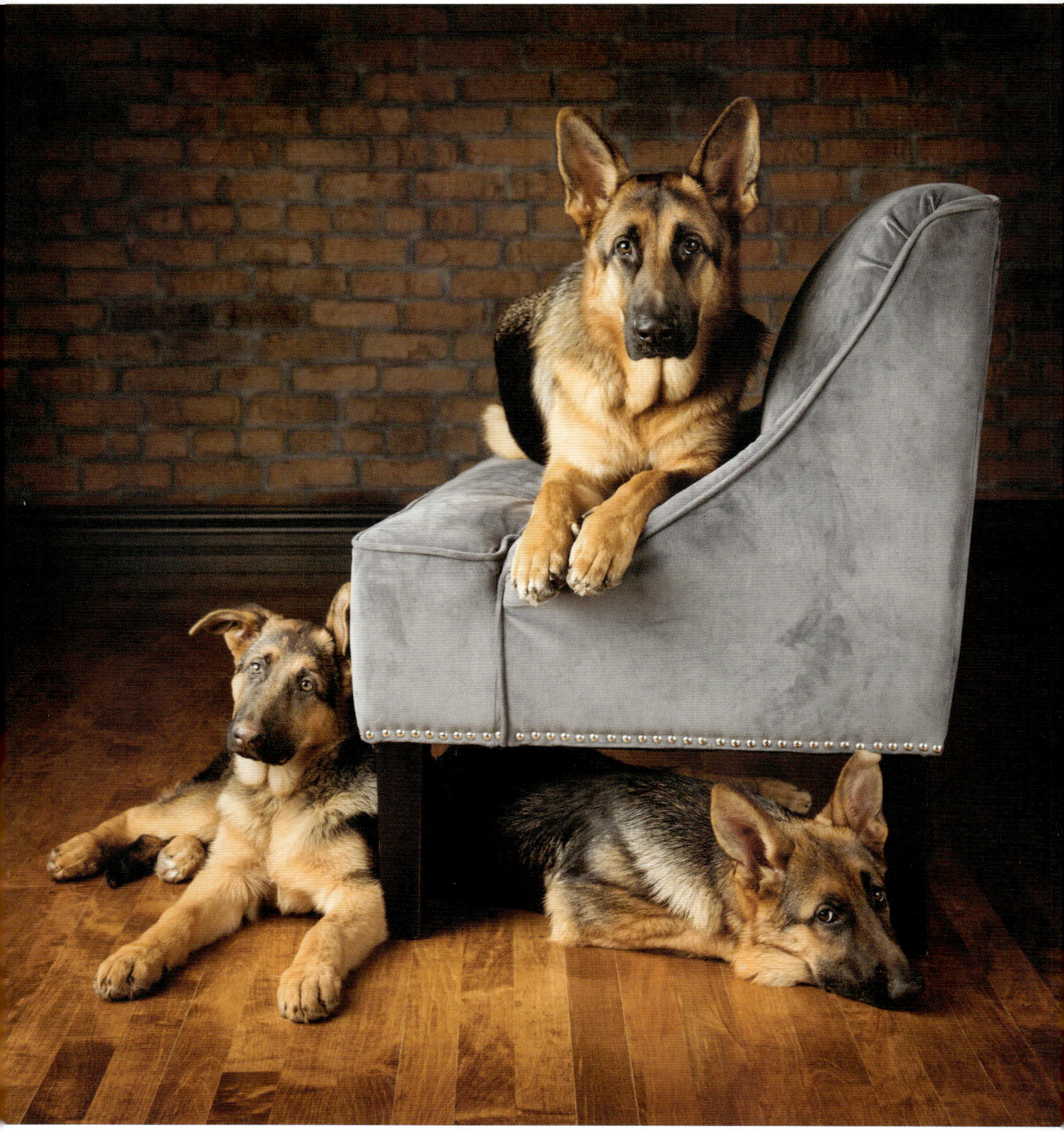

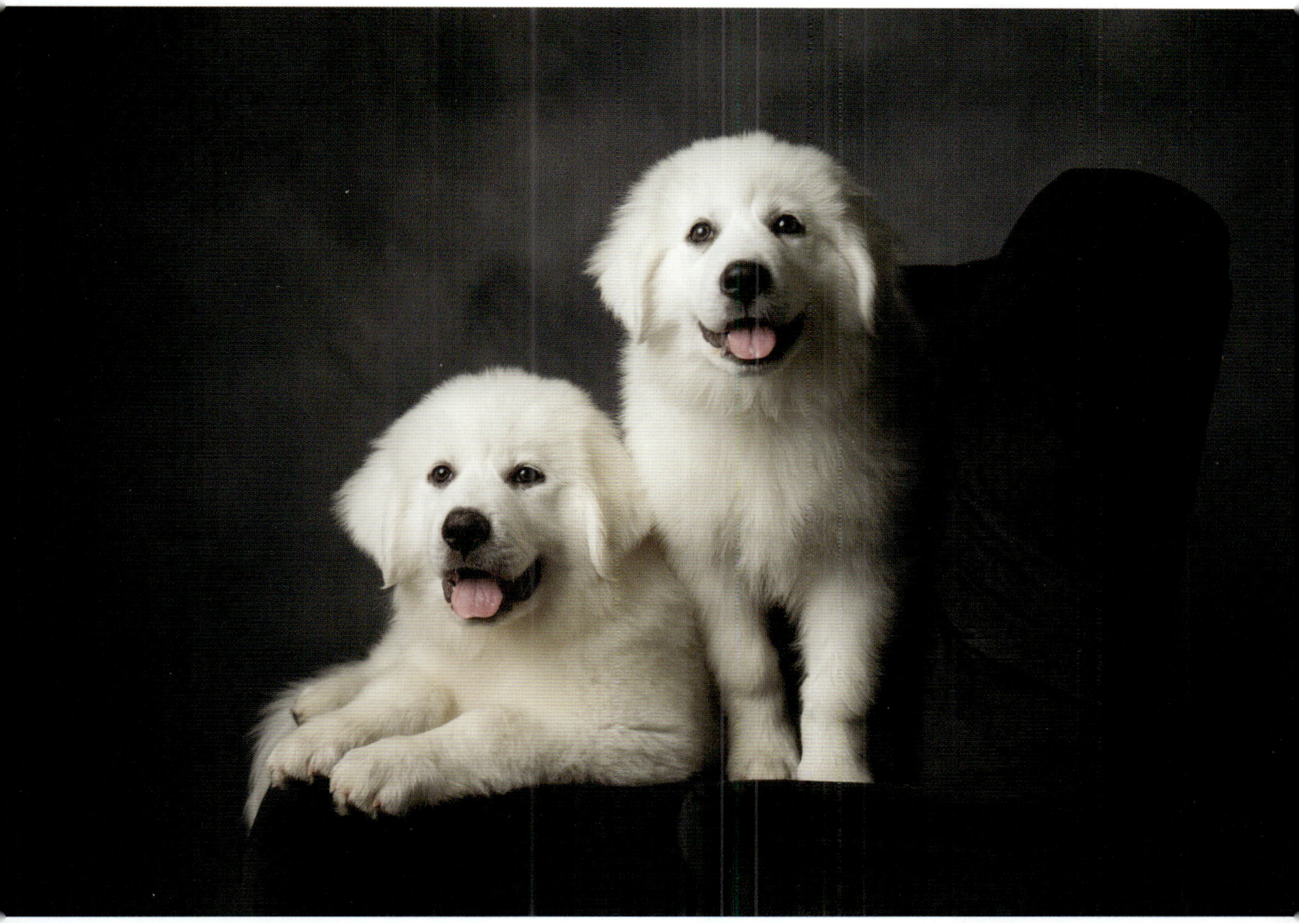

Don't be afraid to try new things. Think out of the box. I photographed these three Shepherds on one of my armless sofas, turned it at and angle, and used it to get one of the three dogs off of the floor. This created a fun, dynamic look.

Here *(above)* is another great pose when you are working with more than one dog. Have one sitting and one standing. Just getting one up and one down to get their heads on separate levels creates a much more interesting photo. You can also do poses in which both dogs are sitting, both are lying down, one is up and one is down, and so on, to get work more variety into your sessions.

"Make sure the subjects occupy different planes in your images."

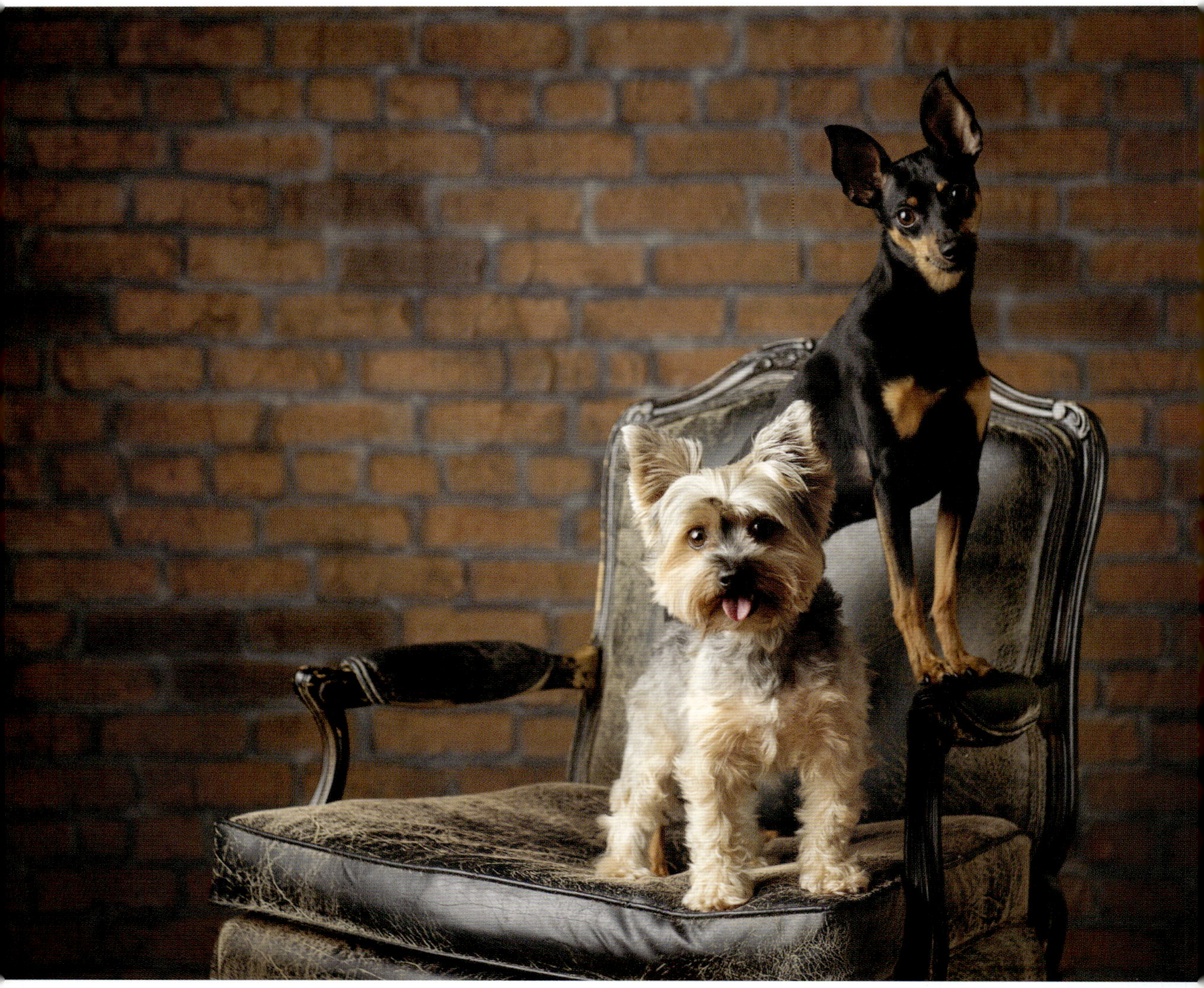

Sometimes you get lucky enough to photograph a dog who is pretty cool when it comes to trying most anything. If so, have fun with it!

This little guy was fine with perching his front legs on the arm of this chair. It helped to get him up and out from behind the Yorkie, so both dogs have good light on them, and the pose is different than what you would normally expect to see.

Of course, in a perfect world, I would have switched the position of the two, since the one perched on the chair is much darker than the dog closest to the light, but as I have mentioned before, you have to go with the flow when you are working with pets.

Not all of your pet portraits need to have the subject facing the camera and making eye contact with the viewer. Yes, there are a lot of owners who feel that's all they need, and sure, you do need to create some of those images—but you also should change things up and add in some out-of-the-box poses that your clients don't expect to see.

I love posing animals and then having the owner stand off to the side and call to them. It causes them to look toward their owner, rather than at the camera. I'm able to get beautiful profiles that tell a different story about the dog.

"Have the owner stand at a 45-degree angle to the camera so that your pet looks at him or her while in a profile pose."

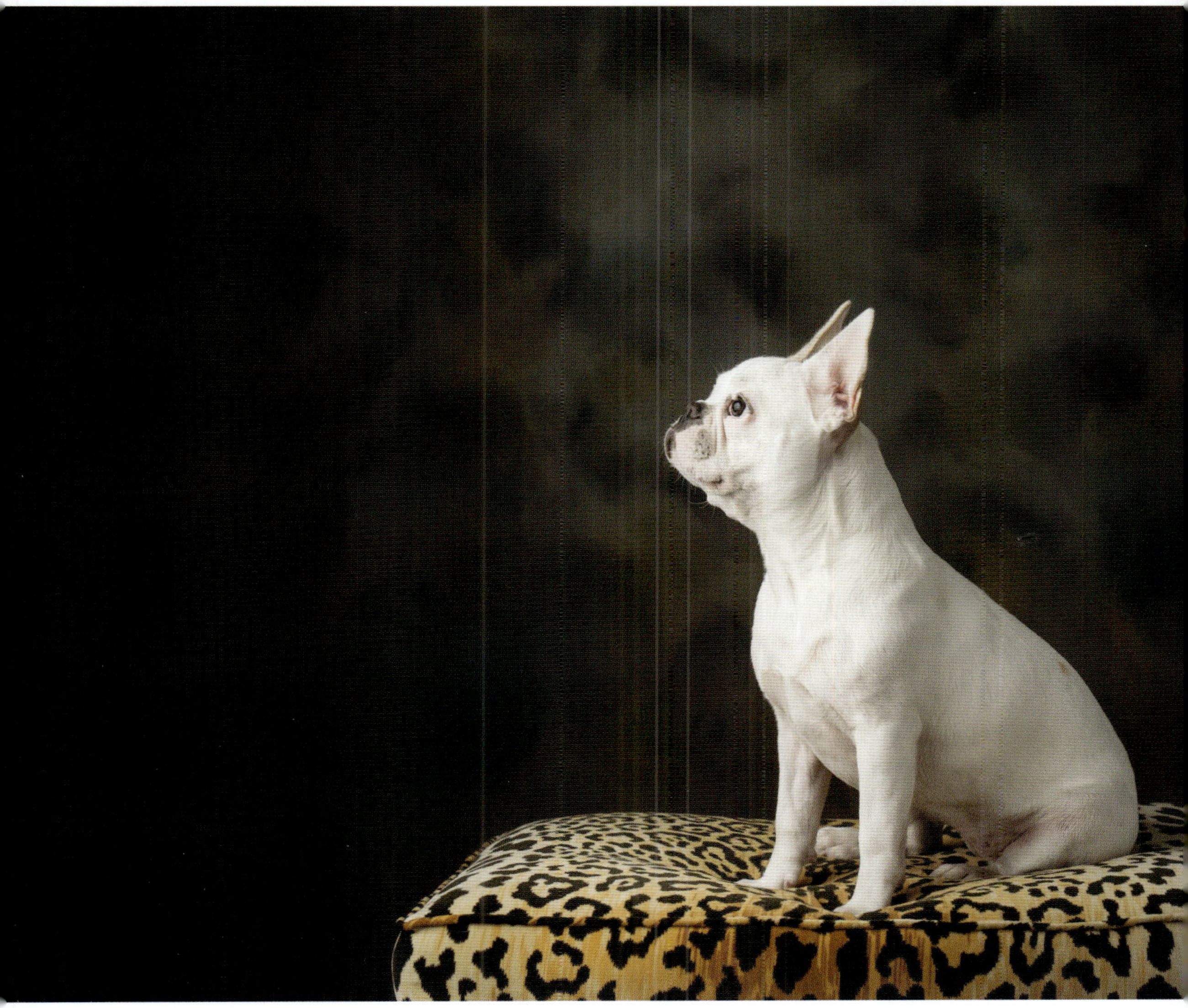

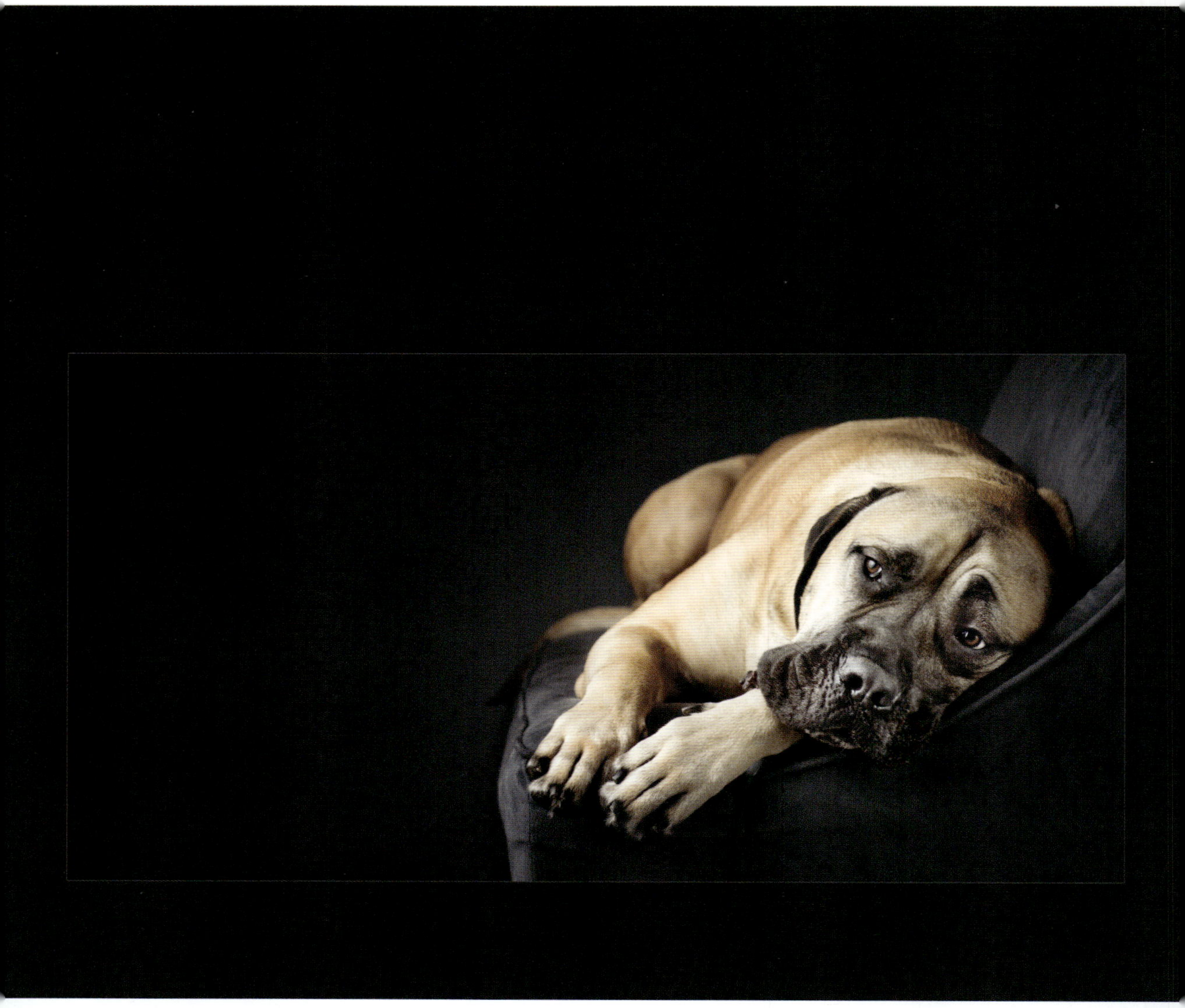

Here's another example of an unconventional, creative pose. This guy was tired from jumping on and off the furniture and was pretty much done. You can tell in his face that he is over it!

I love his expression with the one eyebrow raised. It's so cute, and it really told a story about him. Don't be afraid to take "offbeat" images and show them to your clients. You have to remember that they want you to photograph their pet as they see them, and this may be how this guy hangs out at home.

"Take advantage of natural poses that show a dog the way his owners may see him at home."

With two dogs, if you can get one to put his paws on the arm of a chair, you'll establish different levels in the image—and create a portrait that doesn't look like everything else. This is easier when you have the owner stand to the side of the pup to get the dog up, and then you get the subject to turn their head back toward you by making a noise.

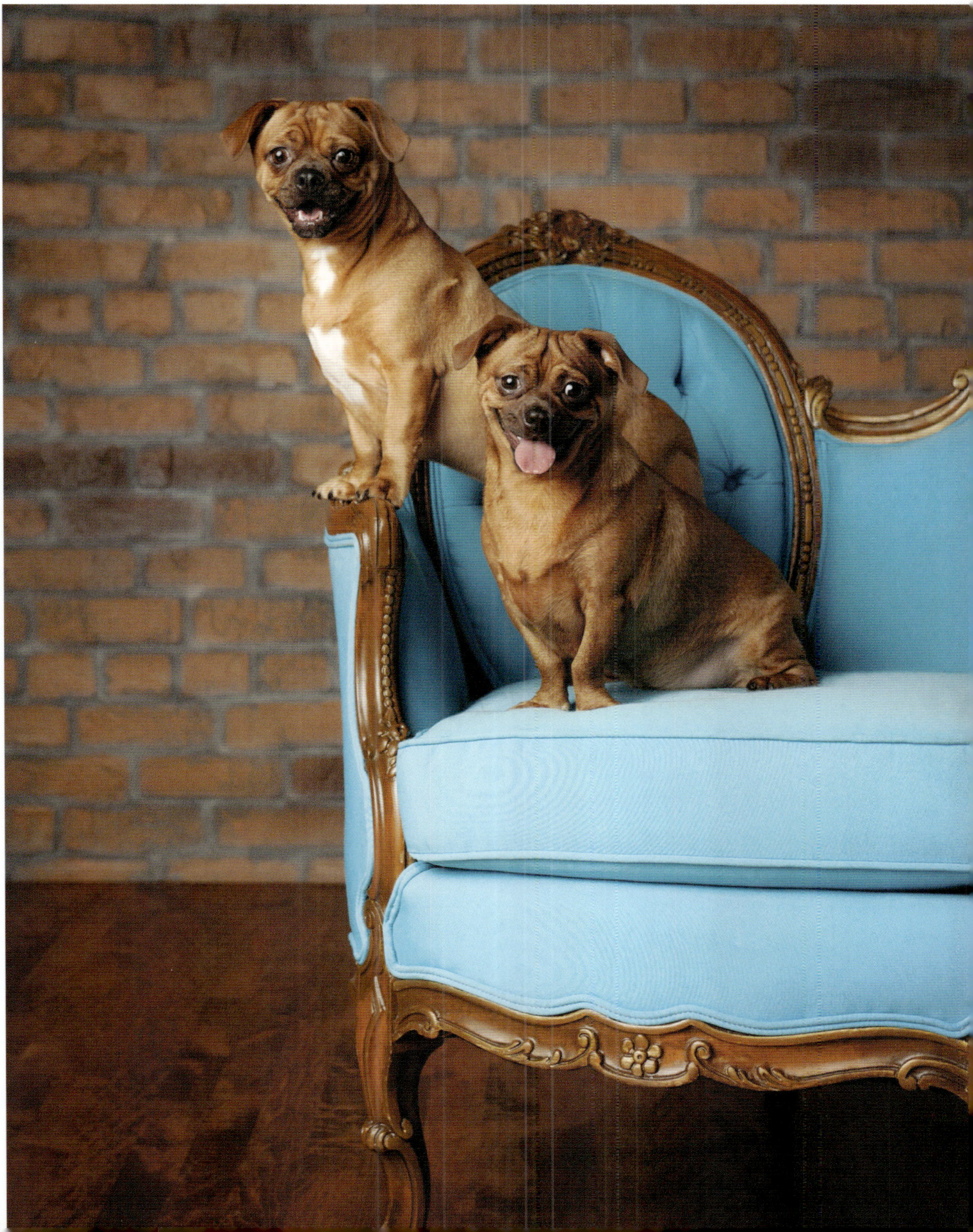

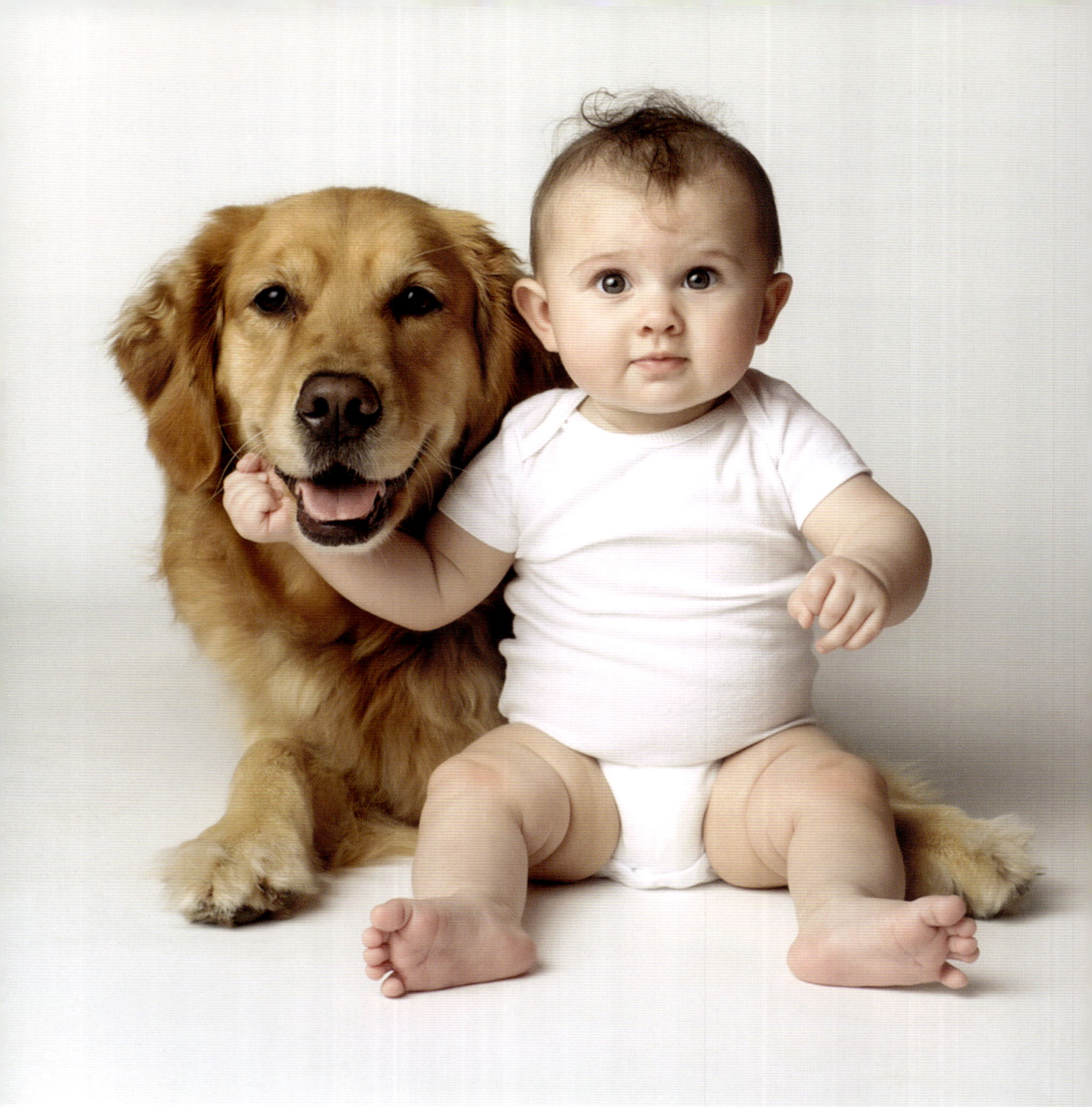

I have always said that my dog didn't become the family pet when my daughter was born, but she became a big sister. I truly believe that. It's amazing how many people don't understand the relationship people have with their pets, but our pets are also our children. Understanding and showing that relationship is such a strong tool to have at your disposal when you are creating images for your clients.

"Dogs are part of the family. Create images that illustrate that point."

Here is another example of all the kids together! The same principles apply here, except baby gets placed first and dogs get placed around. Notice that I've put the darkest-colored dogs closest to the light. I did have to use leashes on these pups to keep them in place (as seen in the top image), which I then retouched out. Mom and Dad are holding the leashes. Note that the everyone's head is on a different plane, as well!

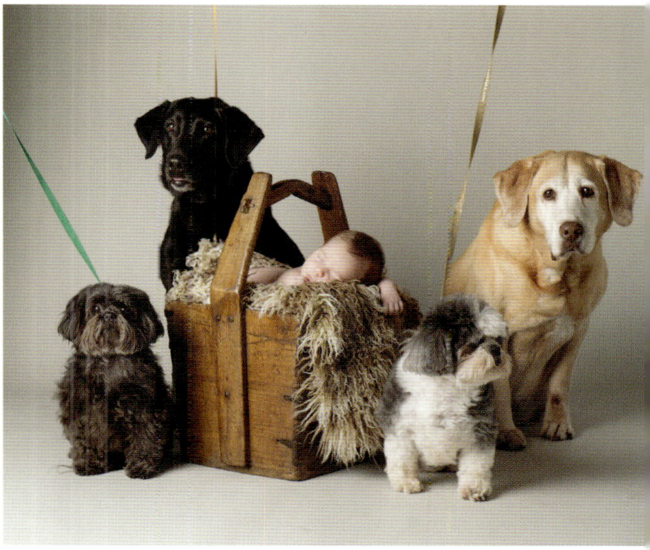

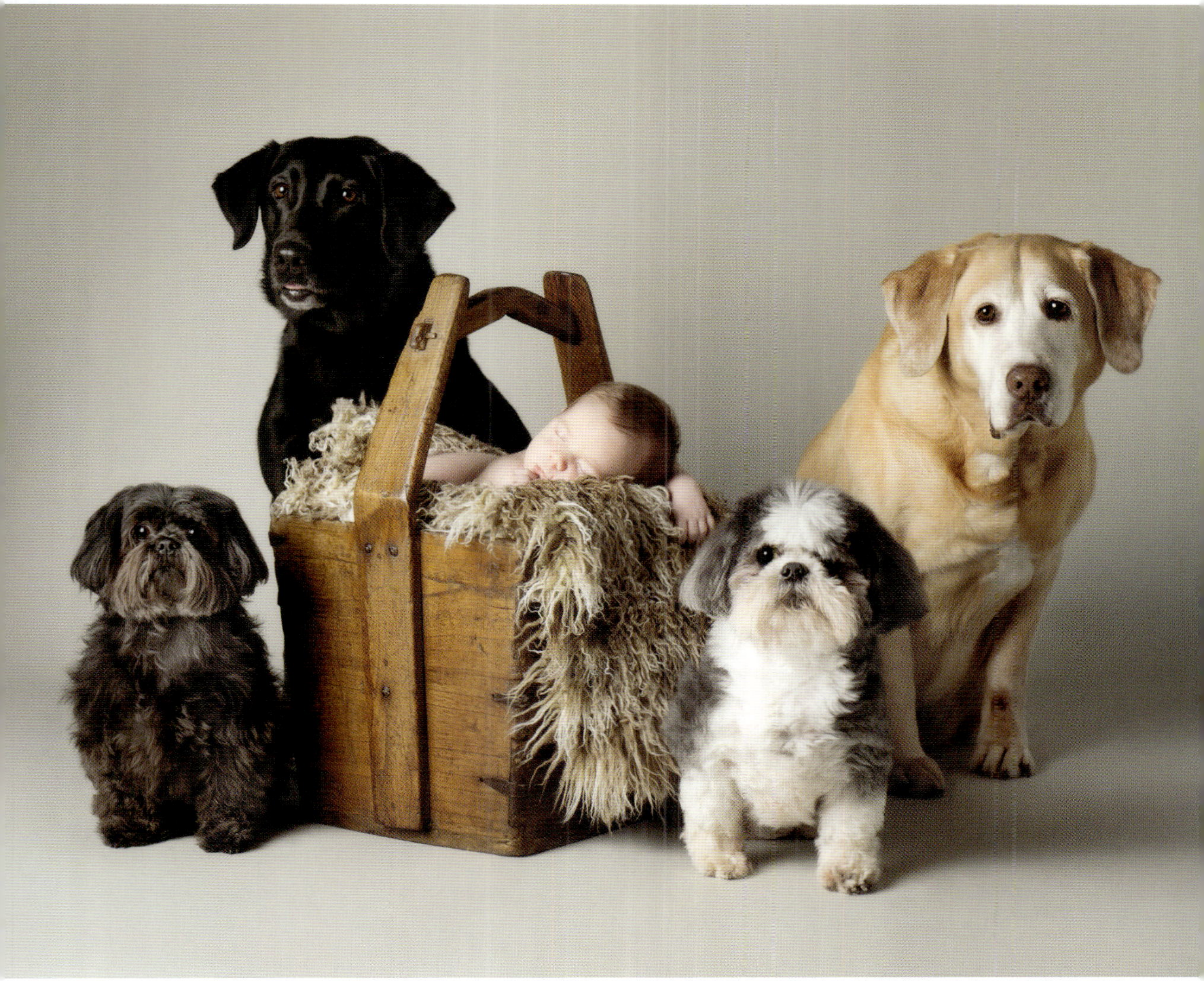

A pose like the one in the image below is another popular option that allows you to include the pet parents in the image, without making them the main focus of the photograph.

I personally love this pose because it allows me to portray the family without the owners having to worry about how they look. We still get a clear sense of the relationship here.

I love how the Husky pops out against the blue jeans in this shot. The great contrast helps to make him the main focus of the image.

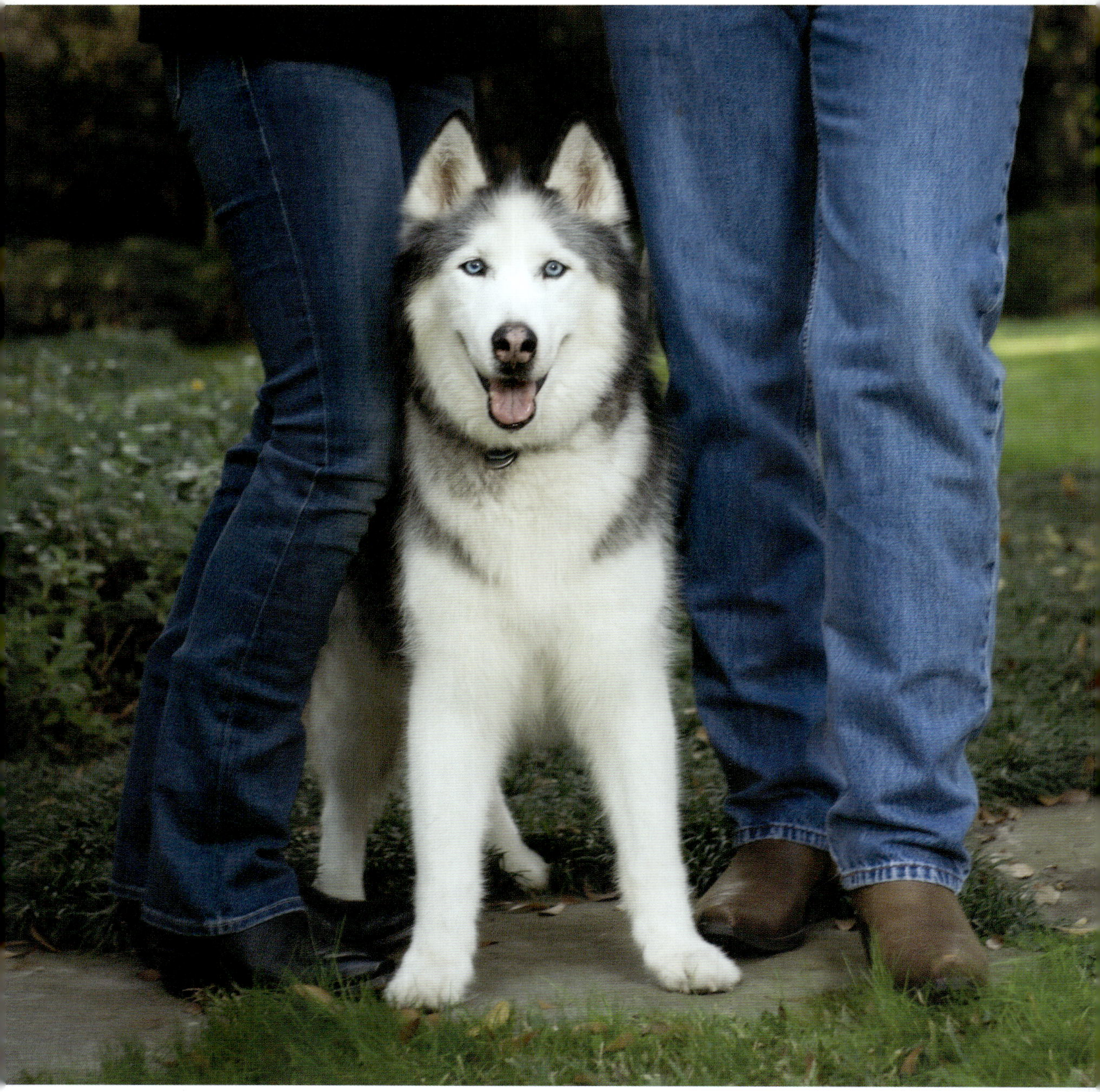

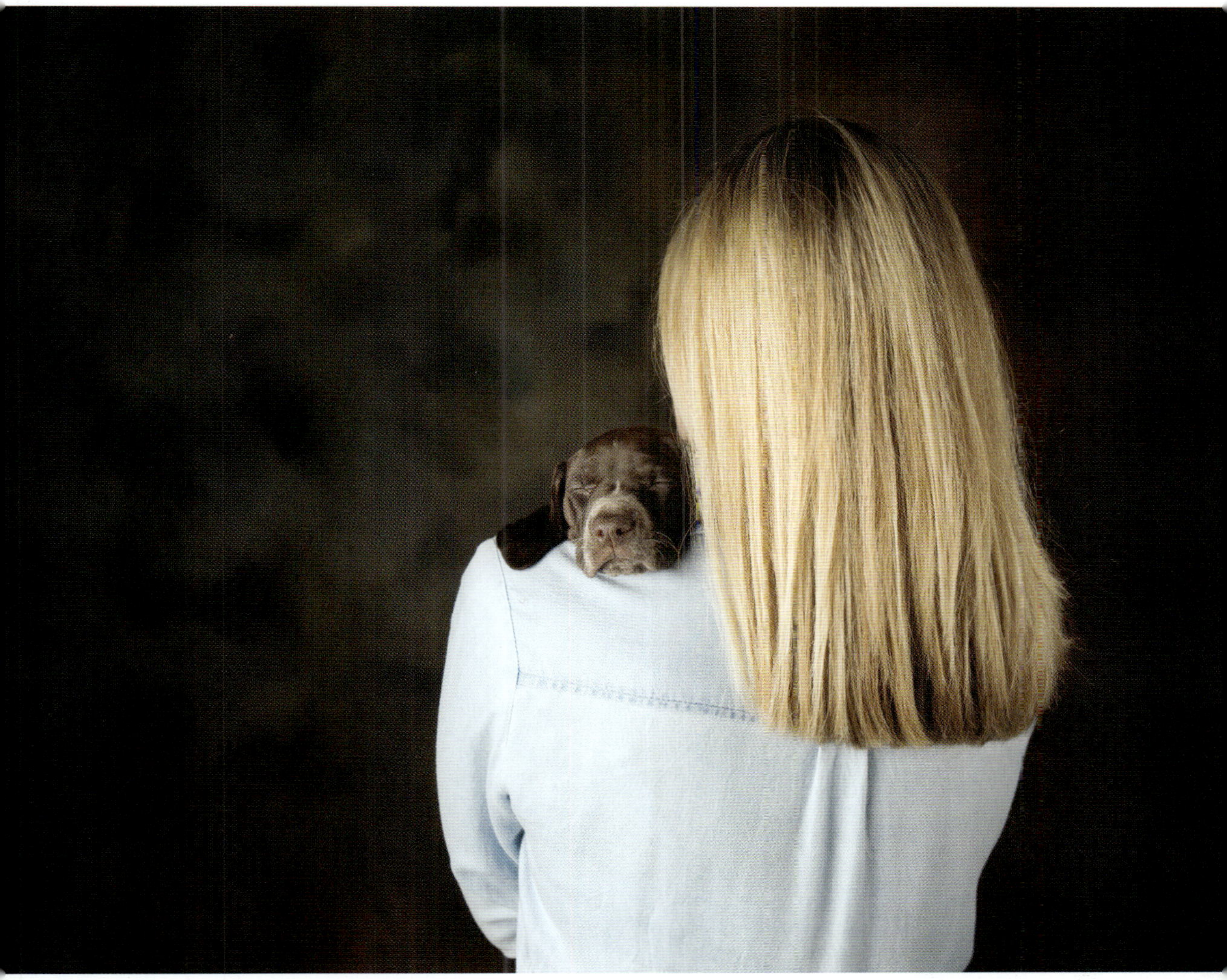

Here is another great pose that you can rely on if you are met with a self-conscious owner. I always talk to my pet parents in advance and tell them to bring clothes/shoes to the session in case we do add them in the images.

This approach is a great option when you have a "Velcro" dog who wants only to be next to their owner. You can have the parent "in but not in" the photograph by having him or her act as a prop for you.

Showing relationships between multiple subjects in an image is so important, and it is something that we shouldn't overlook when photographing pets.

"Use people as props in your images to show the bond in the family unit, while keeping the focus on the dog."

CHAPTER FIVE

Artistic Vision

Let's talk about how to create photos that are much more than a snapshot.

There are several things you can do in your images to elevate the artistry in your portraits. The four elements I like to highlight are composition, color harmony, expression, and simplicity, and you can use these aspects to sculpt your own creative vision. This image has all of these elements.

"Use the tools at your disposal to craft a work of art."

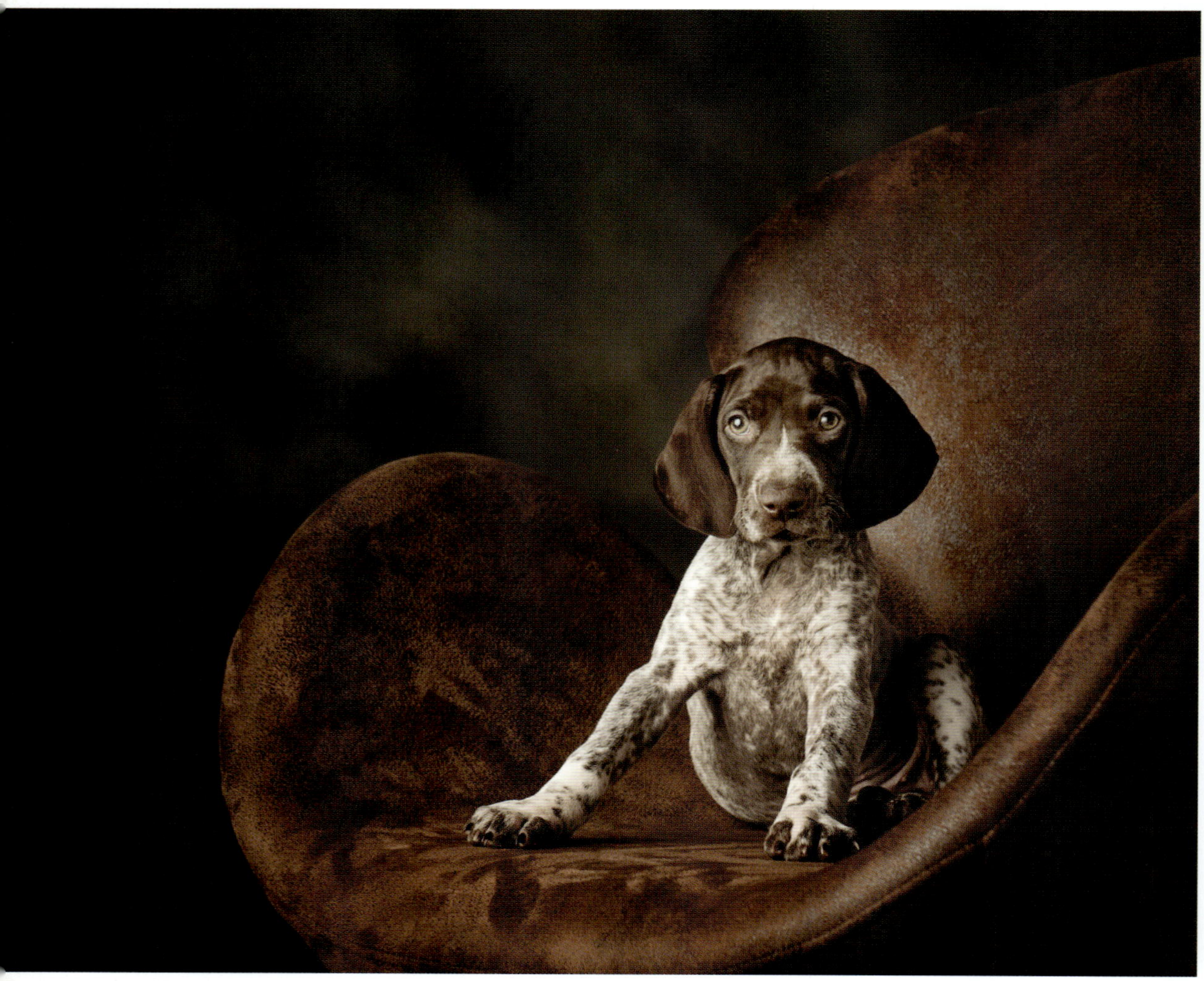

Color Harmony

Let's consider color harmony first.

I love to incorporate as much color harmony as possible in my images. I knew the coloring of the little guy in the top image in advance of the session and set up an earth-toned backdrop, then brought in this brown chair to complement his fur. If I had picked a really bold color chair in this instance, it would have been distracting. Having color harmony helps to let the props and background fall away so that the pet really shines in the portrait.

Another advantage to using color harmony in your photos is that it is easier for someone to hang an image like this on their wall versus one with lots of different and/or bold colors.

You can ask the owners, prior to the shoot, about colors in their home so you can have the image complement the tones in their home. An added benefit? This will also make it easier to sell the art work as a wall portrait.

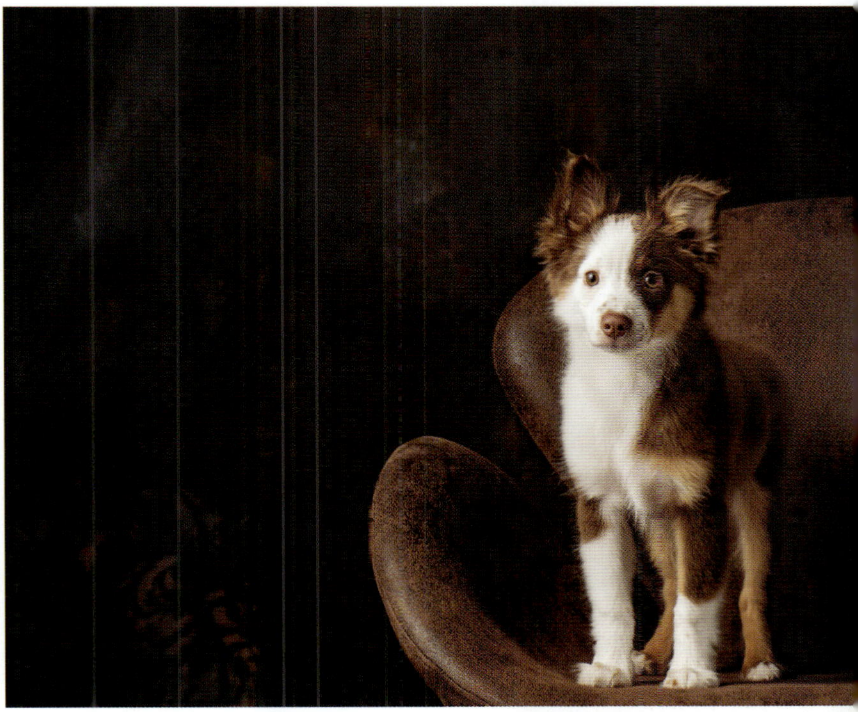

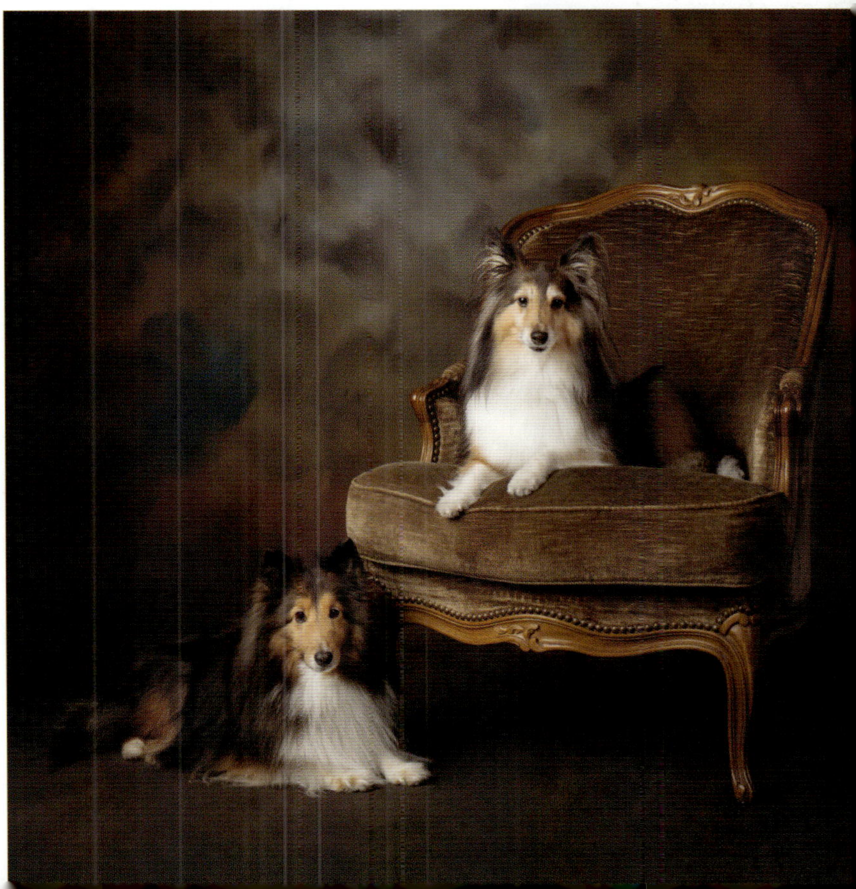

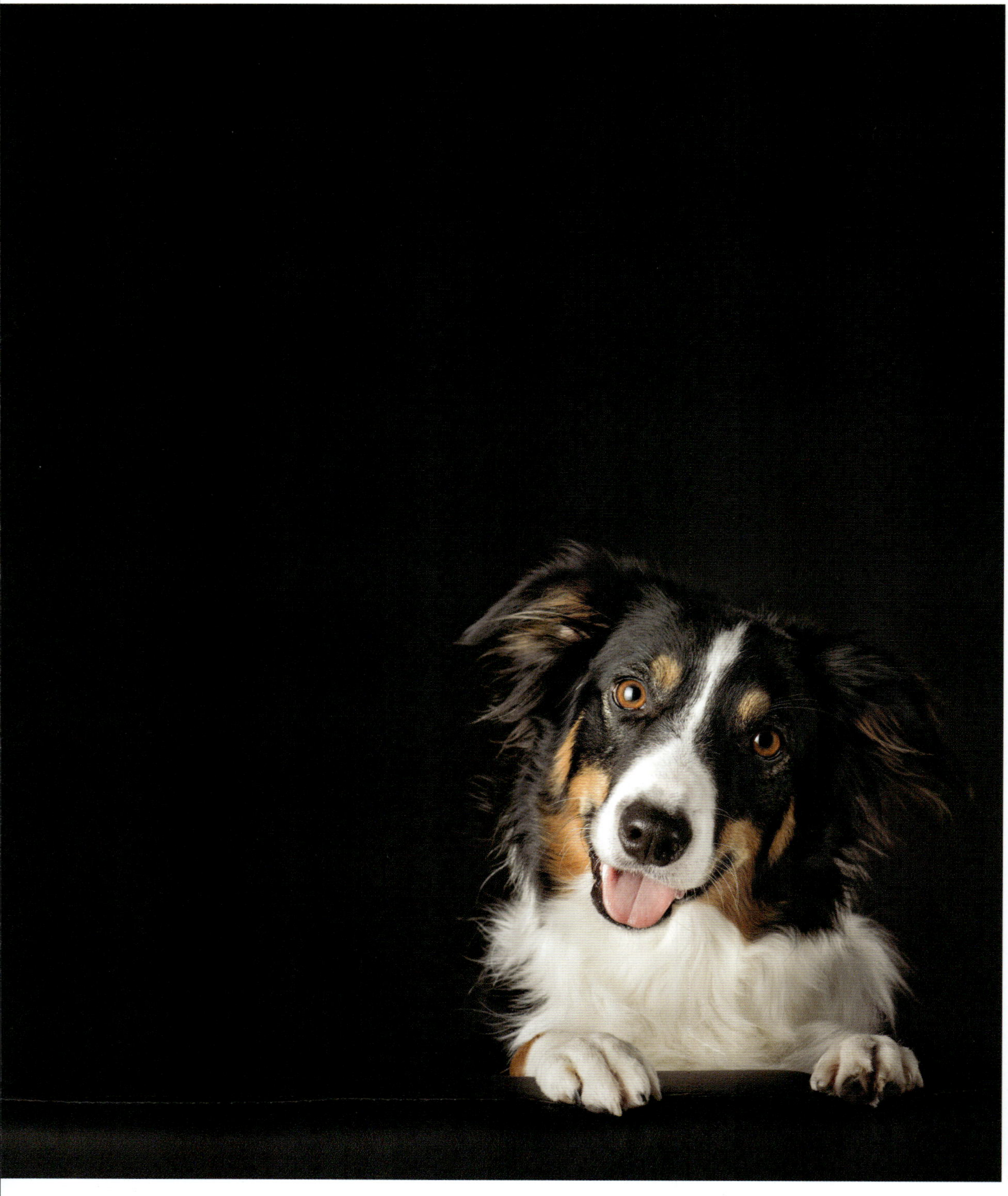

"Build negative space into your composition to draw the eye to the subject."

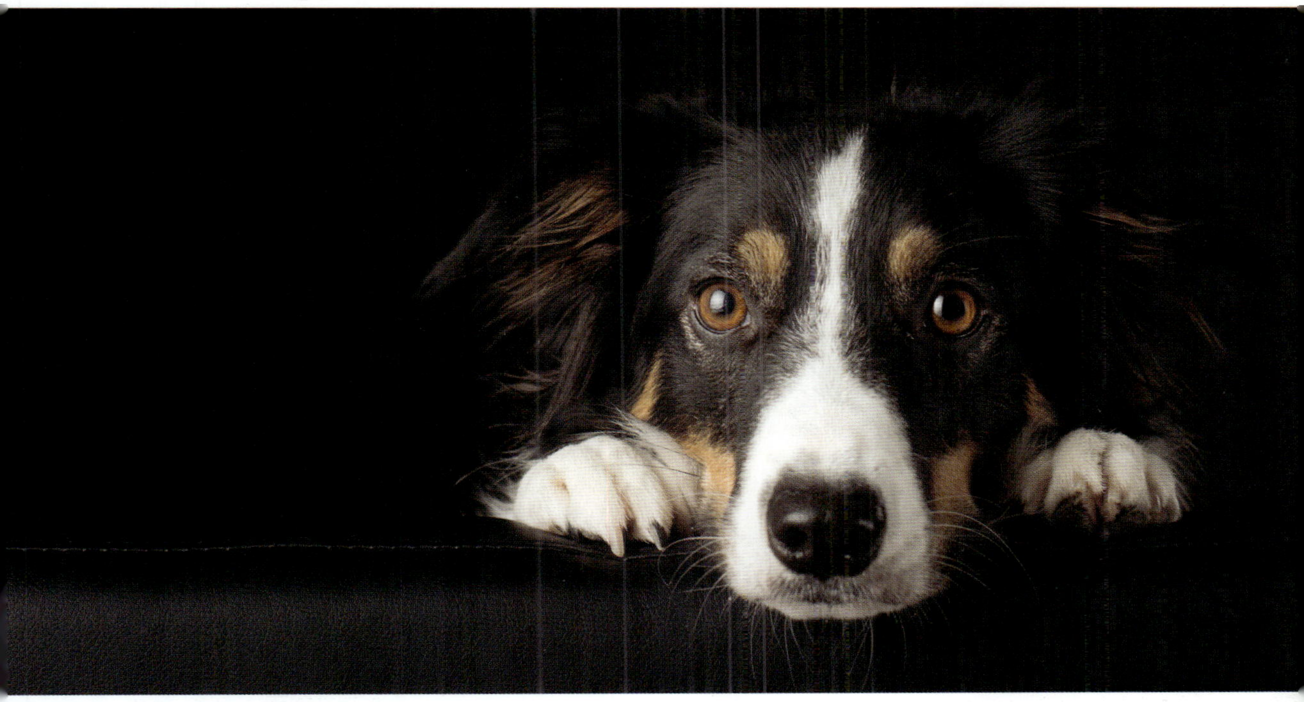

Composition

The photo on the previous page is one of my favorite images. This pup belonged to a dog trainer, so my subject was ridiculously well behaved!

This is a peeking-over-the-prop pose, but her expression is what makes it perfect. I also placed her specifically in the bottom-right corner of the frame so she popped out. The color harmony is on point, but it is mainly the composition that makes the image interesting.

I could have positioned the dog anywhere in the frame, but it's a playful image, so I wanted to put her in a place that was a bit unexpected and untraditional. I personally love negative space, and you will see that a lot in my work.

Above, you can see another example from the same session with Gilly. In this case, too, I chose to take advantage of negative space in the composition to draw the viewer's gaze right to the pup.

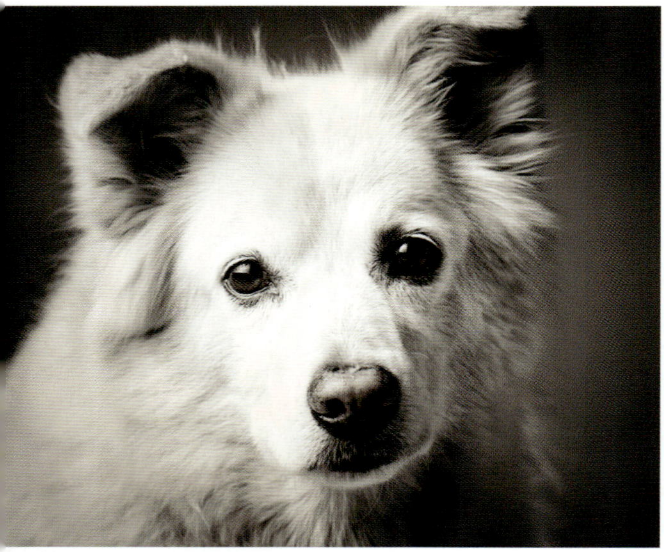

Expression

Expressions sell your images. Capturing a great expression is key to creating an image with impact and meaning. It's hard to do this without a planning session where you can meet the pet and learn about them. Understanding what a pet likes and dislikes, what they best respond to, and if they respond to any keywords will be hugely beneficial in getting a personality-filled expression when you photograph them. Do your homework up front, because it will pay off in your images.

Keep it Simple

Nowadays, you see so many props in images. It's cute in some cases, but in others, it's a distraction. My vote is to keep things simple and highlight the pet you are photographing. An owner is more likely to put a subject-centric portrait like this on their wall versus something that is super trendy with 100 props in it.

"Create a classic, simple portrait that withstands the test of time."

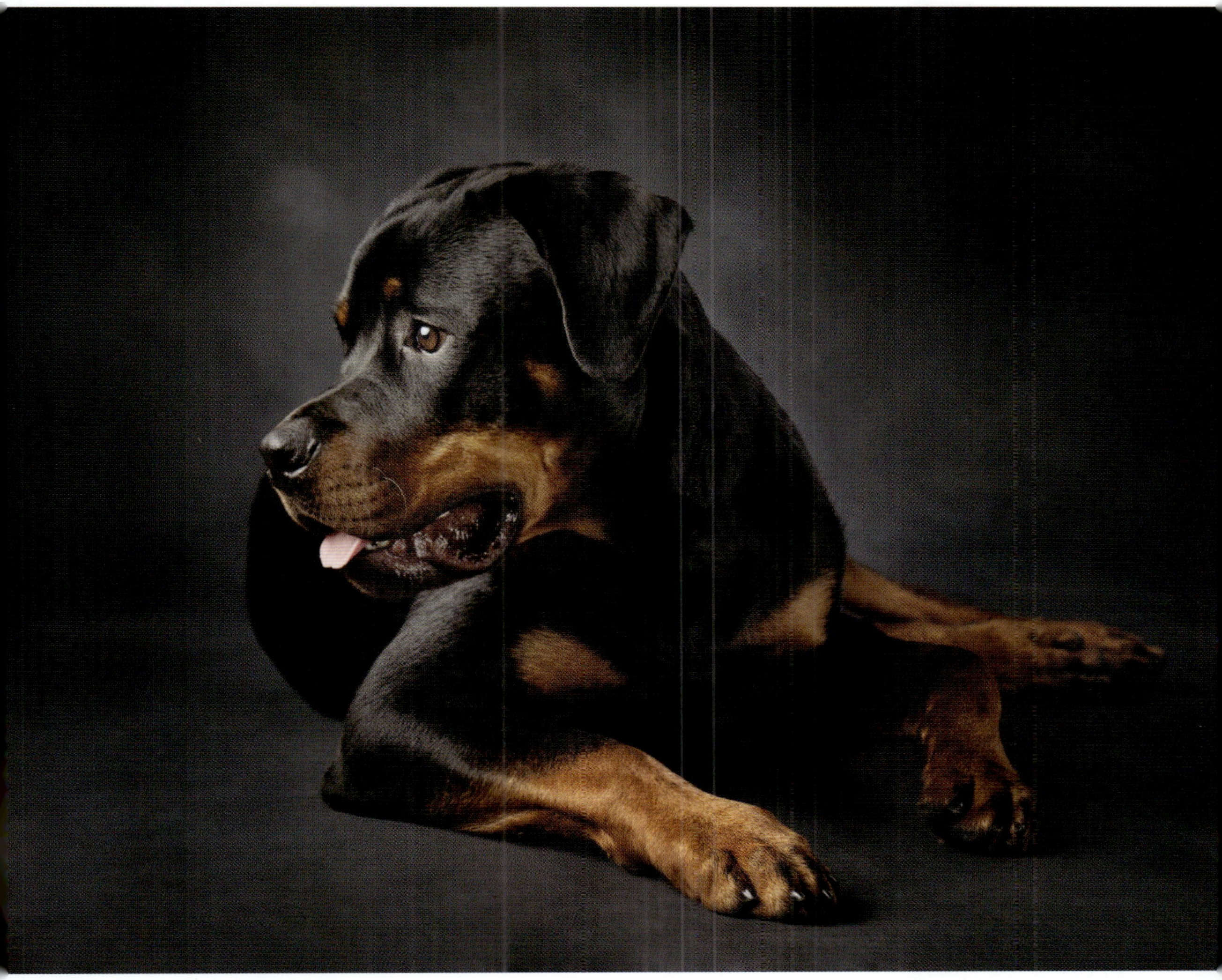

Moving On

We've covered a lot of information about studio lighting, posing, props, and how to take your images to the next level. All of this information will translate to working on location, as well.

When working outside of the studio, the lighting is a bit different, because we have to work on balancing the natural or ambient light with the light from our flash. We don't want the lighting to look too flashy, but natural with just a little pop of flash.

We're going to dive right into incorporating off-camera flash in the following chapter.

CHAPTER SIX

Location Sessions

Equipment

The majority of pet owners use only natural light when photographing their animals outdoors. For more professional and artistic results, therefore, it pays to use off-camera flash in your portraits to create a work of art that really sings.

Using off-camera flash is a simple technique to add in. The photo on the following page, probably taken around 2011, shows my first real try at off-camera flash. I used to practice on Ruby and Agador all the time when I was starting out in pet photography, and they were always willing models!

Looking at this image now, I would have made some adjustments to this image (like minimizing the light spill in front of the chair), but overall, I think it came out pretty good!

This image got me hooked on off-camera flash because of what you could create with it. I love the layers of light in the foreground and background, which add a sense of depth and interest.

"Use off-camera flash to add depth and interest to your outdoor shots."

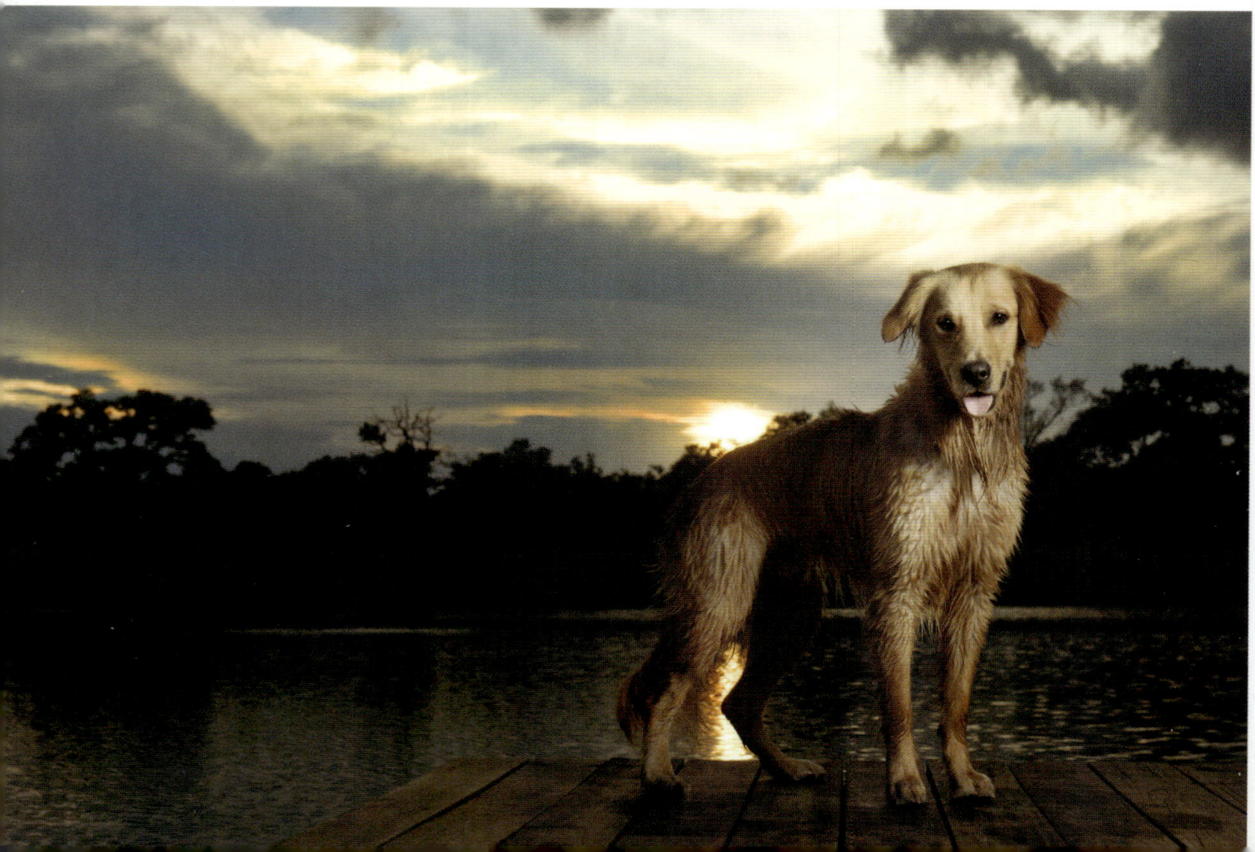

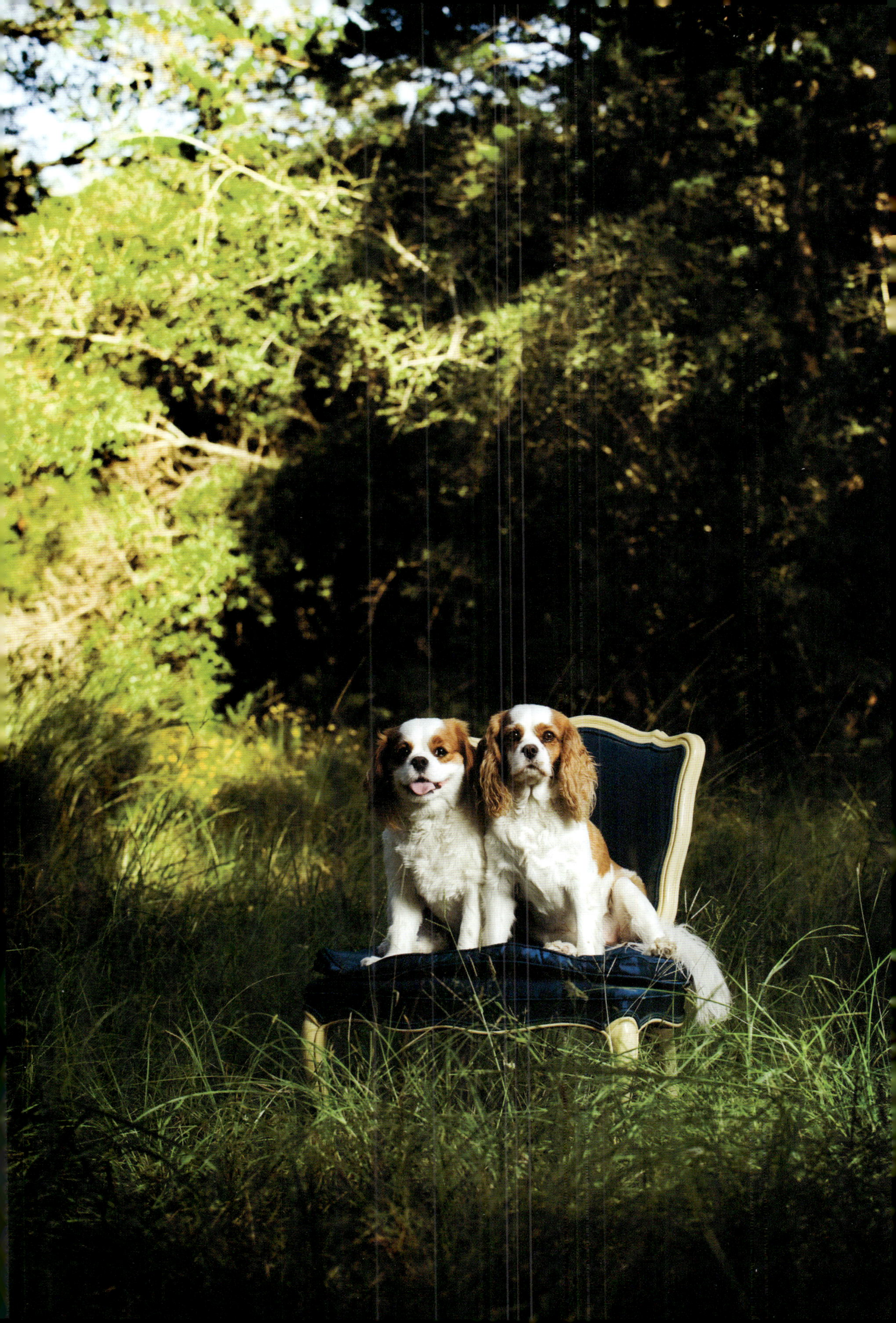

One of the best things about using off-camera flash outdoors is that you can balance the natural light with your flash to ensure that everything in the frame is properly exposed. No more blowing out backgrounds to get the right exposure on your subject! Plus, you can photograph at any time of day. No more early-morning or late-afternoon shoots. Plus, it's hard to get the kind of depth and dimension that working with off-camera flash delivers when you are working with natural light alone. Don't get me wrong, natural light is beautiful if you catch it at the right time of day, but using off-camera flash will give you that capability any time of day.

"Master off-camera flash so that you can create magical portraits at any time of day."

You have a lot of options when it comes to choosing equipment for on-location sessions. I've used everything from a speedlight to high-speed sync strobes. Ultimately, what works best comes down to what you're comfortable using as well as what you're trying to achieve. There are pros and cons to each type of light as well that you need to consider, including size, cost, and flash recycle time.

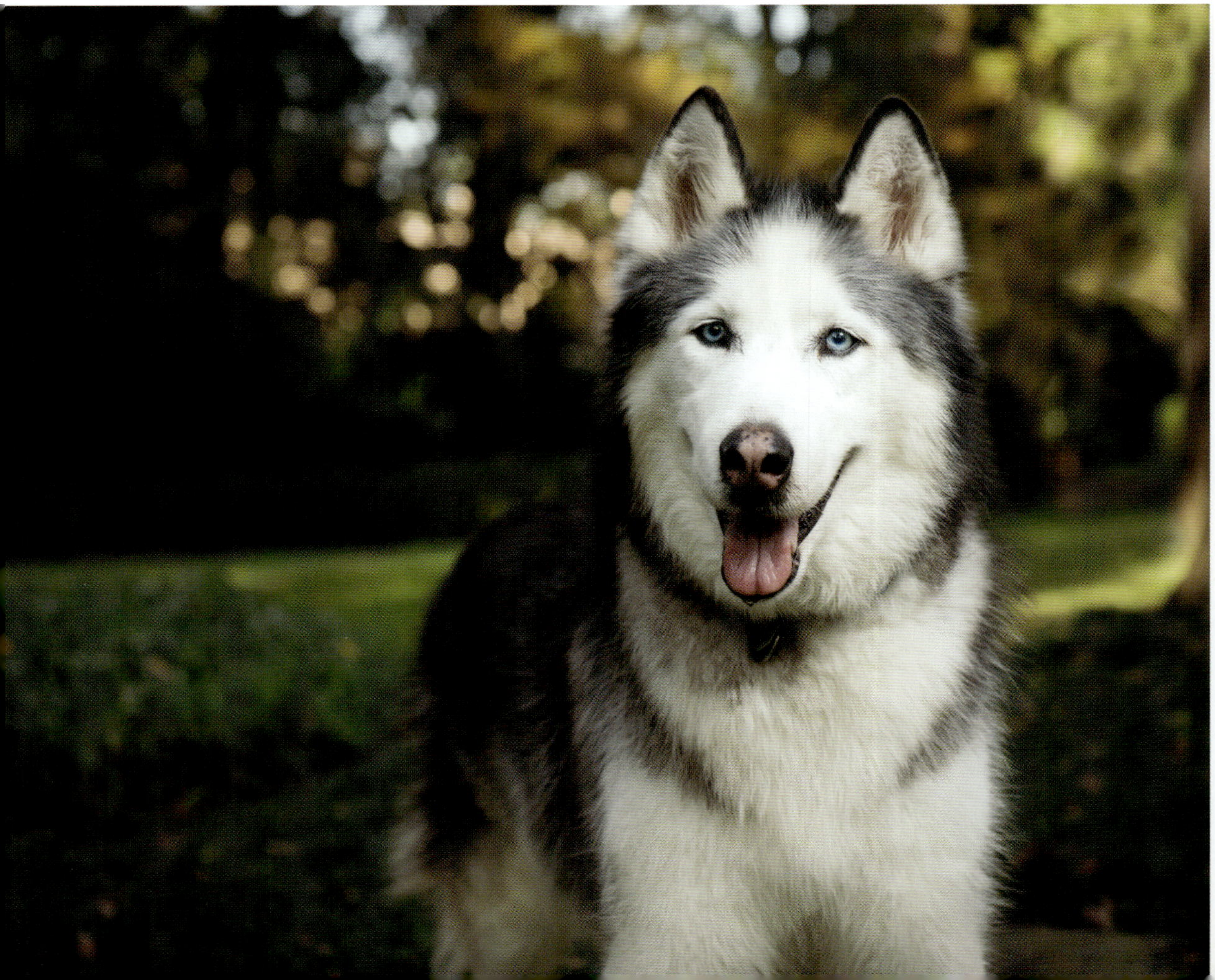

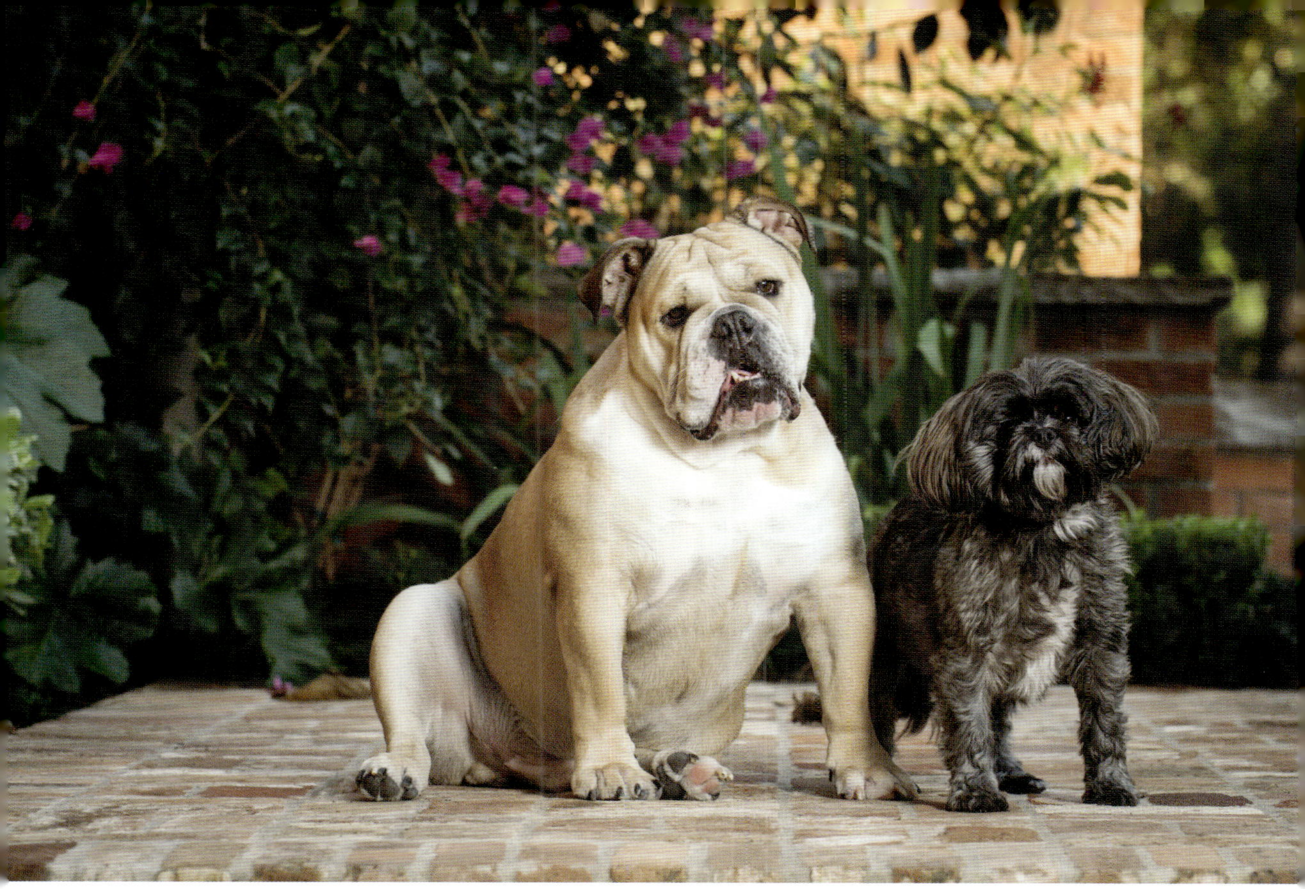

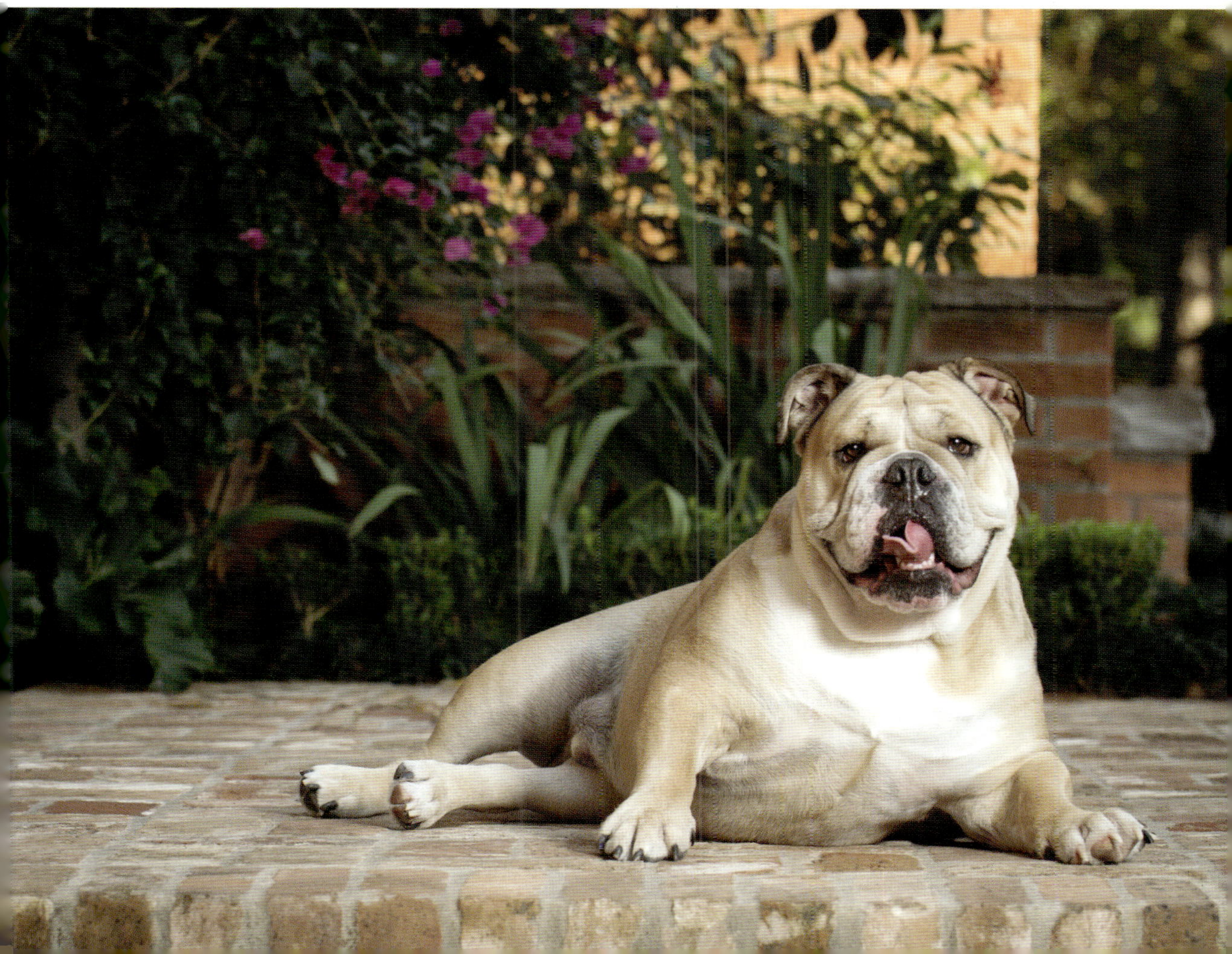

Speedlights are a great option because of their portability, but they are not nearly as reliable as a studio strobe on location. However, if you're using a studio strobe, you will need a lot more equipment, like a portable battery pack, which will increase your cost up front but will save you a lot of headaches down the road. For example, I was on a shoot with a client for engagement portraits and my speedlight overheated. I had to put it in a cooler between locations and hope it would cool down enough to get a few more flashes out of it. That was the last time I ever used it for my off-camera flash setup. Still, you can see from this image that a speedlight can get the job done if that's all you have to work with. Sorry there isn't a pup in this image—there were no puppies allowed on the golf course where we shot!

"If you're using a studio strobe, you will need a lot more equipment . . . "

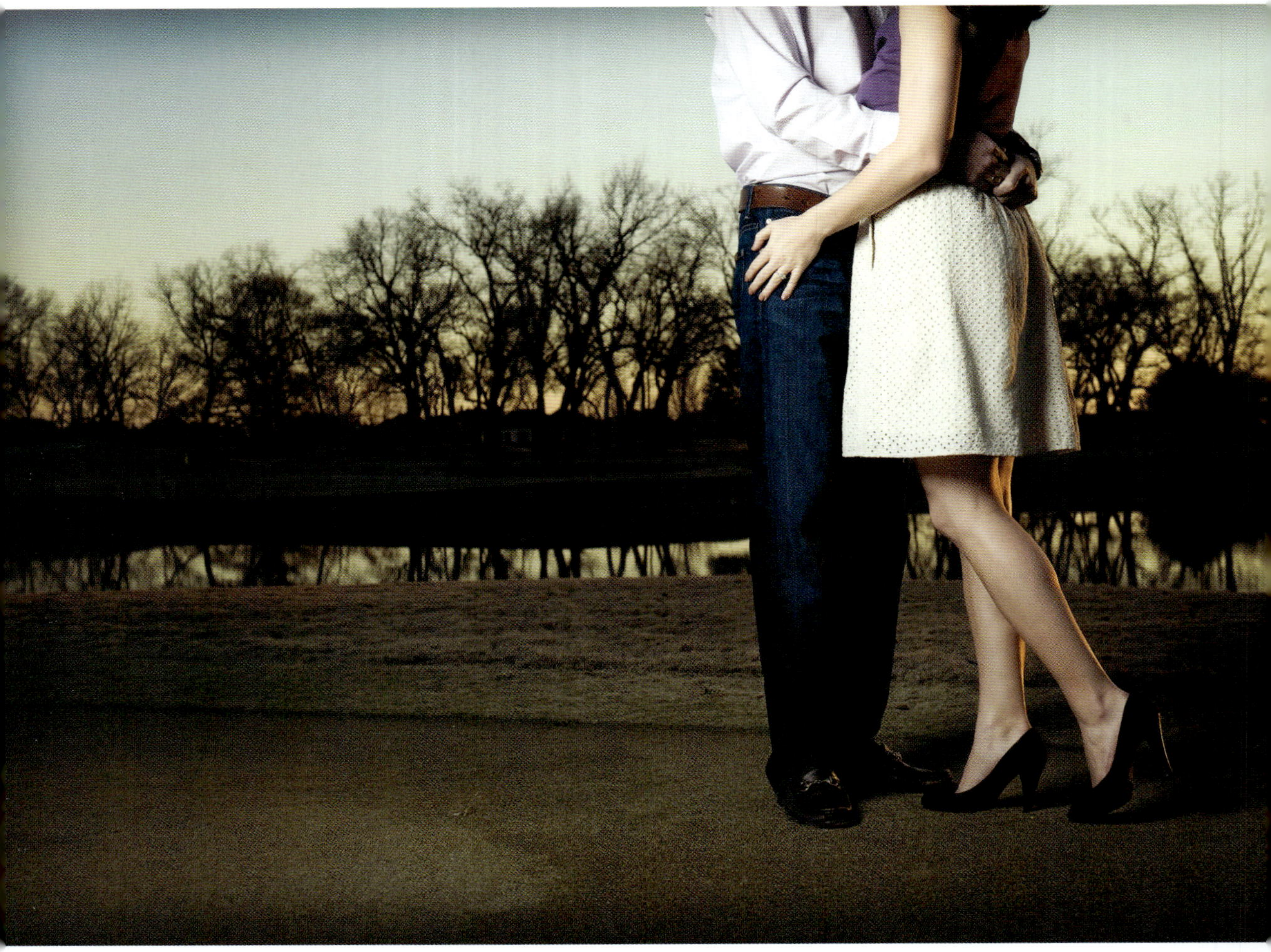

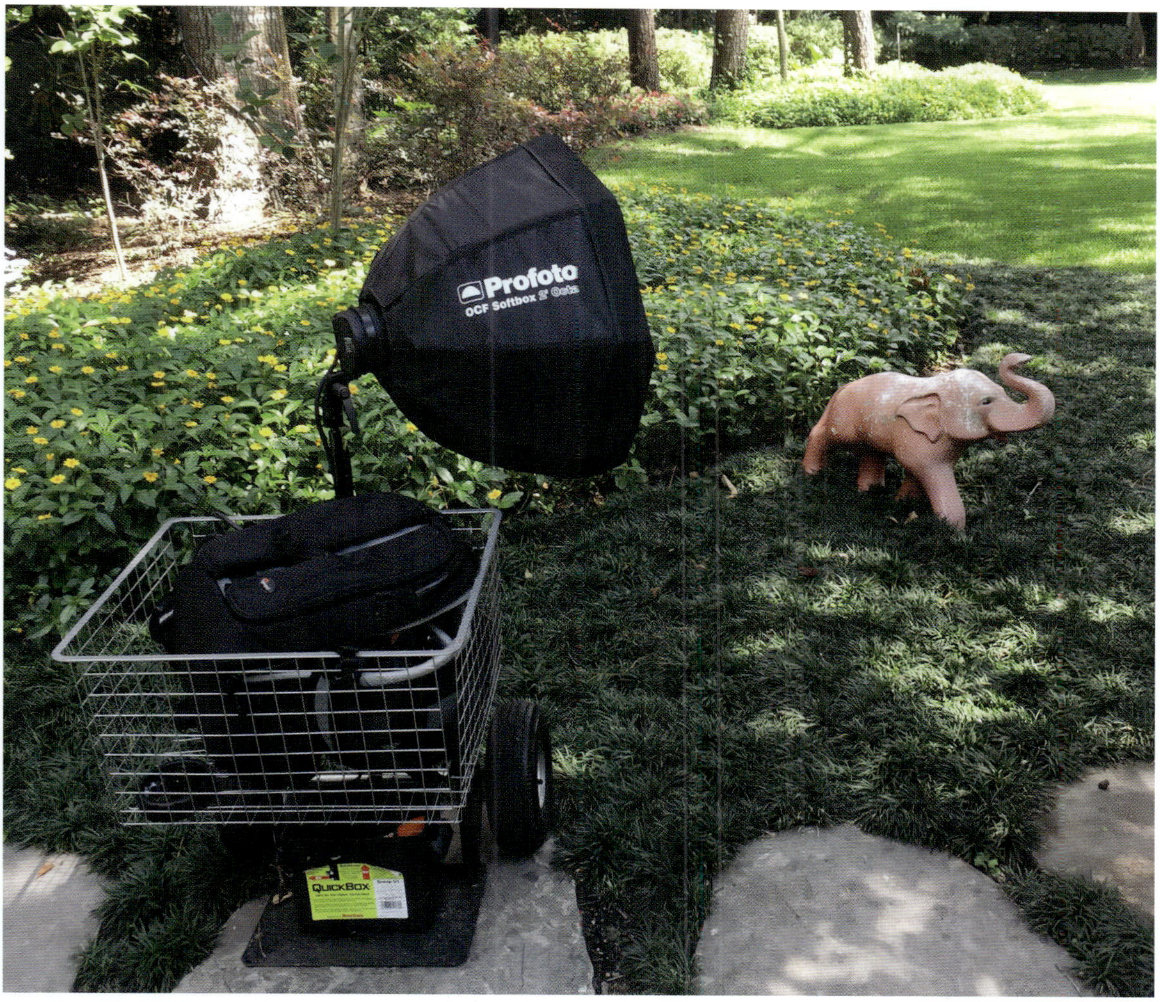

Another point to consider when you select your equipment is that, if you are working without an assistant, you will need a setup that you can easily carry on your own.

I use the LR-02 from Blair Phillips (http://www.blairphillipsworkshops" .com/store/lighting/lr-02?imageID=0). It is a light stand built into a dolly. It's great because it allows me to take all my gear and have my light without relying on an assistant. I added a basket to the front of my stand to hold my camera bag, waters, and bug spray, and it also helps to weigh the cart down.

You also need some sort of light modifier on your light. You have options for both your speedlight and studio strobe—you just have to decide what works best for you. I get a lot of use out of a 2-foot portable beauty dish with a silver interior.

You will also need a set of triggers, like Pocket Wizards or an equivalent, to trigger your lights.

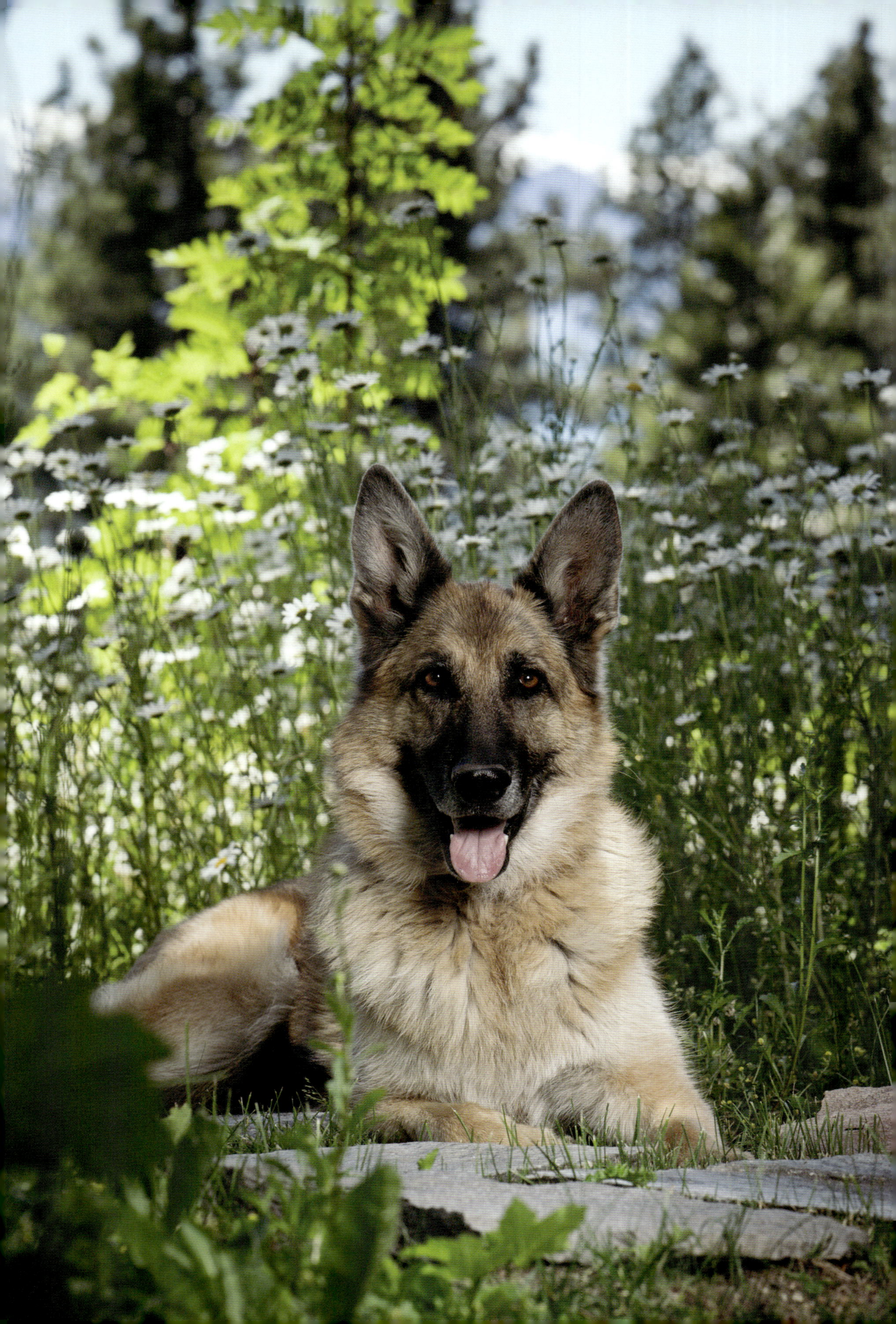

Off-Camera Flash Techniques

Using off-camera flash is actually quite simple. The key to balancing the ambient light and the flash is making sure you understand which camera components control what. Just as a reminder: the shutter speed controls the amount of ambient light and the aperture (or f/stop) controls the flash output. Most likely, you will be adjusting your shutter speed to let more light into the background and your aperture to increase or decrease your flash output. You can adjust your ISO as well, but it will affect the entire light output in the image.

I typically use a shutter speed of about $^1/_{125}$ second because it allows for enough ambient light to come in. If you get closer to your shutter speed sync in the $^1/_{200}$–$^1/_{250}$ second range, you will notice that your photo will seem very dark with a flashy area. You want to balance the light sources as much as possible by using a slower shutter speed to let in more light. Of course, you don't want too slow of a shutter speed because you will get camera shake if you're hand-holding your camera. We want a nice balance so the background is still lit without being blown out and distracting from the subject.

This image of Sammy is straight out of camera with zero edits, so you can see how spot-on you can get images using off-camera flash.

"Balance your light sources as much as possible by using a slower shutter speed to let in more light."

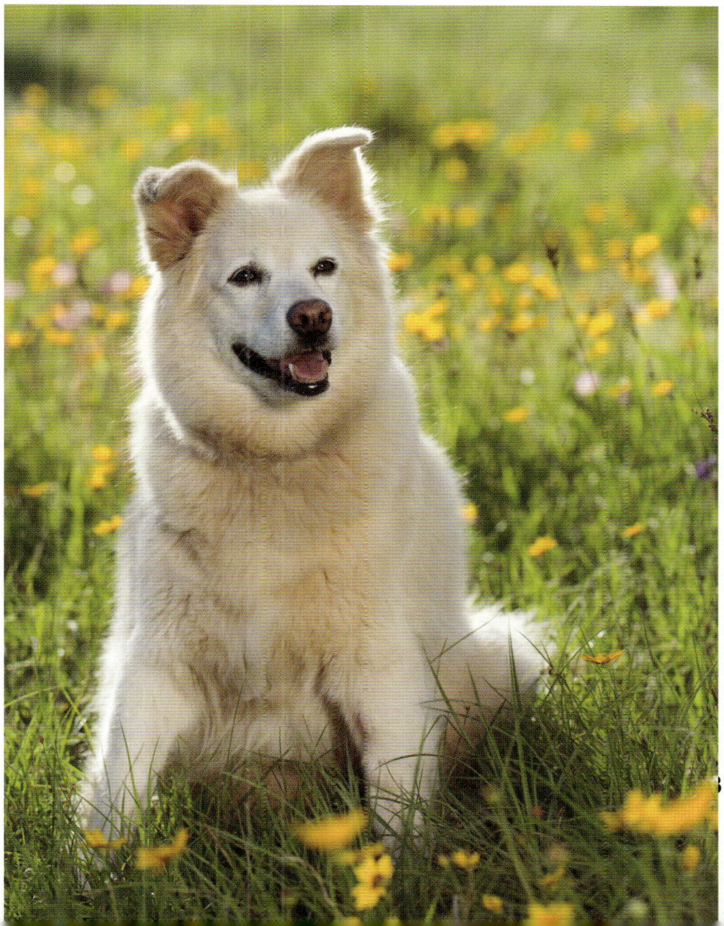

Let's talk about the basics of off-camera flash. I will break it down into a few simple steps for you.

First, you will want to position your pet with their back to the sun. You will achieve a beautiful rim light that way.

This image was taken in the middle of the day when the sun was its strongest. In the image below, you can see how your image will look without using off-camera flash. If you're not working with a flash and photographing at midday, your lighting options will be limited and most likely very harsh unless you're working on a cloudy day or in open shade.

Look at the image on the following page. See what happens when we add off-camera flash? Now, the dog is properly exposed; there is really nice texture and dimension in her fur, and the background is properly exposed, too.

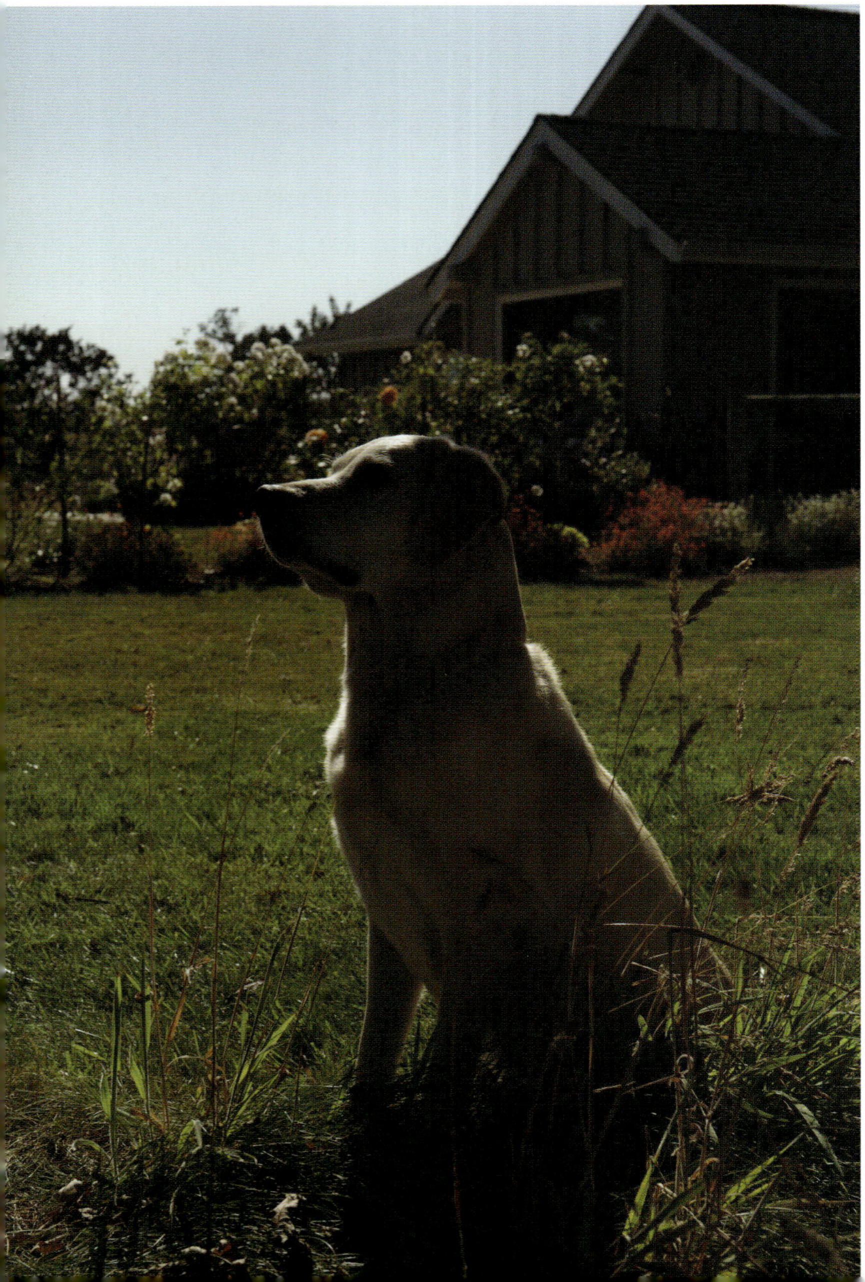

Using off-camera flash will give you a lot of flexibility in terms of your creative expression in your images. It can allow you to book more clients, too, as you can shoot at any time of day—not just at prime times, like early in the morning or at sunset. This photo, for example, was taken at midday.

"Work with off-camera flash and schedule more sessions throughout day."

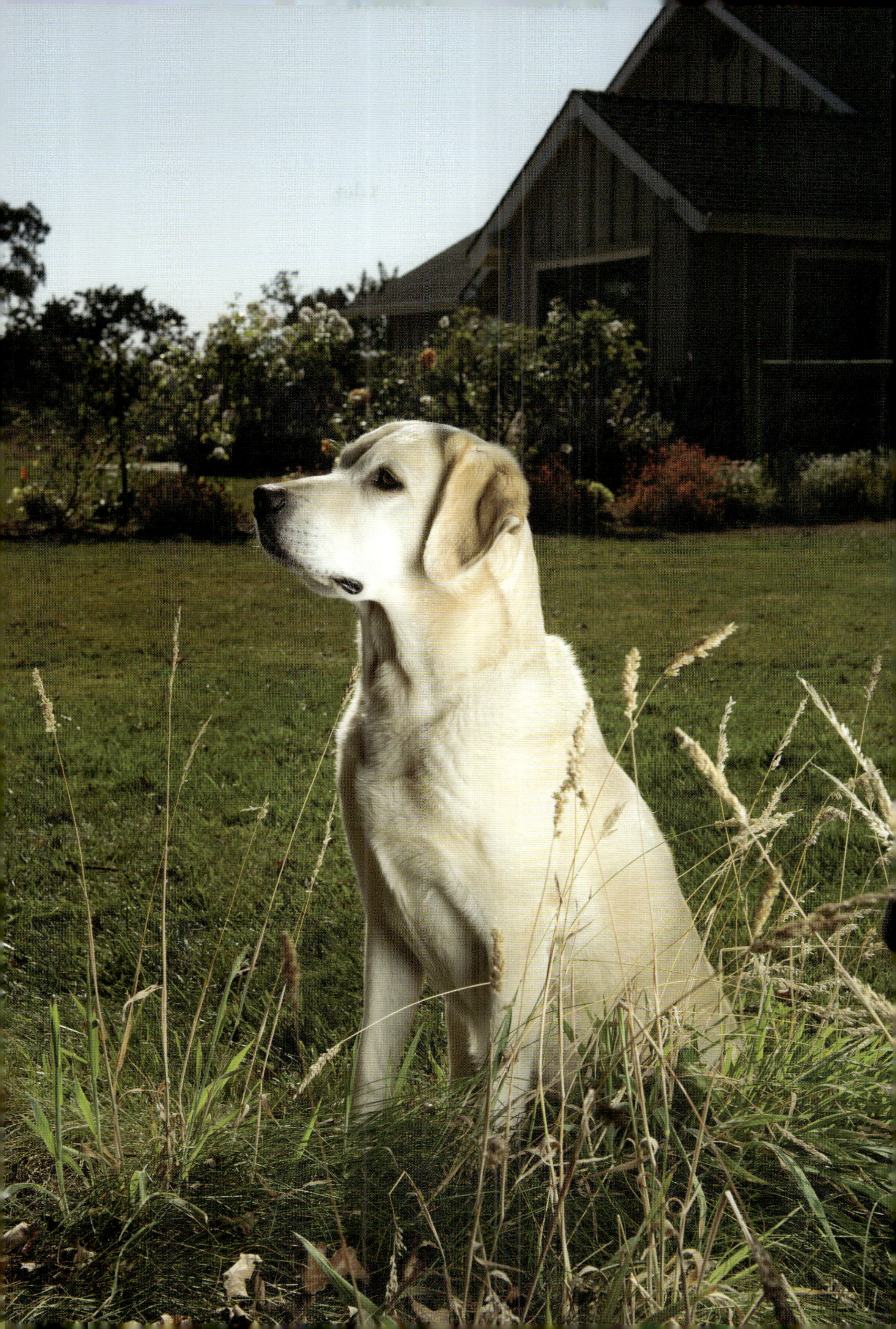

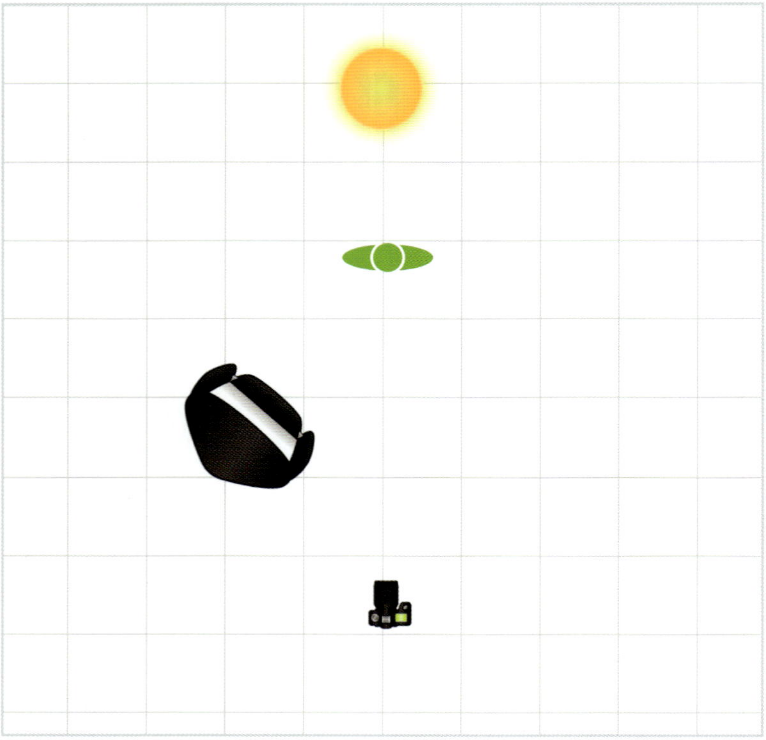

While you can work with your flash mounted on the hot shoe on your camera, you'll achieve the best lighting results when you get the flash off of your camera—hence the name, "off-camera flash." With the flash on top of your camera, you will get flat and unflattering light on your subject. By taking it off of the camera and positioning it at an angle to the dog, you will bring in directional light, just where you want it, to create flattering lighting that brings out the very best in the subject.

The best way to get your flash in position is to use a light stand. I recommend placing your light at a 45-degree angle to your pet, similar to a studio setup.

You can see what I mean by checking out the lighting diagram above. It shows how I set up my off-camera flash about 95 percent of the time. I may change which side I place my light on, but the angle of the light relative to the subject remains the same.

"Place the flash on a light stand and at a 45-degree angle to the subject."

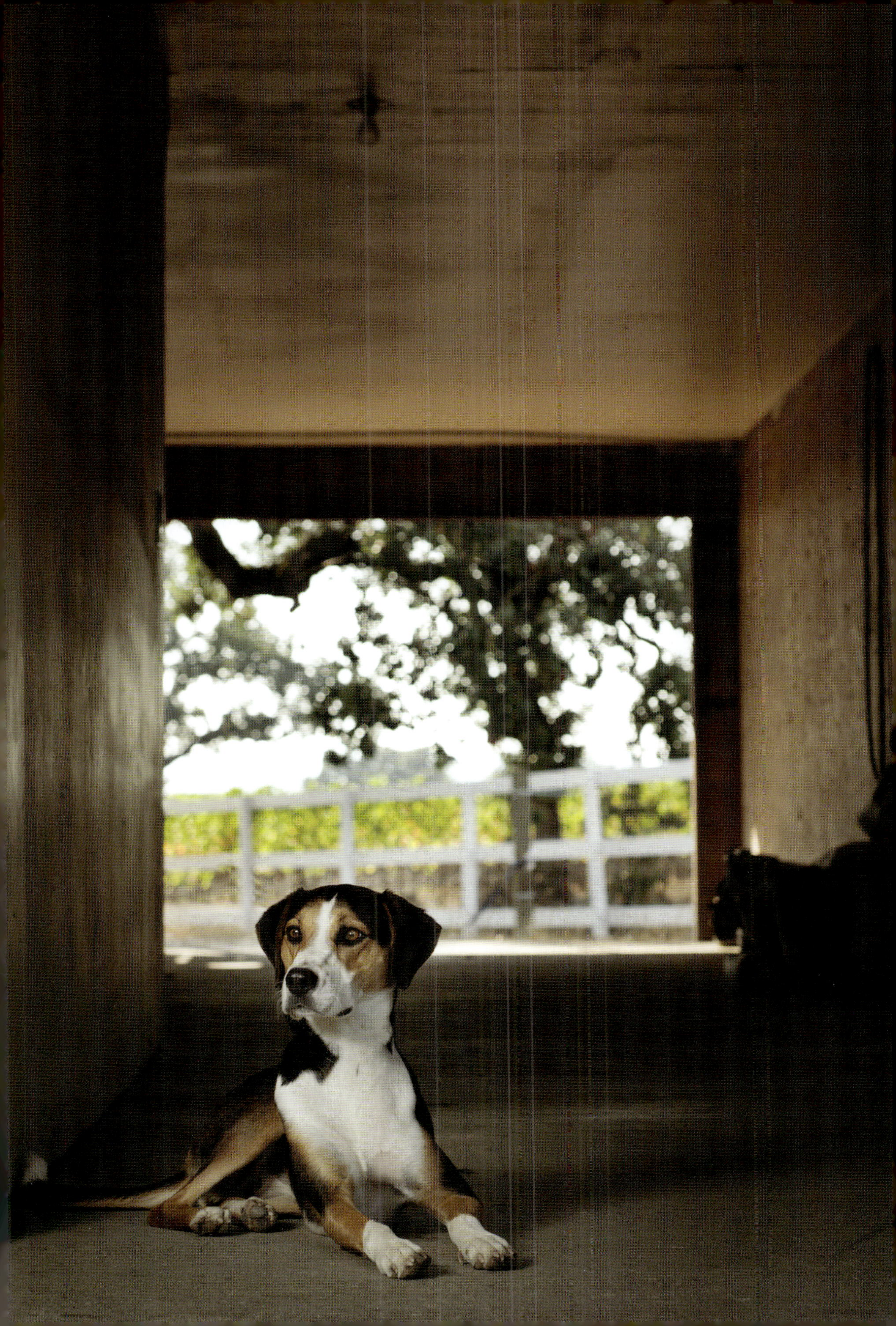

Let's talk about how to balance the flash with the ambient light, because that is key to creating portraits that don't look too flashy. The first thing I do is meter for the background in-camera. I want to make sure I properly expose the background first, with no flash, before I add that in. Again, the ambient light is controlled by the shutter speed, and the flash output is controlled by the aperture. So, first, I meter for the background and figure out what that exposure should be. Once I know that, I make my image a tad bit darker (a personal preference)—just by one stop—by adjusting my aperture. So, if I metered at f/5.6, I would set my aperture to f/8.

Once I have properly exposed for my background, I add in the flash. This part is definitely more trial-and-error than an exact science. You want to have your flash on manual mode and start off with it at about 1/4 power. Take a test shot to make sure you get enough light before you start trying to get expression. You want enough light to pull the subject out, give it dimension, add texture, and get catchlights in the eyes.

You may have to keep tweaking the light, depending on where and when you are photographing. If you're working at noon, you are definitely going to need more light than you will if you are shooting at the beginning or end of the day, when the ambient light level is lower and the background is less bright.

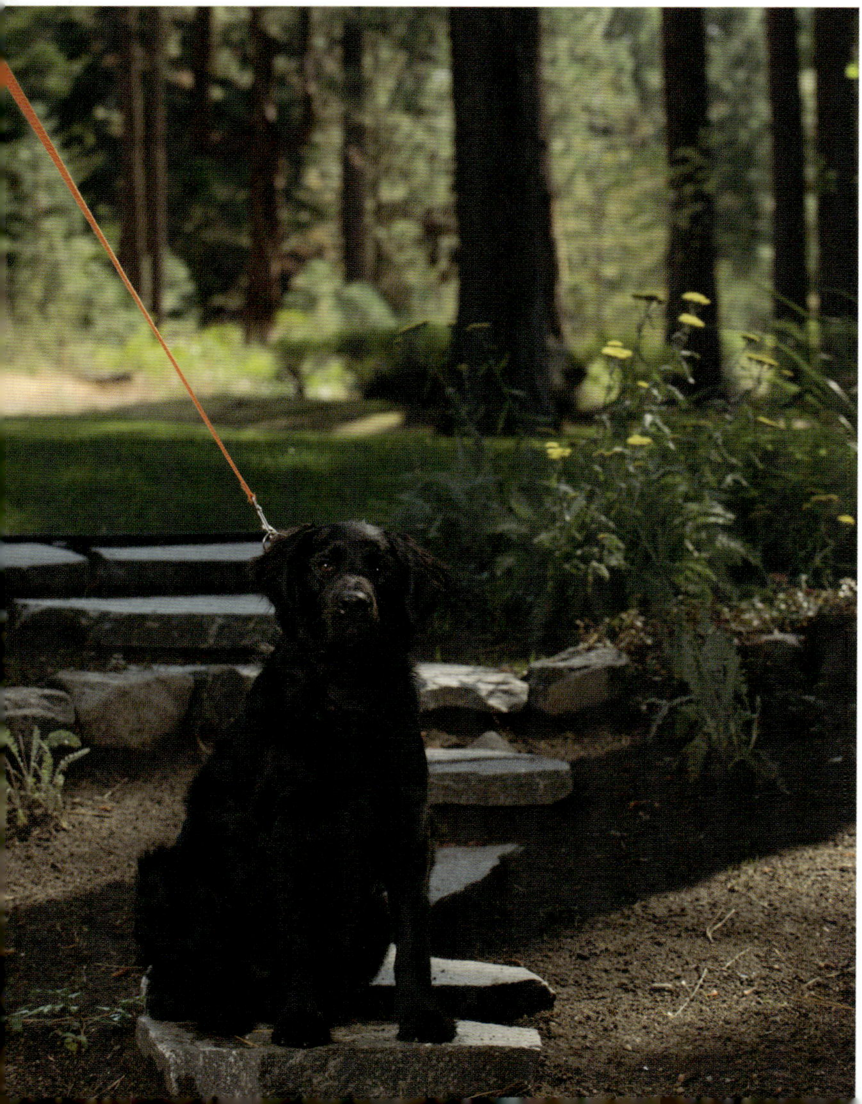

"Take a test shot with your chosen settings and evaluate the light."

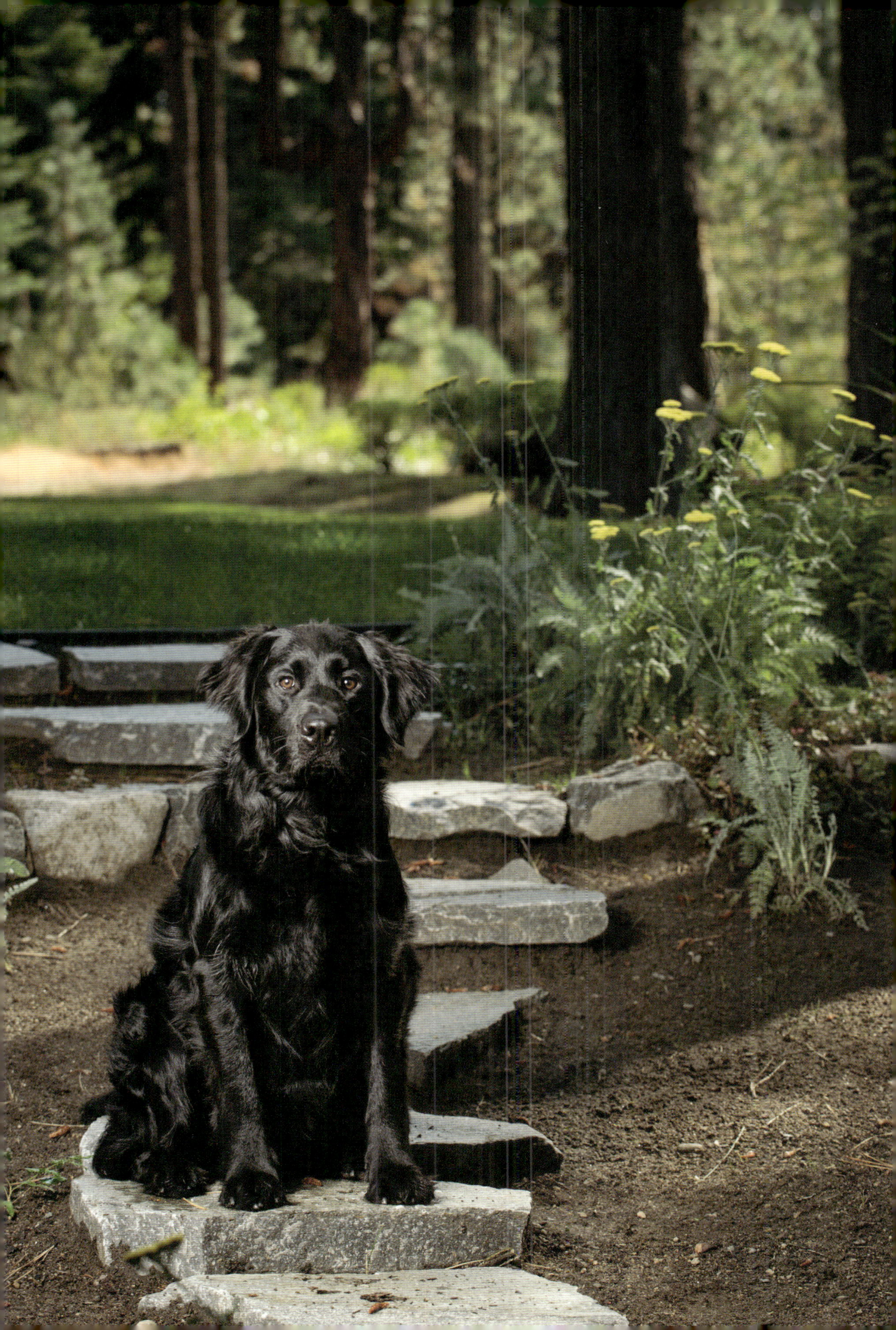

Here is another example of a session done in the middle of the day. Below is the image without the flash added in. You can see how the background and sky are properly exposed, but the dog is too dark. We do have a nice rim light on her from the sun, though.

See the difference *(following page)* once we add the flash back in? Since this was photographed at midday, the flash had to be a bit stronger to pull her out. Look at how beautiful this image is, even without any retouching. The light is perfect on her. It pulls her out of the image, making her the focal point. Her fur is not blown out, and we still have different highlights and shadows in her fur, giving the image more depth.

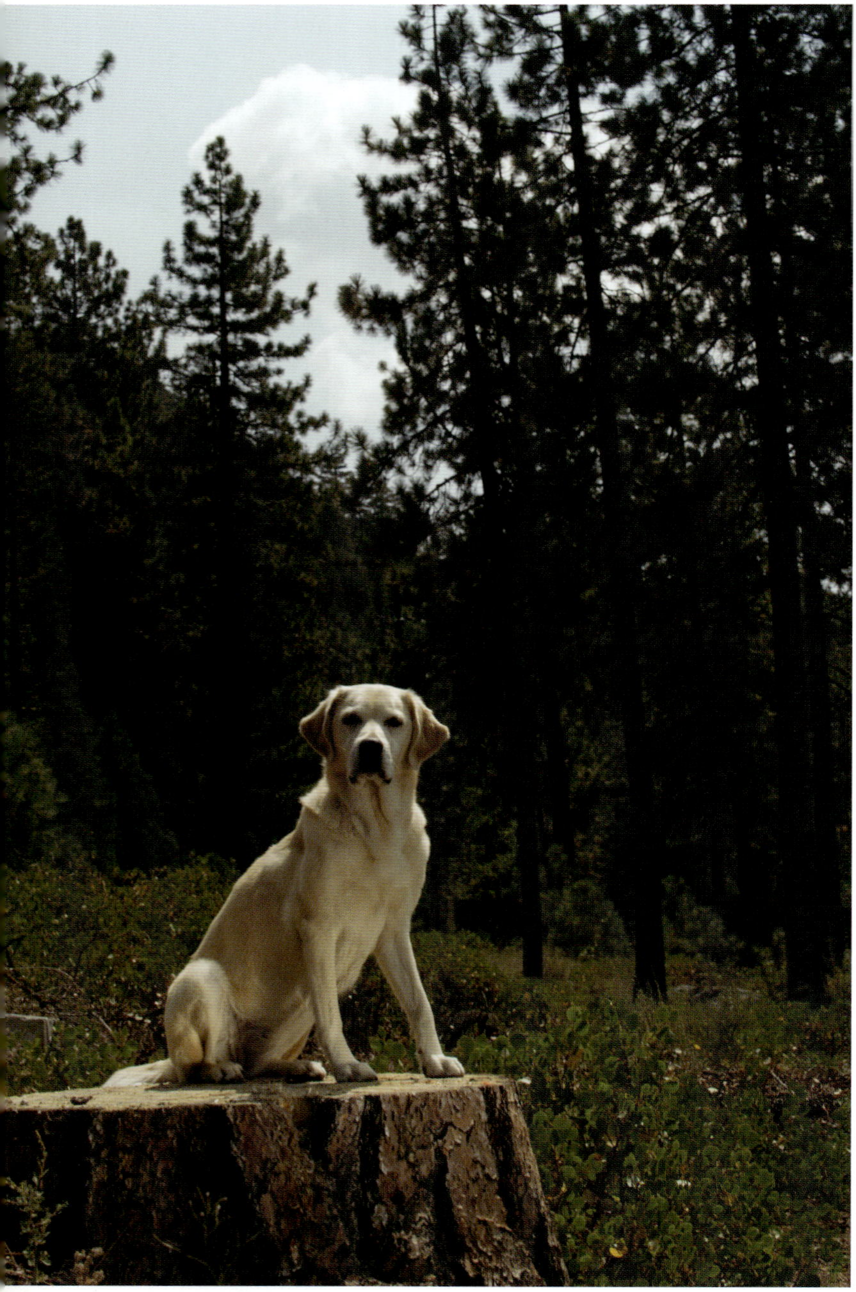

"Notice what a big difference adding a little flash makes."

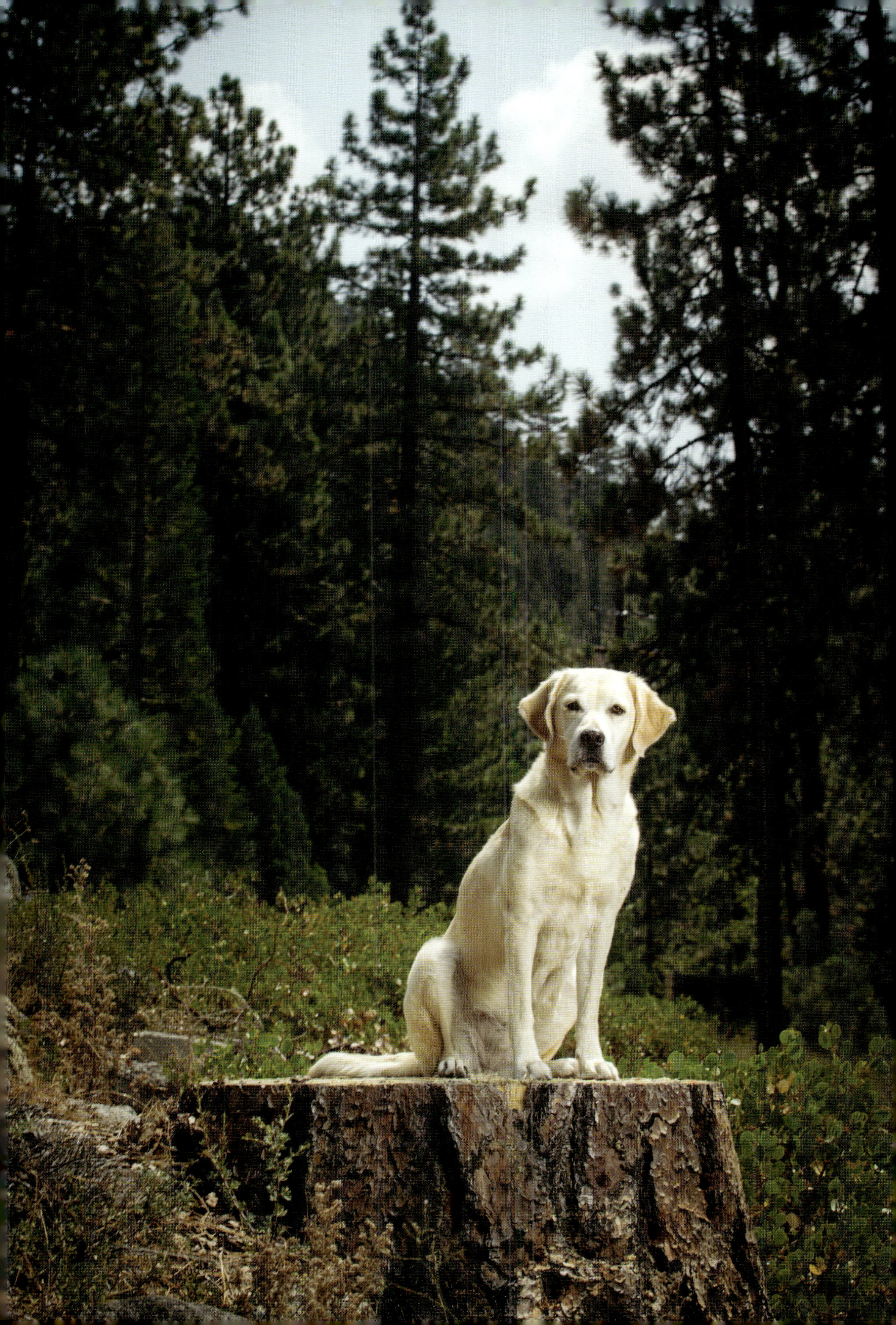

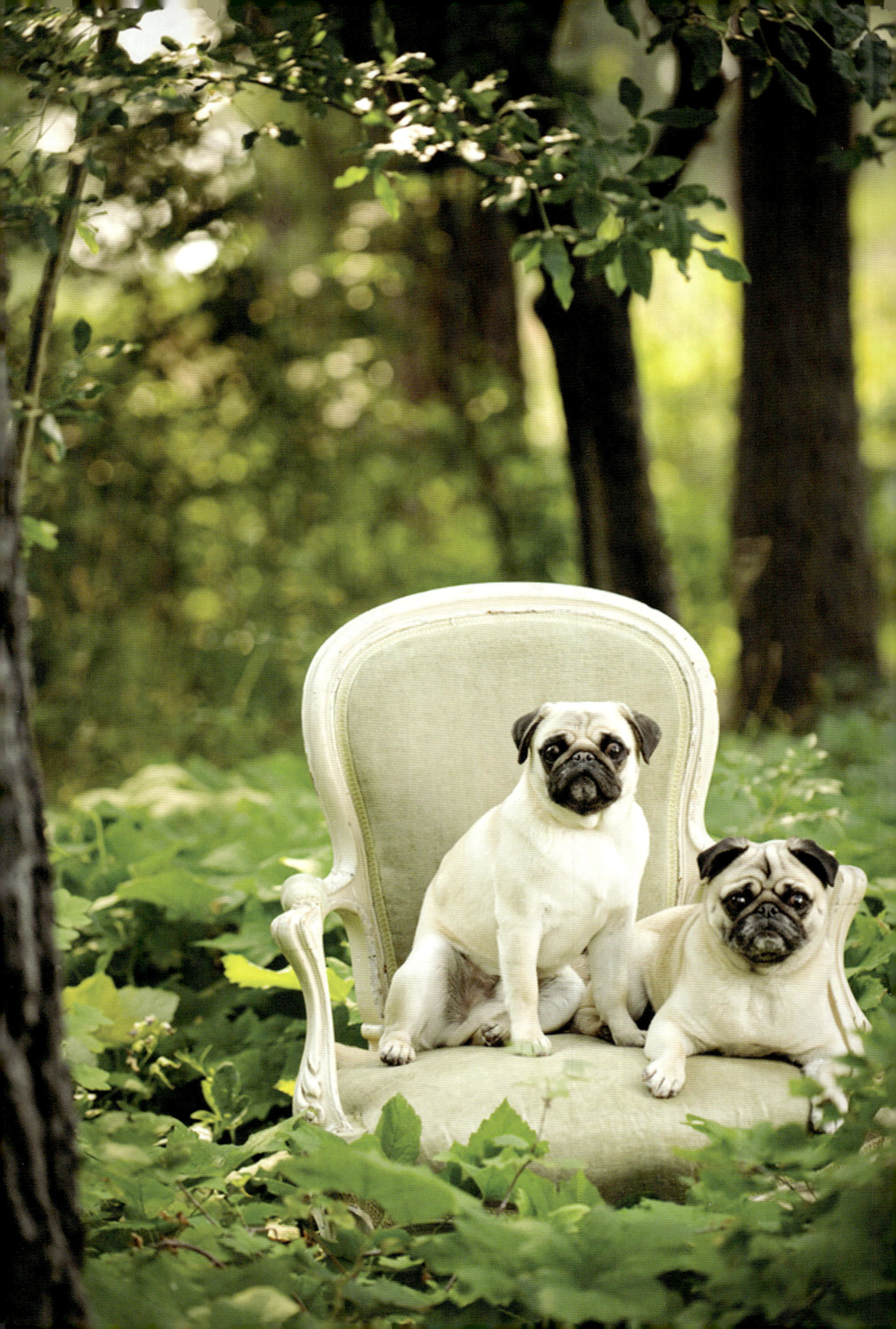

If you find that the background is properly exposed but there is too much flash on your subject, adjust your aperture to let in less light, thereby making your light a bit softer and less flashy. So, if you were at f/5.6, you would want to adjust your aperture to f/8 or so. Like I said, this is not an exact science; you may have to play around with your settings. If you do this right, you may not even be able to tell that you used a flash at all, like in this image. I most definitely used off-camera flash here *(previous page),* but I did it in a way that makes it less noticeable. The flash did add interest in the image by getting all the layers of light, texture in the fur, and catchlights in the eyes.

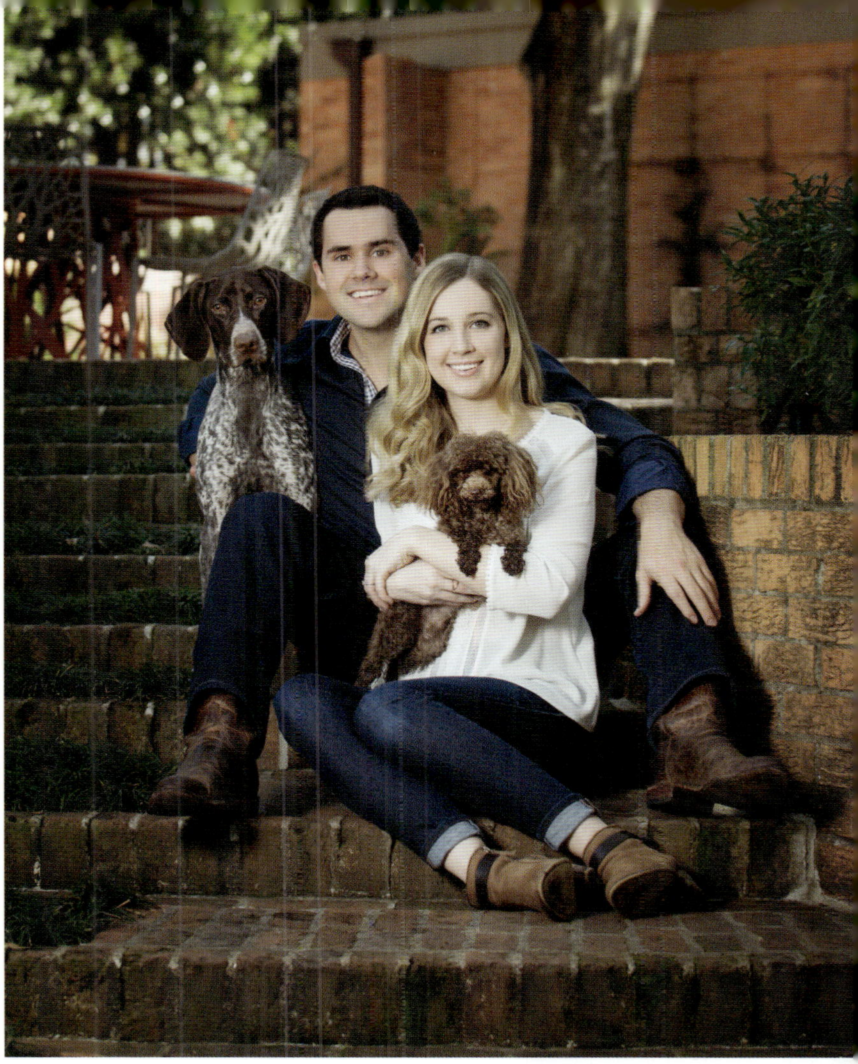

"To control the light, adjust the aperture of change the output on the flash."

If you have too much flash but don't want to change the aperture because you want a certain depth of field in your photograph, you can adjust the output setting on your light, instead. Start at $^1/_4$ power, then slowly bump it up or down and take a test shot. At midday, you may be photographing with your light at full power. If you're photographing in open shade with lots of ambient light, you may need a $^1/_4$ power.

I typically adjust the power output on my light rather than changing the aperture. It's my personal preference.

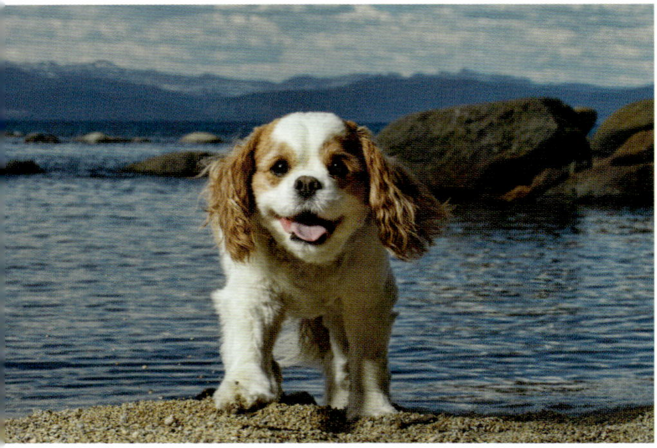

High-Speed Sync

I want to briefly touch on using high-speed sync. This is a great option when you're photographing motion. High-speed sync allows you to photograph with a flash while using a faster shutter speed than is normally possible. To do this, you need special equipment, like Radio Poppers or Profoto lights that

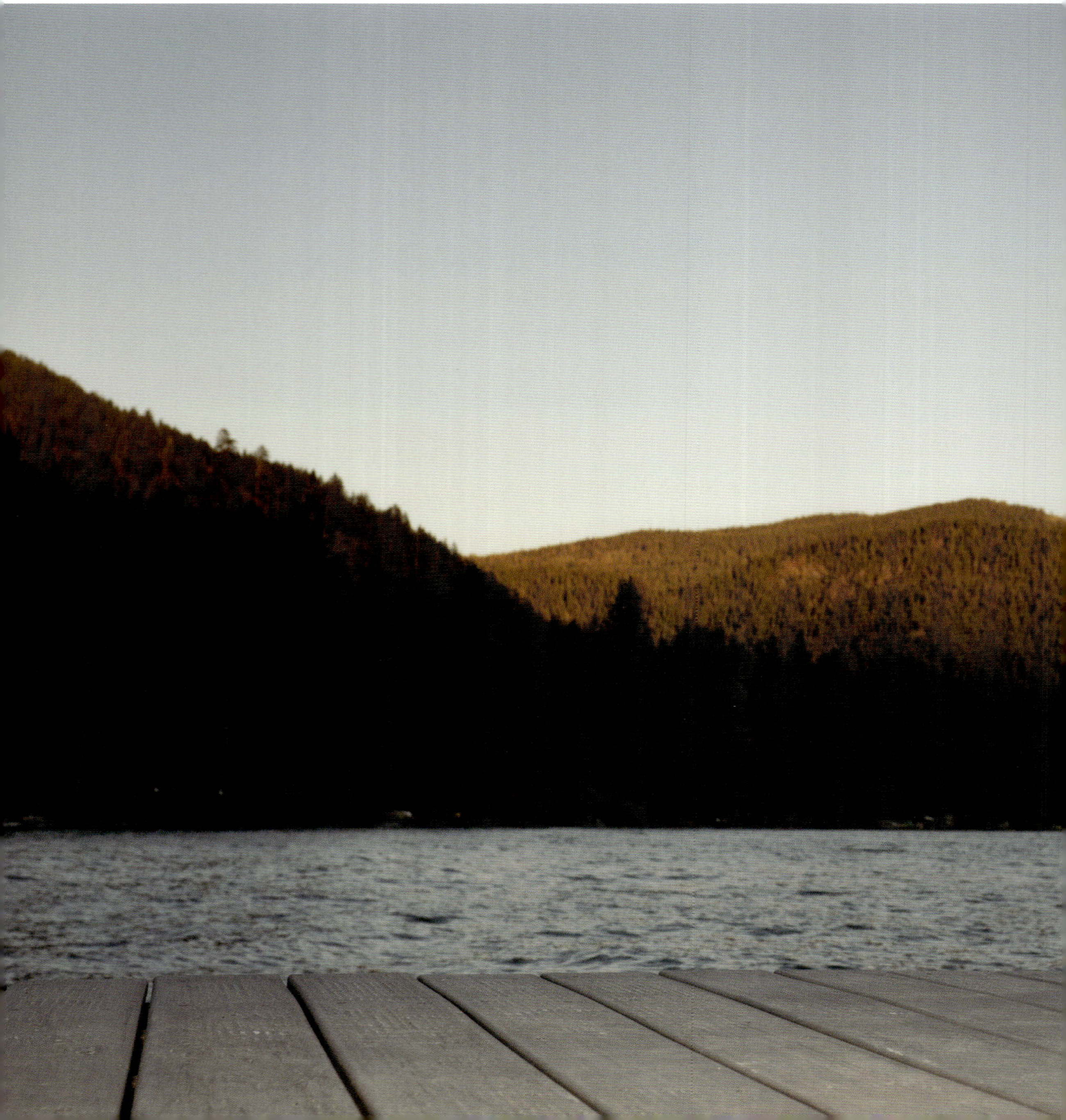

are high-speed sync compatible. All the steps remain the same, but you have to adjust as much as you can to allow in more ambient light, which is difficult if you're photographing at a high shutter speed. This is something to keep in mind if you're looking to photograph dogs running or something like agility training or sessions.

I think working with a reliable assistant is wonderful. However, with my schedule, it is tough to find someone when I need them, which is why I invested in a "portable assistant" that I can take anywhere. It makes scheduling sessions easier, and I know my light will be right where I need it when I need it.

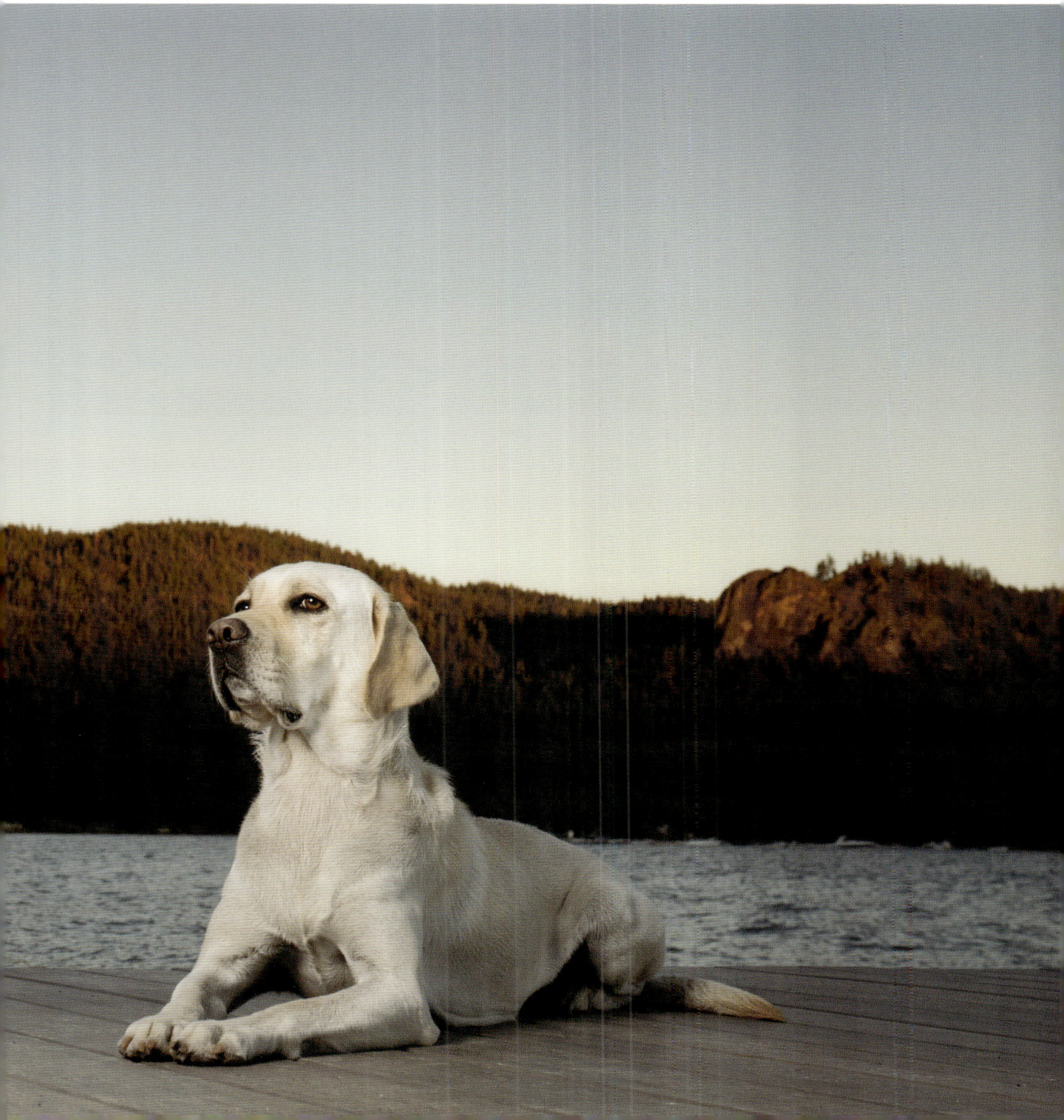

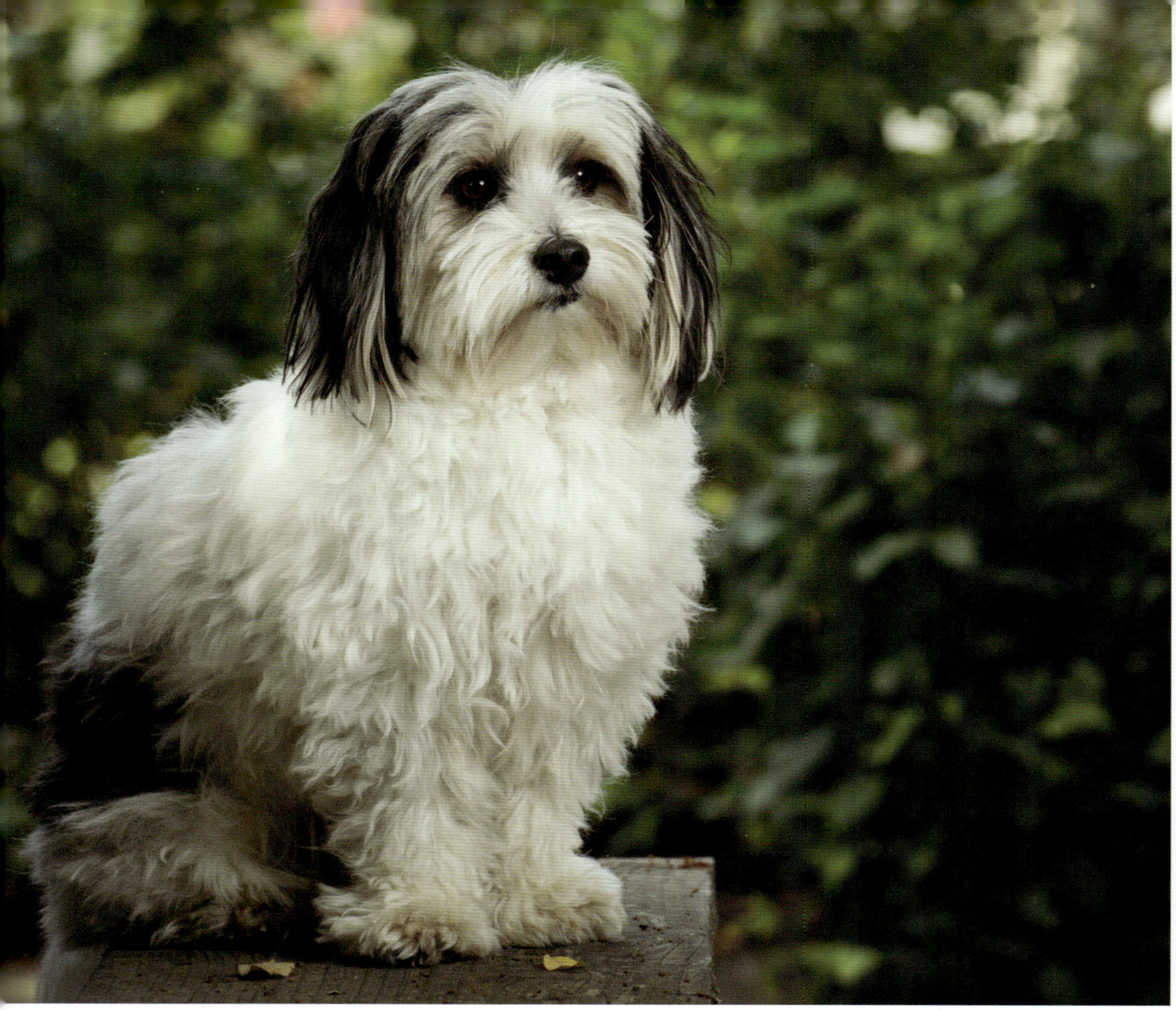

Incorporating off-camera flash into your work is not as difficult as you think. Once you have your setup and understand the basics, it's pretty easy to use it during your sessions.

When I have a session scheduled at a client's home, I always bring a light. I suggest you do the same, because you never know what opportunities may present themselves. For example, this home was especially beautiful and offered so many areas to photograph outdoors. I would not have been able to achieve the properly exposed background and a beautifully exposed pup without a pop of flash here. Using it made a tremendous difference. There are so many layers in this image, from the light in the background, to the middle ground, to the foreground with the pup.

"Always bring a flash along when you have a session at a client's home."

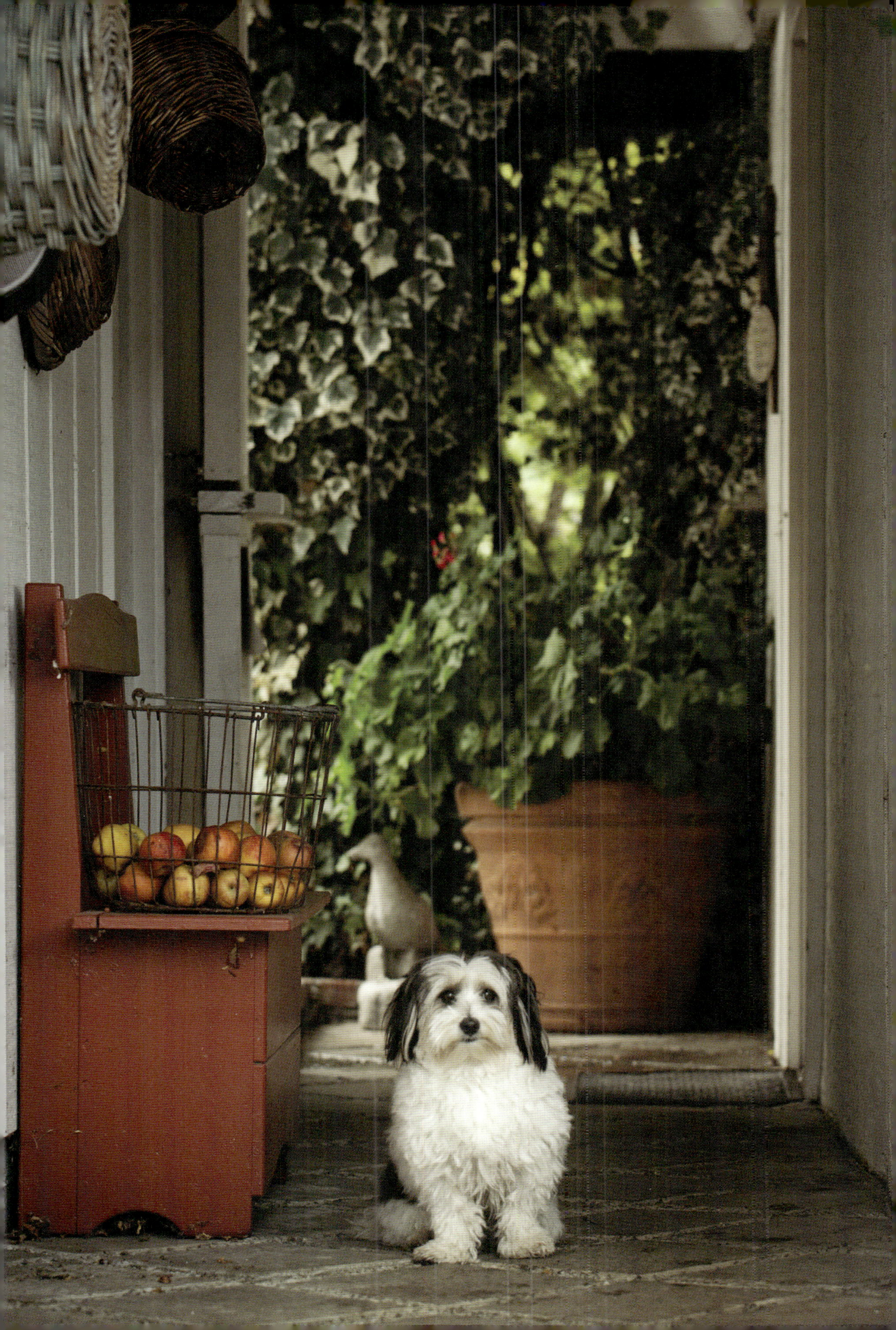

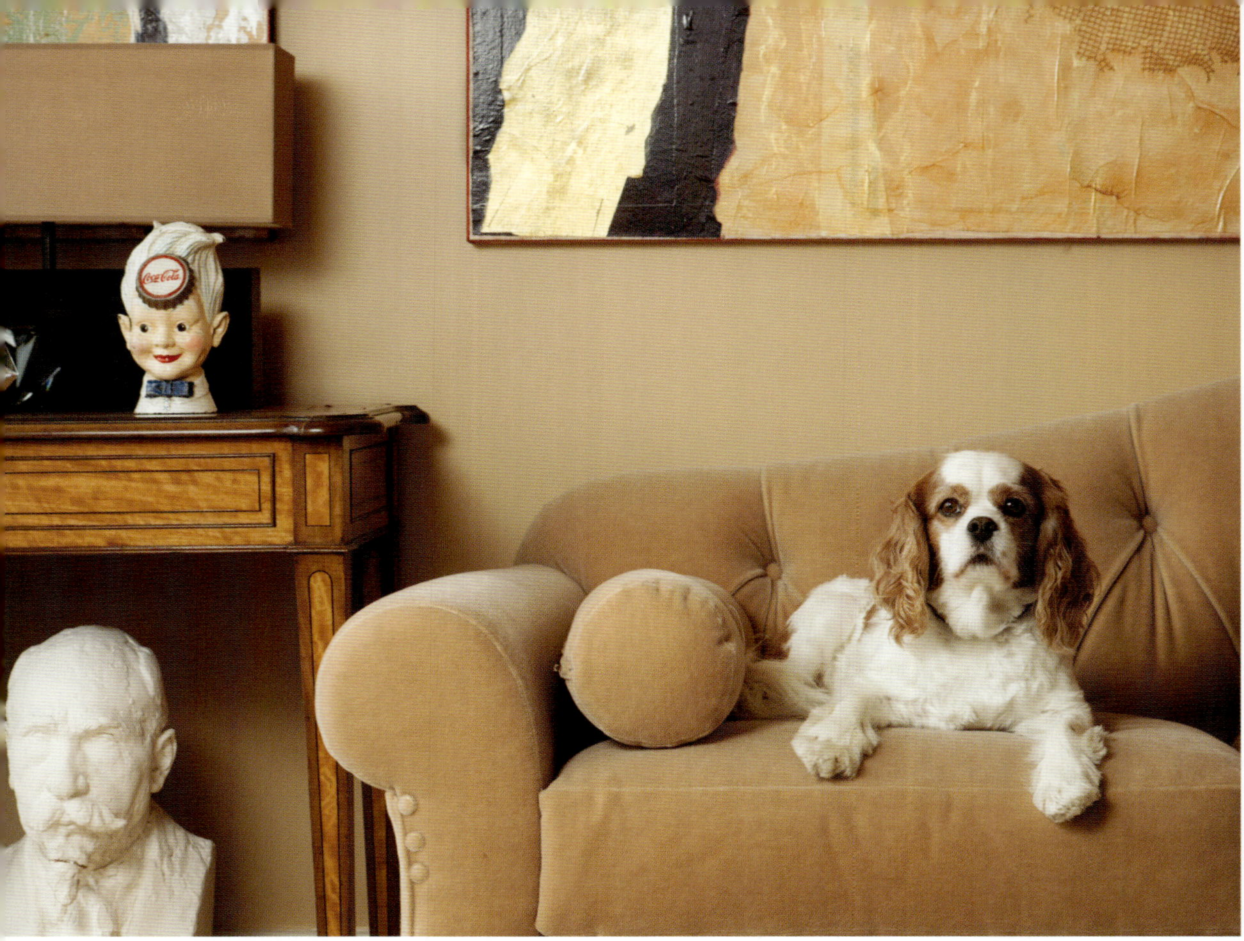

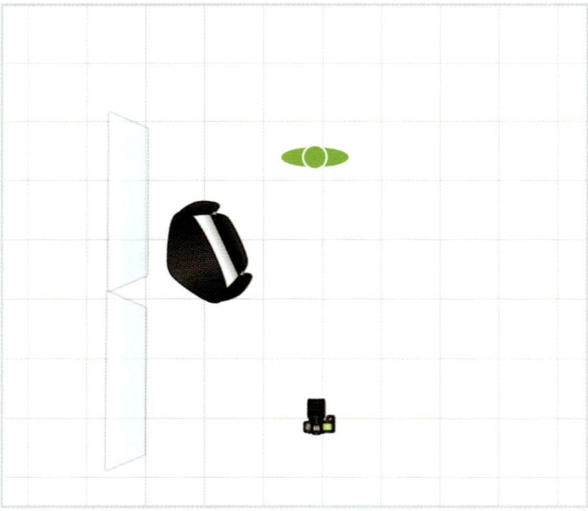

When you bring a light with you to photograph in a client's home, creating effective lighting can be a bit trickier because, if you're working in a small space, it may get flashy quickly. Yes, balancing the light in a client's home is more difficult, but just stick with the basics and use a minimal amount of flash. The key to making the scene look natural is to position your light as if it is natural light coming through.

For the image above, I used off-camera flash to provide an additional pop of light. The flash was positioned to allow it to come from the same direction as a large window, so the illumination just added to the natural light that was already present. If you don't have space inside the house, you can always position your light outside a window pointing indoors, instead.

Adding off-camera flash to your location work will allow you to create images like you can create in the studio. For the image below, you can see that I still used a prop outside, and both dogs have beautiful details in their fur and catchlights in their eyes.

Look at how these two adorable dogs positioned themselves. They are brother and sister, and I love how they snuggled together. The pop of light from the flash helped to visually bring them to the forefront of this image.

Adding a light to your on-location work can also cut down on your retouching. I usually don't have to adjust the exposure, bring back highlights and shadows, or add in catchlights in postproduction when I use off-camera flash.

"Use flash to reduce your postproduction work."

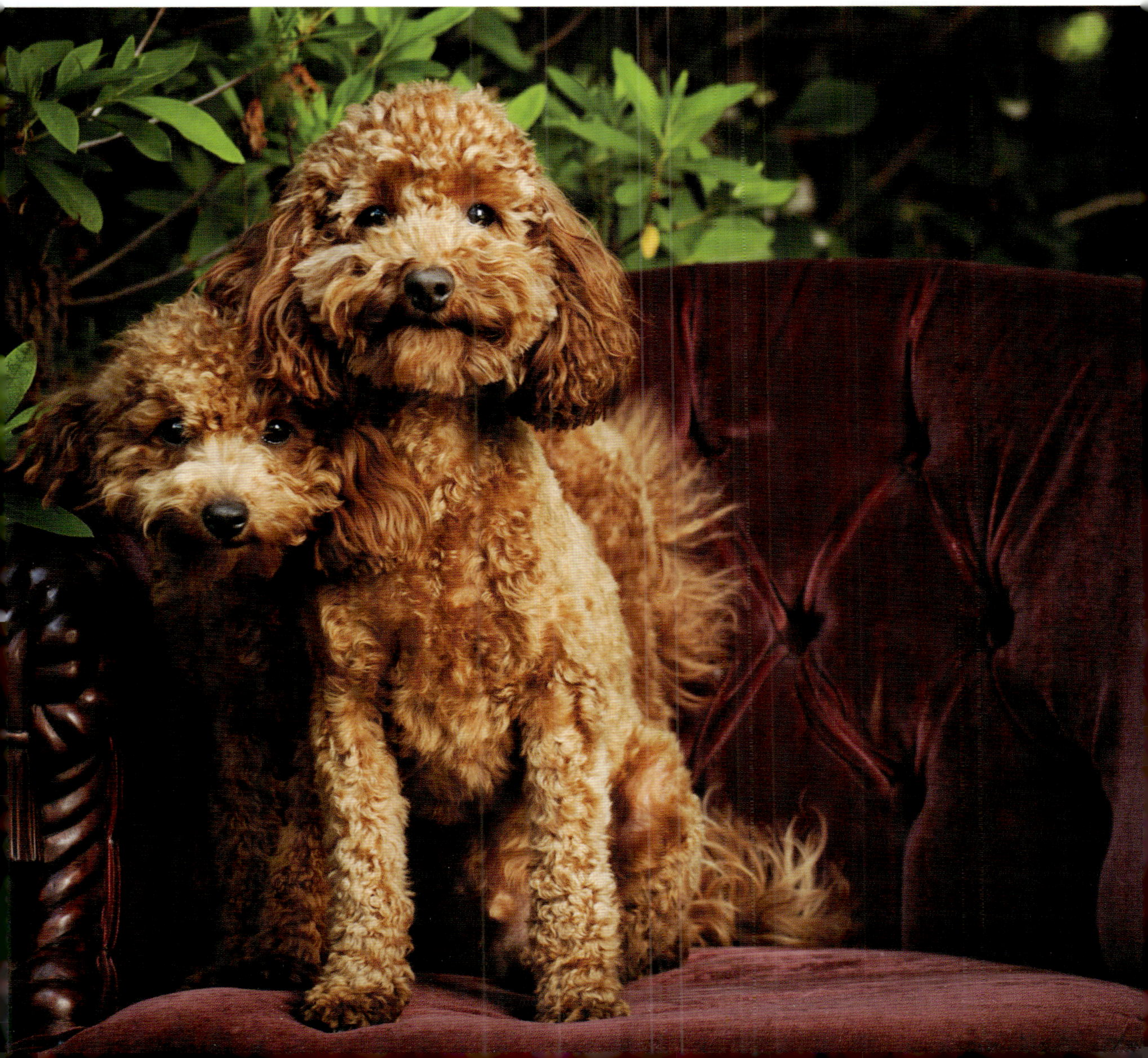

For the image below, I used the setup illustrated in the diagram on page 106, except that I placed the light on the right side of the dog, rather than the left. You can see lots of detail in her fur and eyes, and there are layers of light in the background. If I had used only natural light, her fur might have appeared flat, and the light in the background may have been overexposed.

The layers in this image give it a more interesting look and more depth.

The image on the following page is one of my favorite environmental images. It easily proves that you can capture amazing portraits at a client's home, in a park—in fact, just about anywhere.

I love what adding a bit of flash did for this portrait. It brought out those gorgeous Labs enough to show all the beautiful texture in their fur, and added catchlights in the eyes. It also added depth between the dogs and the background, making this two-dimensional image appear three-dimensional.

A fun little fact about this image: the bow ties belong to their dad, and he hand-tied each one!

Each time I made a noise to get the pups' attention, the black dog came barreling toward me and licked my face all over. These two were lots of fun to work with!

"Explore locations with confidence, knowing you can create exquisite light."

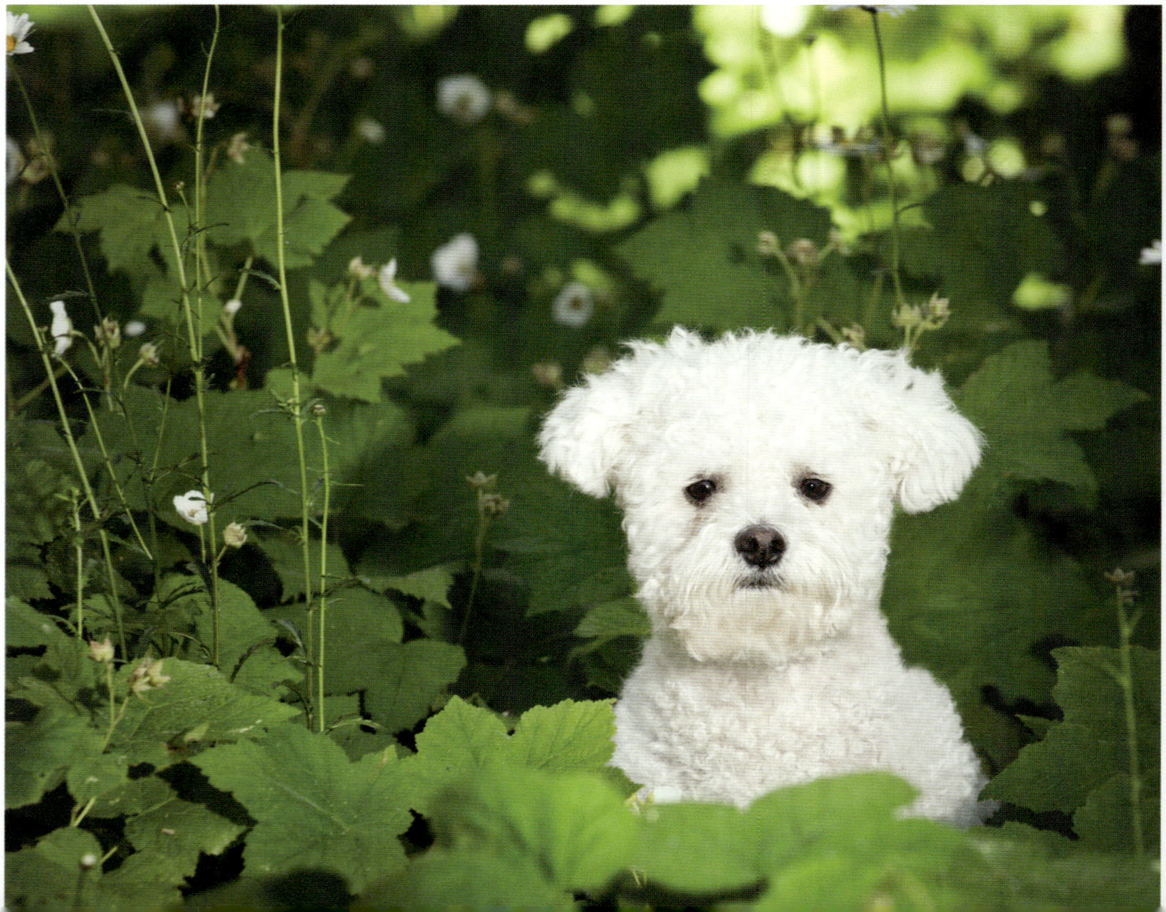

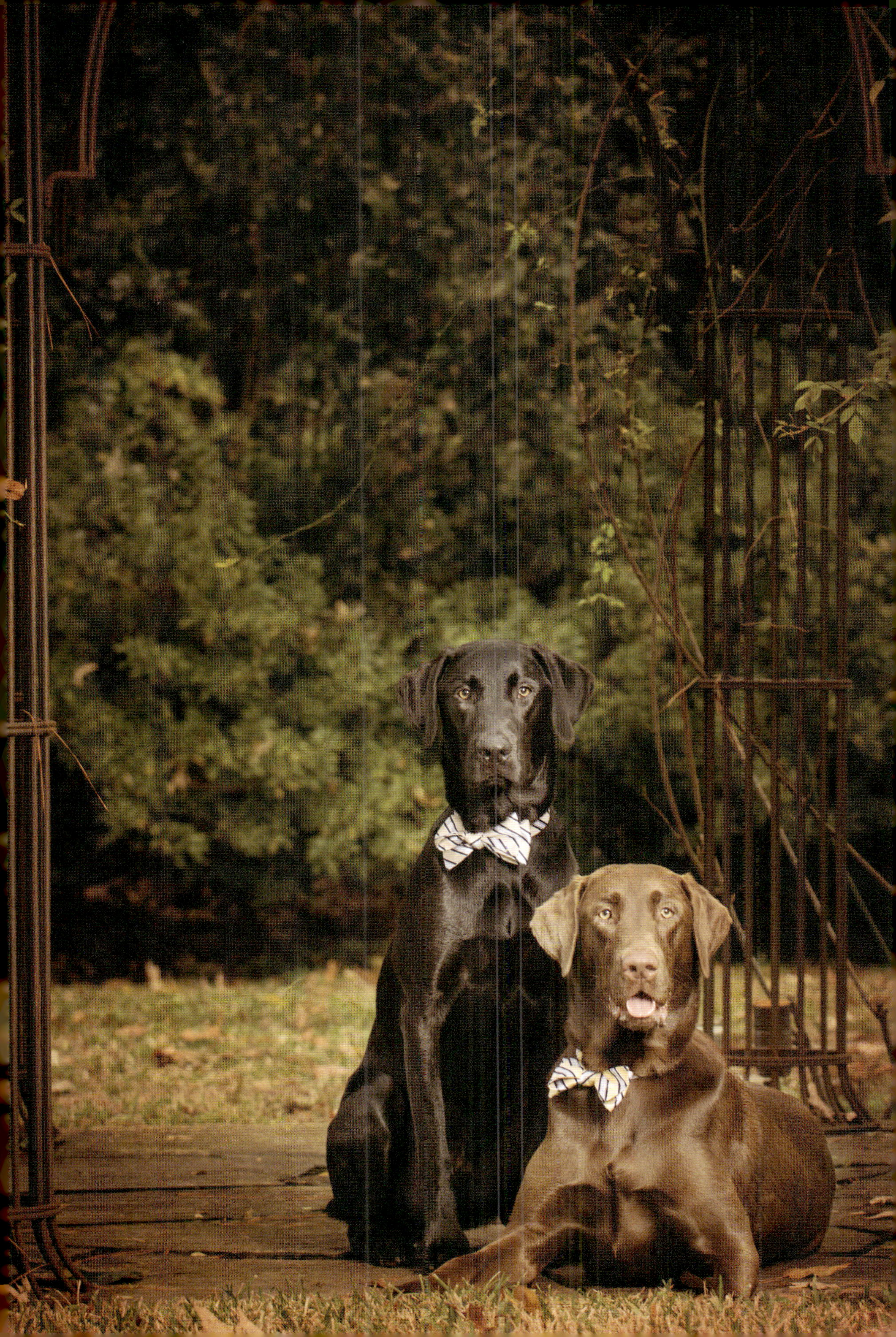

Conclusion

Understanding the principles of how to light fur is key to capturing amazing pet portraits. These lighting methods are the same in-studio and on location, so having a solid understanding of how your aperture, shutter speed, and ISO work together will help you to work and problem solve quickly. Sometimes

I only have a few minutes to set up and shoot. You have to be quick and be ready to take the shot.

It's also important to remember that every situation on location will be different, and sometimes you have to go with it.

The portrait below was photographed in a location in which there was very little ambient light, which is why you see more flash. However, that was the situation I was presented with, so I'm okay with the photo having more flash in it. Plus, it's a pretty cool night shot. Always be flexible, and don't forget to get the shot, even if it isn't the one you planned, because it may be the only one you get!

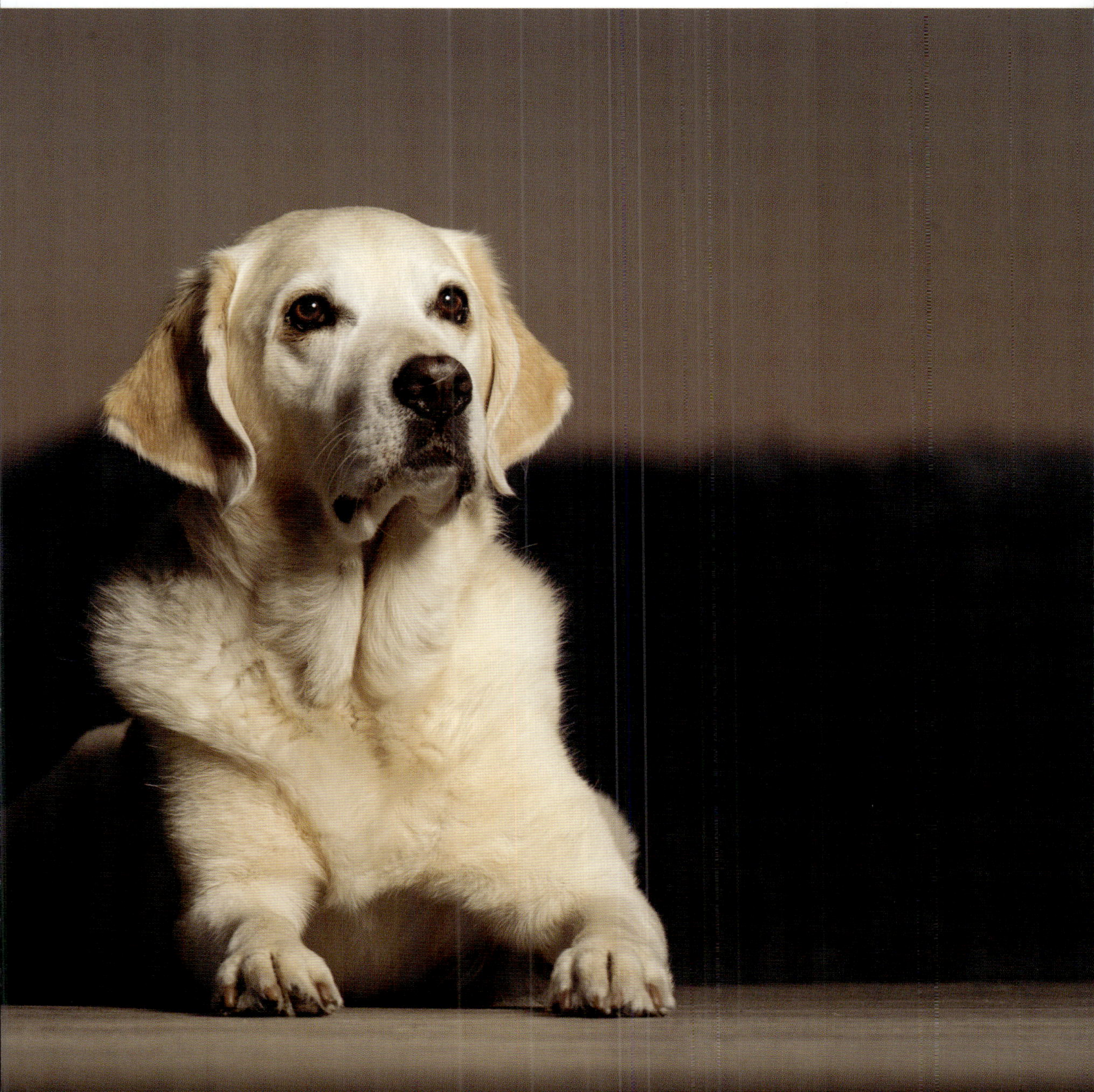

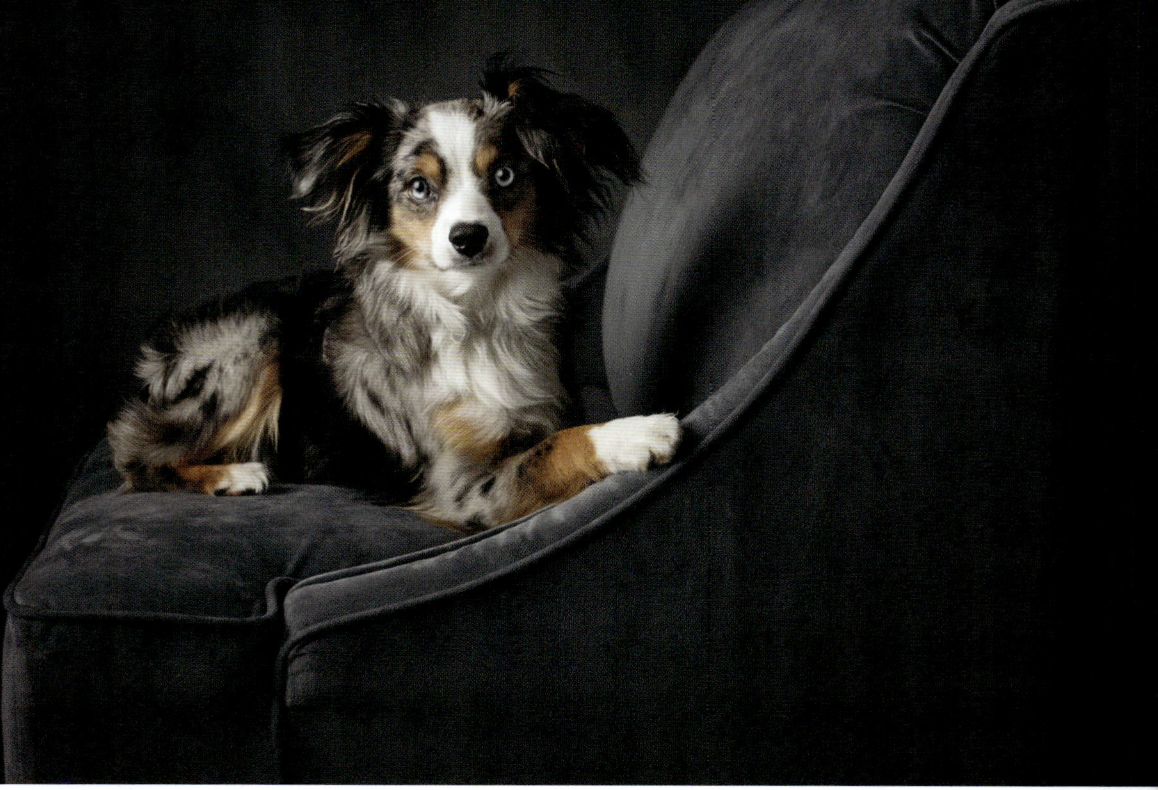

The key to mastering light for dog photography in studio and on location is to practice, practice, practice! My work has changed dramatically since I first opened my studio back in 2010, and I continue to evolve my style based on what I want to shoot and what my clients want as their finished pieces. Don't be afraid to try new things, and continually work to improve your lighting, posing, and composition for ever-better images.

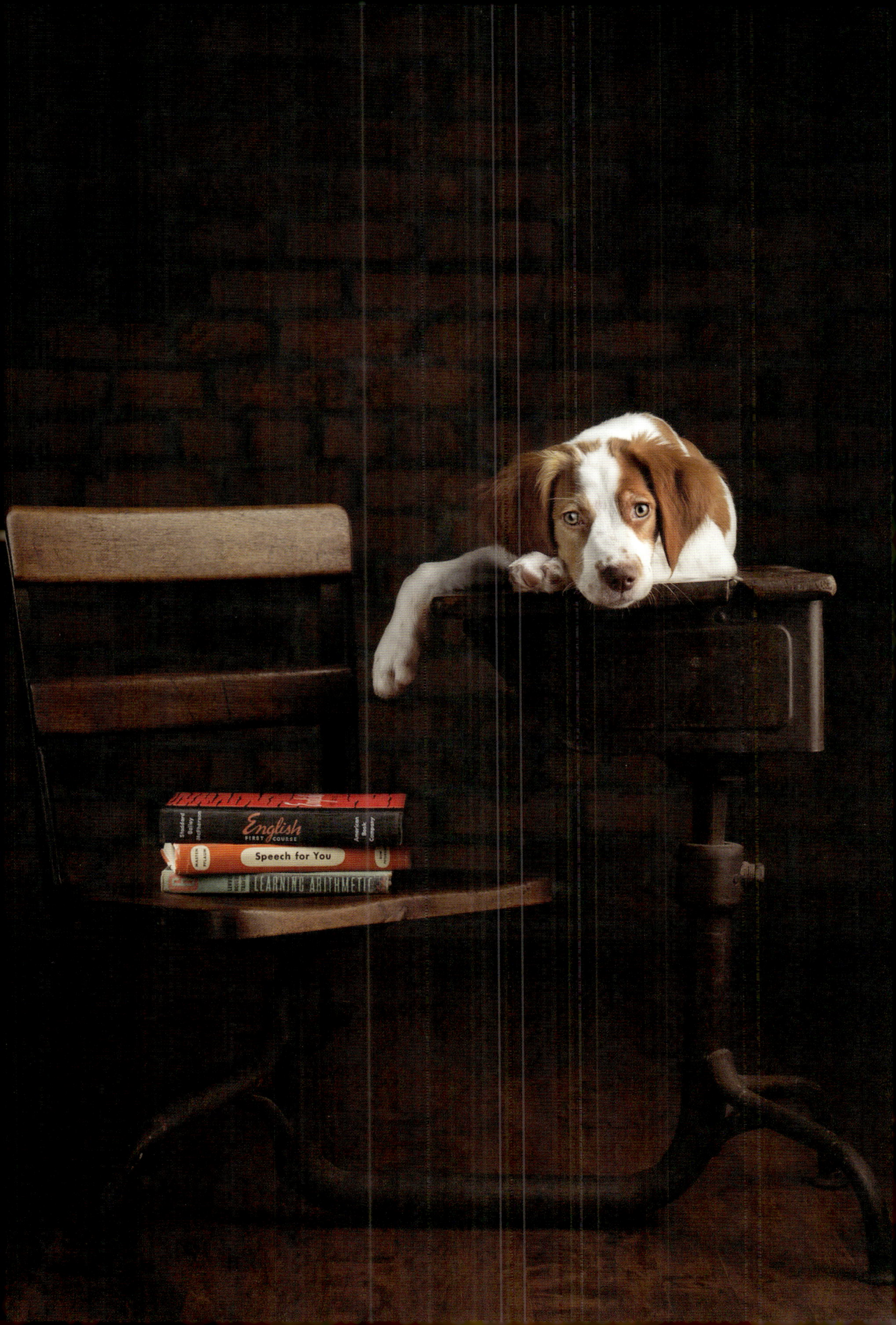
English
FIRST COURSE
Speech for You
LEARNING ARITHMETIC

Index

AmherstMedia.com

- *New books every month*
- *Books on all photography subjects and specialties*
- *Learn from leading experts in every field*
- *Buy with Amazon (amazon.com), Barnes & Noble (barnesandnoble.com), and Indiebound (indiebound.com)*
- *Follow us on social media at: facebook.com/AmherstMediaInc, twitter.com/AmherstMedia, or www.instagram.com/amherstmediaphotobooks*

Create Pro Quality Images with Our iPhone Photography for Everybody Series

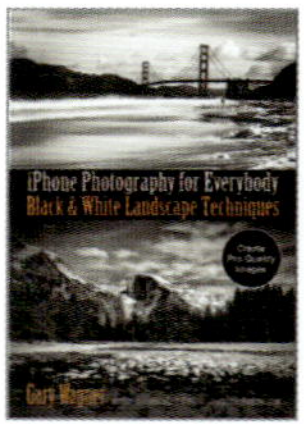

iPhone Photography for Everybody

Black & White Landscape Techniques

Gary Wagner delves into the art of creating breaktaking iPhone black & white landscape photos of seascapes, trees, beaches, and more. $29.95 list, 7x10, 128p, 180 color images, ISBN 978-1-68203-432-3.

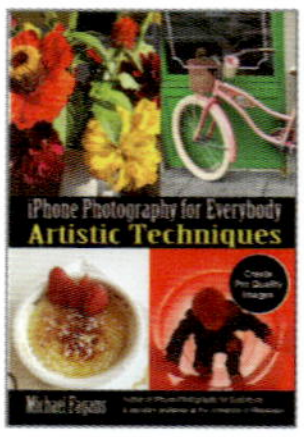

iPhone Photography for Everybody

Artistic Techniques

Michael Fagans shows you how to expertly use your iPhone to capture the people, places, and meaningful things that color your world. $29.95 list, 7x10, 128p, 180 color images, ISBN 978-1-68203-432-3.

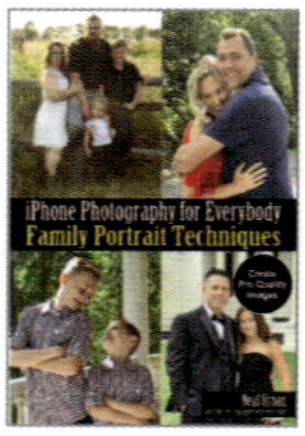

iPhone Photography for Everybody

Family Portrait Techniques

Neal Urban shows you what it takes to create personality-filled, professional-quality iPhone family portraits. $29.95 list, 7x10, 128p, 180 color images, ISBN 978-1-68203-436-1.

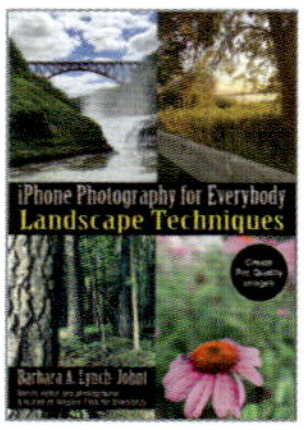

iPhone Photography for Everybody

Landscape Techniques

Barbara A. Lynch-Johnt provides all of the skills you need to master landscape photography with any iPhone. *$29.95 list, 7x10, 128p, 160 color images, ISBN 978-1-68203-440-8.*

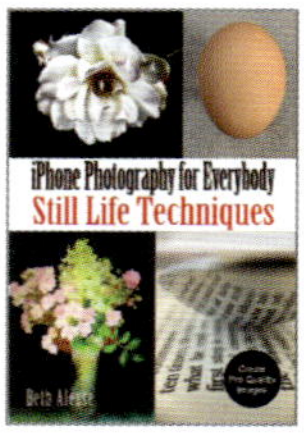

iPhone Photography for Everybody

Still Life Techniques

Beth Alesse provides creative strategies for artfully photographing found objects, collectibles, natural elements, and more with an iPhone. $29.95 list, 7x10, 128p, 160 color images, ISBN 978-1-68203-444-6.

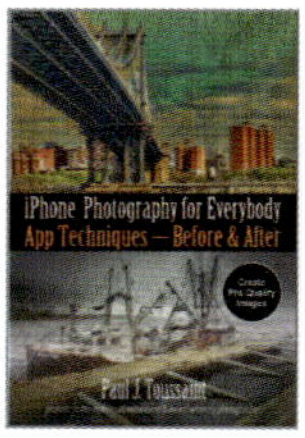

iPhone Photography for Everybody

App Techniques—Before & After

Paul J. Toussaint shows you how to transform your iPhone photos into fine art using an array of free and low-cost, simple apps. $29.95 list, 7x10, 128p, 160 color images, ISBN 978-1-68203-451-4.